AN INTRODUCTION TO PUBLIC SECTOR MANAGEMENT

AN INTRODUCTION TO PUBLIC SECTOR MANAGEMENT

Edited by

IAN TAYLOR & GEORGE POPHAM

LONDON
UNWIN HYMAN
BOSTON   SYDNEY   WELLINGTON

Published by the Academic Division of
Unwin Hyman Ltd
15/17 Broadwick Street, London W1V 1FP, UK

Unwin Hyman Inc.,
8 Winchester Place, Winchester, Mass. 01890, USA

Allen & Unwin (Australia) Ltd,
8 Napier Street, North Sydney, NSW 2060, Australia

Allen & Unwin (New Zealand) Ltd in association with the
Port Nicholson Press Ltd,
60 Cambridge Terrace, Wellington, New Zealand

First published in 1989

British Library Cataloguing in Publication Data
Taylor, Ian
An introduction to public sector management.
1. Public sector. Management.
I. Title. II. Popham, George.
350
ISBN 0-04-350076-5
ISBN 0-04-350077-3 pbk

Library of Congress Cataloging in Publication Data
An Introduction to public sector management /
[edited by] Ian Taylor and George Popham.
p.   cm.
Bibliography: p.
Includes index.
ISBN 0-04-350076-5 (alk. paper).
ISBN 0-04-350077-3 (pbk.: alk. paper).
1. Administrative agencies – Great Britain – Management.
2. Government business enterprises – Great Britain – Management.
3. Public administration.
I. Taylor, Ian. II. Popham, G. T.
JN425.I57   1989.
354.41–dc19   88-31367 CIP

Typeset in 10 on 11 point Bembo by Computape (Pickering) Ltd,
Pickering, North Yorkshire
and printed in Great Britain by Billing & Son, London and Worcester

Contents

Notes on contributors

KEITH BARNARD is currently Guest Professor at the Nordic School of Public Health in Göteborg, Sweden. Previously he was Head of the Nuffield Centre for Health Service Studies at the University of Leeds.

TONY BOVAIRD is Lecturer in Public Sector Management in the Public Sector Management Division at Aston University's Business School.

ROGER BUCKLAND is Lecturer in Finance in the Corporate Management and Finance Division at Aston University's Business School.

HOWARD ELCOCK is Professor of Government in the Department of Economics and Government at Newcastle Polytechnic.

MARTIN GROCOTT is Senior Lecturer in Public Administration at Wolverhampton Polytechnic.

SANDRA NUTLEY is Lecturer in Public Sector Management in the Public Sector Management Division at Aston University's Business School.

GEORGE POPHAM is Senior Lecturer in Government in the Public Sector Management Division at Aston University's Business School.

IAN TAYLOR is Lecturer in Government in the Public Sector Management Division at Aston University's Business School.

MARTIN UPTON is Assistant Treasurer to the Nationwide-Anglia Building Society, having previously held the posts of Group Accountant at Coventry City Council and Lecturer in Economics at Aston University.

Preface

British government and public sector management are now assuredly amongst the most centralized in the Western world. Elected local authorities have been squeezed financially, by-passed by a plethora of ad hoc agencies and in some cases abolished. Ministerial patronage in the Health Service and other fields has reached new heights. Since 1975/6 it has been the primary concern of central government to contain inflation by reducing government borrowing. Managers have therefore been forced to operate in an atmosphere of crisis and to try to make the best (although not necessarily most desirable or effective) use of available resources. The steady erosion of social security benefits and services, high unemployment and cuts in public sector housing pose serious problems for maintaining a sense of social solidarity. Cuts in manpower, accompanied by cash limits, are not going to make the task easier whatever the techniques, skills and technology available. In view of the many, often radical changes that have occurred in the public sector during the past ten years there is considerable scope for reviewing the impact of change on organizational structures and procedures.

This text is addressed primarily to students and practitioners of public sector management seeking an introductory guide. The scope of public sector management is so wide that omissions were inevitable if selected aspects and services were to be considered more than superficially. It is hoped that an insight into the general character and context of public sector management is provided which, together with examples from specific services, will illuminate the tasks of those employed in fields not directly confronted.

We are indebted to Shirley Wilkes of Aston University who typed the draft chapters and the final manuscript. Jenny Hipkiss, also of Aston University, was of considerable assistance to us.

Introduction:
Issues and trends in public sector management

IAN TAYLOR

Management has become a vogue term in British government since the late 1960s, and the notion of 'efficient management' as an approach to running organizations, solving problems and providing services is being applied more rigorously throughout the public sector than ever before. However, the notion or idea of management or a more managerialist approach to running and organizing public bodies is by no means new. In their study of the British civil service from the period 1850–1970, Richard A. Chapman and J. R. Greenway (1980, p. 184) argued that 'the growth of more positive government gave rise to questions concerning the relationship of management efficiency to the political goals and objectives of government'. Desmond Keeling (1972, p. 18) has argued that a 'growing awareness of the relevance of management in the civil service owes much to the Plowden Report of 1961'. Certainly since the Maud Report on the 'Management of Local Government' (1967), the Fulton Report which observed that 'too few civil servants are skilled managers' (1968, p. 12), and the Bains Report (1972) which focused on a corporate approach to strategic management in local government, there has been greater emphasis on the need for senior officials in central and local government to pay more attention to clear objectives and organizational principles.

While it is important to recognize the vogue usage of management, managerialism has recently taken on a more ideological and prescriptive form to complement the cost-saving policies of Conservative governments since 1979. Consequently, public sector managers at all levels and in all forms of organization are expected to operate their departments and provide services on the basis of traditional private sector notions of, for example, value for money

(VFM) and economy, efficiency and effectiveness (3Es), in the face of cuts in levels of funding, privatization, and the threat of increased competition for service provision from the private sector. The following comment by Shan Martin (1983, p. 46) is particularly appropriate. 'As the non-government sector becomes increasingly more service producing than goods producing, the opportunities for utilising similar management techniques in both public and private enterprises increase.'

An introductory text should allude to the differences between management and administration, consider conceptions of management, forms of management, notably strategic and operational (functional) management and assess the applicability of techniques from the private sector. It is also necessary to consider the wider environment of the public sector and evaluate how public policy can influence management, and to look at recent trends in public policy. Public sector management is a function of organizations which are publicly accountable for their actions in the light of their statutory obligations and fulfilment of expectations of the citizens they serve. The political, social, economic and cultural environment in which they operate is crucial to all forms of strategic and, increasingly, operational management.

Management and administration

There are many definitions of management and administration. Managers may undertake administrative functions and administrators may manage. Fulton's observation (1968, p. 12) that too few members of the administrative class of the civil service actually saw themselves as managers is significant. Rosamund Thomas's observation (1978, p. xvi) that most Americans 'feel that the term "management", is a dynamic sounding word whereas "administration" is wooden', suggests that imagery rather than substance separates the words. However, her notion that administration is 'cultural' and 'philosophical' (p. xv) can be associated with the historical development of the British civil service, its institutional position and the conventions that determine the relationship between politics and administration. This view is supported by Christopher Hodgkinson (1978, p. 5) who defined administration as 'those aspects dealing more with the formulation of purpose, the value-laden issues, and the human component of organizations', and management as 'those aspects which are more routine, definitive, programmatic and susceptible to quantitative methods'. This approach is somewhat narrow in that it excludes the possibility, indeed, likelihood of overlapping of administrative and managerial functions. Those who consider themselves to be managers in central government, local authorities, the National Health Service and public corporations are often just as concerned about ends as means. Desmond Keeling's view (1972, p. 35) that administration is conceptually distinct from management in that administration is an activity 'in which the best use of resources does not lie at the centre of the task', whereas management is less concerned with procedure and more concerned with innovation, is probably more appropriate. Certainly his view that the objectives of management, which consist of broad strategic aims supported by more detailed short-term goals, provides us with scope for attributing broad as well as specific functions to managers in the public sector.

While there may be a great deal of truth in Keeling's assertion (p. 103) that the distinction between the administrator and manager is real, it is also true to say that as a more managerial approach is applied to what were considered to be administrative tasks in the public sector, so the distinction is being broken down. The idea that administrators (as opposed to managers) are not time- or cost-conscious, or success seeking is one that is held by many on the political right as well as a number of management theoreticians, notably Peter F. Drucker (1973) and more recently Tom Peters and Nancy Austin (1985, p. 265) whose notion that management is concerned with 'shaping values, symbolising attention – and it is the opposite of "administration" and, especially "professional management"' highlights a more irrevocable difference. Even if there are, as Keeling asserts, conceptual differences between management and administration, when it comes to performing tasks administrators may be creative and innovative and managers may be narrow and relatively passive. The constitutional notion of the thoughtful and active administration of the state's activities through the civil service may be seen to complement the role of strategic management in government yet at the same time contradict it, if we are to think of senior civil servants as thinkers, advisers and delegators rather than doers.

The debate about the difference between management and administration and managers and administrators is likely to continue, and may gather momentum in the light of proposals to reform the civil service. There is a sense in which managerialism, in the shape of approaches and techniques incorporating the values of the private sector, is undermining the notion of a neutral public service sector committed to service provision on the basis of justice, need and demand. Various definitions of and approaches to managment may be entirely at one with more traditional ideas about public service. It is perhaps appropriate to follow the advice of Robert M. Fulmer (1978, p. 48) that 'to seek a one-and-only doctrine of management is foolhardy'. It is useful to consider a number of definitions and approaches because this shows the variability and flexibility required to approach the study of management as a descriptive and analytical discipline as well as a practical activity. For example, John Bourne (1979, p. i) described the study of management as 'the systematic examination of the ways in which groups of people organise themselves to achieve goals by co-operative action'. Dalton E. McFarland (1974, pp. 6–10) focused on the versatility of the use of management, which he described as a 'process, a discipline, people and a career'.

In many respects, there is little new in management thinking. A great deal of management theory and practice whether advanced thirty years ago or today may be described as 'common sense'. For example, William H. Newman (1958, p. 341) defined the objectives of management as the formulation of priorities and plans, the development of a plan of organization, the development and administration of a constructive personnel development plan, the accomplishment of duties and responsibilities fully, effectively and harmoniously, the control of costs and manpower, updating procedures and encouraging good employee relations. As if to prove that there is little new in approaches to management, the Audit Commission's handbook for 1983, *Improving Economy, Efficiency and Effectiveness in Local Government in England and Wales*, recommended that managers should adopt the McKinsey '7s' framework which appeared in an earlier work by Thomas J. Peters and Robert H. Waterman (1982, p. 10). Their framework sought the integration of vision, strategy, structure, systems, staffing skills, style, which the authors considered to be essential to any 'intelligent approach to organising'. This is in keeping with E. F. L. Brech's view (1972, p. 19) that management is a unified process whose several aspects are *inter-dependent* rather than merely inter-related.

Distinctions between titles and job descriptions as well as functions often become blurred and distorted in the performance of tasks. The notion that 'we are all managers now', even though we may call ourselves professionals, technicians or administrators, is one which many public sector employees have come to accept reluctantly, welcome with enthusiasm or even ignore. Which ever way, it can be argued that academic concepts of and approaches to management which in the main have been applied to the private sector can also be applied to the public sector, even though the aims and functions of public bodies may be entirely different from those of the private sector. At the same time, it is worth heeding the words of Shan Martin (1983, p. 129) who argued that one of the myths of management was that although it was much revered, a great deal of the work carried out in organizations was undertaken without the actual function of management being exercised at all. Even if management was not as important as managerialists liked to believe, the myth of management still prevailed.

> When things are going well with an organisation, it must be that it is well managed; when things are not going well, it must be that the organisation needs more or better trained managers. (Martin, 1983)

Forms of management: Strategic and operational

Accepting that general conceptions of and approaches to management are adaptable to the public as well as the private sector, it is now necessary to consider some basic forms of management. There may well be differences when we consider strategic and operational approaches and attempt to apply more specific private sector criteria to the public sector.

There are many important differences betwen the forms and obectives of management in the public and private sectors. Public sector management is influenced directly by the political sphere. Public policy defines the objectives and tasks of public bodies, and managers within them are ultimately accountable to politicians or elected bodies. The public sector manager is more likely to be influenced by legislation and constitutional considerations than his or her private sector counterpart. Statutes determine what public bodies do, if not the form they take, so that the organization has an obligation to respond to changes in existing law or new requirements and regulations. Although the private sector manager will also be influenced by legislation and public policy, particularly with regard to trading and safety standards, trade policy, fiscal policy and environmental controls, the life of the organization does not depend upon implementing the policies of democratically elected politicians.

There are other important differences. The public sector is the main provider of services which are regarded as vital to state security, the maintenance and promotion of public health, social and education provision, the environment and the running of industries and services which are considered to be strategically vital but not economically viable as far as the private sector is concerned. However, to argue that the public sector provides what people need and the private what they want is an over-simplification, just as it is inaccurate to argue that the *sole* aim of management in the public sector is to provide a service whereas in the private sector it is to make a profit, although it is undeniably the main objective. Possibly the main difference between public and private sector bodies is that the public sector depends heavily on public funds and is more constrained by fiscal policy which is part of the political sphere. Drucker's argument (1973, p. 141) that business is paid for by the customer while service institutions are usually paid out of a budget allocation is probably over-simplifying the position. The services provided by nationalized industries are in part paid for by the customer, and consumers of services such as education and public transport have already partly paid for the service they receive through various forms of taxation. However, Drucker's contention that managerial autonomy and competition are not feasible in traditional public sector activities, such as the administration of justice and defence is certainly valid, and does point to a major difference between private sector organizations operating in the market-place and some (although not all) public bodies whose tasks can only be defined by government and the constitution. The extent to which this situation remains is one which many public sector managers now face, as what have been regarded as traditional and important public sector activities become candidates for privatization or competitive tendering.

Any analysis of management in the private and public sector must take account of the two main forms of management – strategic and operational or functional, although these are umbrella terms which frequently overlap. In the private sector, strategic management is often associated with corporate strategy, as the decisions are taken by senior management with regard to 'how a business organisation should relate to its product market environment' (W. Stewart Howe, 1986, p. xiii). La Rue T. Hosmer's view that the most meaningful definition of strategic management in the private company sense is 'probably the method of competition to be followed by the business' has traditionally differed sharply from considerations of strategic management in the public sector. H. J. Claycamp (1985, p. 10) observed that strategic management in business was 'to a large extent a new catchphrase coined to describe what CEOs have always been paid to do'. Claycamp identified three key aspects of the role of strategic managers: making decisions about objectives and major resource allocations, motivating the organization to implement them and making sure that desired results are achieved. Strategic management in the public sector may well conform to the private sector notion described above, although certain objectives such as the need to increase profits, changes in marketing strategy and identifying and keeping ahead of competitors are examples of some strategic issues which strategic management in the public sector has been less concerned with until recently.

As in the private sector, strategic management in the public sector takes account of a wide range of functions and is more concerned with policy objectives, the role of the organization in the process of government, its relationship with other organizations and the impact of policy than with the way in which the organization operates or functions on a day-to-day basis. In central government, ministers, senior civil servants and policy advisers play a key role in strategic decision-making, which is generally concerned not only with policy, but with the way in which government departments should respond to the implementation of policy, indicating an operational role as well. At the local level, committee chairpersons, Chief Officers and the departments of Chief Executives are most directly concerned with strategic decision-making and management. To some extent it could be argued that the owners of corporate business make policy and the senior executives manage its execution, and that governments are the trustees of public bodies which are owned by the public. It is also important to stress that within government each department has its own organizational and implementational approach, which may be independent or separate from the overall management of the public sector which is the ultimate function of elected governments.

In view of this, a key difference between strategic management in the public and private sectors relates to the dual issues of accountability and autonomy. Most private sector conceptions of strategic management confer considerable policy-making functions upon senior managers, allowing them a great deal of autonomy to interpret what has to be done as well as how to accomplish it. Policy-making in the public sector belongs to the political sphere, and although senior civil servants, Chief Officers and professionals within government influence policy, their influence does not always extend to the objectives of policy, although they are concerned crucially with its implementation. In other words, they have less opportunity to utilize their values and opinions to the same effect as in the private sector, a factor which affects their autonomy. Conversely, implementation may affect policy, which is where public sector managers may be most influential in a strategic and operational sense. As Hosmer (1982, p. 418) has pointed out, service orientation, non-market pricing, external funding, professional personnel and multiple constituencies influence strategic management in the public sector. According to Peters and Austin (1985, p. 4) at the broadest level, the concerns of strategic management may well be similar:

> In the private or public sector, in big business or small . . . take exceptional care of your customers (for chicken, jet engines, education, health care, or baseball) via superior service and superior quality. Second, constantly innovate.

If strategic management is concerned primarily with the management of organizations, operational management is concerned more with day-to-day management *within* organizations although, as has been pointed out, organizations may contain departments and divisions which adopt their own strategies. In its widest sense, operational management is concerned with the actual production of goods and services. In this context, Roger G. Schroeder's definition (1981, p. 10) is particularly appropriate: 'Operations managers make decisions regarding operations functions and the transformation systems used', with particular reference to the production of goods and services (function), the design and management of the productive system and decision-making with regard to process, capacity, inventory, work-force and quality. At a purely functional level, this may be applied to the public and private sectors, since all management is concerned with the inputs and outputs required to run an organization in order to produce a range of goods and services. This includes such key areas of management as personnel, systems, production, financial and marketing. In spite of the narrower or more specific nature of operations management, as Ray Wild (1980, p. 55) has argued, the objectives of operations management will have 'a considerable influence in the choice of strategies and the choice from feasible structures'.

In the case of marketing, with which there are important parallels to be made linking both private and public sector management, the distinction between strategic and operational management is sometimes unclear. For example, the marketing of a product or service may be so vital to the very existence, let alone functioning of an organization, that marketing decisions become strategic level decisions. This is increasingly important in the public sector in view of increased competition in service provision. During the 1980s there has been an increase in the interface between marketing and public policy, and the transfer of product marketing techniques to the public sector. As Philip Kotler (1975, p. 6) has stressed, 'selling is only the tip of the marketing iceberg'. Certainly as Kotler suggests, marketing may be deemed to be sufficiently complex to achieve the status of a managerial process in its own right identifying it as a process as well as a function, as strategic as well as operational. Almost any function can be a strategic or operational matter and while strategic management is usually associated with higher levels of autonomy than operational management, there is frequently considerable functional autonomy at the level of operation, although comparing degrees of autonomy is difficult when strategic and operational management are often concerned with different things.

If it has been the trend since the early 1970s to pay more attention to notions and descriptions of management and managerial functions in the public sector, more recently techniques, approaches and values associated traditionally with the private sector have been applied, particularly in the form of VFM and the 3Es. What constitutes these approaches and their implications for public sector management should be considered particularly in view of the thinking behind them and their impact on operational management in public sector organizations. VFM and the 3Es are not only associated with techniques, but also raise issues of principle and ethics and may be seen as a challenge to some of the long-held values in the public sector. The notion of VFM is a complex one which relates not only to the costing of a service but its value and indeed, *how highly* it is valued and from *whose standpoint*. When applied to the National Health Service for example, its aim is ostensibly to produce lower costs and improve performance, based on the conviction that public sector organizations like their private counterparts should be more conscious of market-related performance and less dependent upon budget allocation. This thinking has a great deal in common with Drucker's argument (1973, p. 142) that in budget-based institutions, the need for economy matters less because, if achieved, budget allocation would as a consequence be lower, so that cost control would not be considered as a virtue. As far as the NHS is concerned, VFM covers all aspects of the service from the merits or otherwise of the 'cook–chill' system, to the advantages of disposable over traditional bed-pans, energy controls, laundry, wards and clinical theatres.

One of the more interesting aspects of the application of VFM to such considerations is that if applied in the private sector, consumer choice and satisfaction may well be taken into account as well as cost-preference in the provision of services. If customers or consumers preferred a more expensive but better product or service, they may be more prepared to pay for it, possibly offsetting any advantages in going for the cheaper system. It is necessary that value for money should not only be judged by the cost-conscious but also by the consumer. If cooking methods and bed-pans are marginal issues when it comes to treating illness, but of some significance in terms of diverting resources to those areas of medical care and innovation which can prevent or cure disease, then there is some merit in applying VFM in hospitals. However, questions of VFM apply across the board and enter into questions of ethics. Are kidney transplants better value for money than heart transplants? Should proportionately more be spent on geriatric care than on the mentally ill? VFM cannot be applied in the NHS in the way it can in other sectors because it is not just the quality of life that is at stake but life itself.

The notion of value for money may well produce positive results for government, the organization, the quality of service, the consumer and taxpayer when applied consistently to all services and when levels of funding are adequate to maintain and if possible improve existing services. However, when the message from government is that budgets will be cut or not keep pace with inflation and the demand for services, the implications of a VFM approach become altogether less tenable, less attractive, especially for professionals in public sector organizations who are unable to offer the service needed by their clients, the general public. In the NHS for example, VFM criteria should relate to value for money for the consumer. The patient will judge the service in terms of quality of treatment and care and should be unconcerned about how much it has cost to save his or her life compared with that of someone else. As Y. Roll and S. Moran have pointed out (1984, p. 450), highly quantitative approaches have to be accompanied by an appropriate 'quality of care' and an awareness of considering the problems in defining output and complexity of treatments. In local government as Brendan McSweeney (1988, pp. 35–6) has shown, the question of comparability in applying VFM and its procedures is only achievable when like is compared with like, something that is highly problematic when comparing different local authorities.

The determination of the present government to encourage a more cost-conscious approach to the management of public sector organizations and provision of public services is also illustrated by the application of the 3Es, which are allegedly practised in the private sector but according to Drucker (1973, pp. 142–3) are sacrificed to budget dependency in the public service sector. However, as John Perrin (1988, p. 10) has argued, a 3Es approach in the public sector may have less applicability. Economy is of 'limited managerial relevance since it takes no account of the outputs achieved', efficiency 'tells us nothing about the need for, or benefit from, any change in output', nor the quality of services; effectiveness requires sophisticated comparative analysis of often different objectives and outcomes.

In his study of the role of the Audit Commission in establishing 3Es procedures in local government, Brendan McSweeney (1988, p. 42) has argued that the commission 'does not merely wish to describe, control, or restrain local authorities but explicitly aims to change them' by insinuating 3Es techniques. Certainly value-judgements are involved. Perrin's summary of the advantages and disadvantages of a 3Es approach highlights some of the problems associated with applying private sector assumptions and techniques to the public sector. The problem for public sector managers whether in the NHS, local government or nationalized industries, is that such exercises create pressures to adapt to more competitive market criteria which may be inappropriate. The determination of the present government to encourage competition for service provision and privatize as many nationalized industries as possible, leads inevitably to VFM and 3Es approaches, which affect the quality of service to the consumer, who is often unable to judge the relative or possible relative quality of service since there is often nothing with which to compare it. Managers in these circumstances are often working in the dark, unable to judge the impact of cost cutting on the quality of services because of the constant need to go on economizing and reorganizing with the ever present threat of privatization and increased competition looming over them. At the same time it must be pointed out that the application of VFM and the 3Es, the prospects of privatization and increased competition are by no means unwelcome to all public sector managers. These procedures are of undoubted value where they lead to more efficient management and a higher quality of service. Ultimately they are linked to questions of ethics and notions of 'public service'. Nevertheless there is a conflict between the managerialist cost-cutting approach and the more traditionalist administrative or professional approach which is more universalist than selective. The application of private sector techniques to the public sector may be of value in a limited sense but only so long as they do not distort the aims of the organizations concerned. Management needs to be put into perspective. As Drucker has recently observed:

> Management is no more of a science than is medicine: both are practices . . . Just as medicine feeds off biology, chemistry, physics and a host of other natural sciences, so management feeds off economics, psychology, mathematics, political theory, history and philosophy. (1987, p. 227)

Drucker's view of management as a form of 'liberal art' is wide-ranging and essentially civilized. It insists that management has different applications in different cases, and is about means *and* ends. If the end of the business organization is to *sell* a product or a service, it is generally the aim of public sector organizations to *provide* a service, to meet need rather than effective demand, whether that service is the education of children or the care of the sick. If private sector notions of economic ends are applied too vigorously in the public sector, the ends themselves are likely to become distorted, and in some cases lost altogether.

Changing attitudes towards the role and nature of management in the public sector, as well as the rigorous application of new techniques and approaches, can only be understood in the context of public policy-making. Policy not only determines what is to be provided, how much and to whom, but is directly related to how public sector bodies organize themselves in response to public policy initiatives.

Public policy and management

The relationship between public policy and public sector management is influenced by the constitutional system as well as by the nature of public policy. In Britain no concerted attempt has been made to divorce the study of policy-making from policy implementation, although there has been a tendency to regard the study of public sector management as a technical exercise in which each branch of the public sector may be understood with little direct reference to political ideology, political activity, social and economic theory and trends. In the USA on the other hand, particularly during the interwar period and immediately after the Second World War, there was a tendency to regard policy-making and implementation as separate processes, which Andrew Dunsire

(1978, p. viii) has described as 'obsolete, mistaken and dangerous'. The so-called 'science' of public administration was in part inspired by Woodrow Wilson's view that administration lay 'outside the proper sphere of politics' and that administrative questions were 'not political questions' (1887, p. 210). This approach acquired a methodological boost with the popularization of scientific management theory, based on F. W. Taylor's work, and in particular the notion that the 'best management is a true science, resting upon clearly defined laws, rules and principles' (1911, p. 7). Herbert Simon's modified scientific approach (1945) produced a theory of 'bounded' rationalism with regard to administrative behaviour, which was popular during the 1950s and 1960s, and contrasted with the incrementalist or 'muddling through' approach advocated by C. E. Lindblom (1959).

There was nothing intrinsically wrong with regarding bureaucrats as careerists operating outside the political sphere while at the same time serving it, a notion very much in keeping with Max Weber's classical view of bureaucracy, nor was it invalid to create a theoretical framework within which to establish procedures for organizing bureaucracies and implementing policy. The main problem with this approach was that it was taken to extremes, as the 'science' of public administration drove a wedge between policy-making and implementation which underplayed the role of bureaucrats in the policy-making process and the impact of politics on their activities. John A. Rohr's view that bureaucrats do 'authoritatively determine the allocation of values' and 'frequently decide who gets what' (1978, p. 28) is a much more realistic one which can be applied to the role of public sector managers in all countries and at all levels of government. Politicians often depend upon the advice of non-elected public officials, advice which influences the content of policy as well as its implementation. Although this advice may not be overtly ideological, it belongs to the sphere of policy-making.

Decisions about how much information to reveal or how much to withhold from government ministers at one end of the policy spectrum, to the allocation of resources to provide services at the other, involve questions of ethics. These relate to notions of justice and fairness, which often have to counterbalance expediency in decision-making. For example, the decision to withdraw or reduce a service may well be influenced by a consideration such as funding, when those involved in administering the service are conscious of the fact that the service is required. The decision and its outcome may well offend or compromise the sense of justice of those responsible for management within the organization concerned. Public sector managers are often in the invidious position of being asked to implement policies with which they disagree. The public servant may be professionally apolitical but subscribe to political values as a private citizen. For those who are conscious of the fact that their personal values may be compromised by their public role, or who realize the adverse consequences of their actions on service provision, life can be particularly harrowing. The fact that government ministers or elected councillors are constitutionally responsible for the outcome of policy, may be no consolation for those committed to the idea of public service. As has been argued, not all public employees are committed to *state-provided* public service, as some senior managers in nationalized industries have shown. Few if any employees of recently privatized public utilities have resigned their posts in protest at government policy, and others have campaigned actively for privatization.

The extent to which a public sector manager is conscious of the implications of his or her day-to-day decisions depends upon a number of factors. These include their role in the decision-making process, the nature of their work and their ideological position. A Permanent Secretary may deal with politicians and policy decisions at the highest level, and play a decisive role in the strategic management of a government department, yet may have little personal interest in the political philosophy of the minister or government that he or she is serving, except in so far as aspects of that philosophy affect the department. On the other hand, a Permanent Secretary may have a strong moral objection to a policy yet be forced to wear the constitutional badge of impartiality. An officer in a local authority may be involved in the implementation of the policies of a Conservative council while being a member of the Labour party. Policies may be deplored by managers who remain powerless to act upon their personal judgement. Thomas Nagel's view that 'public obligations require a sense of impartiality and heightened concern for results' (1978, p. 82) is a pertinent one. However, it may mean that public sector managers conceal strong personal preferences which strain their relationships with both politicians and colleagues.

If public policy is in the forefront of public sector management, it is important for the practising manager to be able to make sense of public policy. This is sometimes a difficult task, given changes in government, and lack of continuity in policy combined with inadequate resources. Policy may be derived from fundamental principles embodied in ideologies or relate to differing conceptions of justice, freedom, equality and fairness. Policy may also be the product of expediency, forced on governments by domestic or international crises. Whatever the origins and aims of policies, public sector organizations are expected to respond. At the very least, this demands flexibility from the organization concerned. Although flexibility is called for, most public bureaucracies operate fairly rigid internal mechanisms, designed to facilitate the most appropriate response to a situation as well as providing for continuity, since some of their work involves implementing long-term policies. In view of this dual function, it is usual for organizations to develop a variety of techniques and procedures to respond to the demands of policy-making and implementation. Rational techniques are generally more appropriate for dealing with the predictable day-to-day situations, while an element of 'muddling through' or incrementalism is often called for in order to deal with the unexpected. Whichever approach is adopted, the words of Aaron Wildavsky (1980, p. 7) should be heeded: 'Every policy is fashioned of tension between resources and objectives, planning and politicism, scepticism and dogma. Solving problems involves temporarily resolving these tensions.'

Radical governments pose problems for bureaucracies, and while an element of stability within organizations is guaranteed, it becomes increasingly difficult to follow standard procedures or expect 'normal' treatment, especially when it comes to funding. Under such circumstances the public sector manager has to operate effectively in an environment which is relatively unstable. A certain level of organizational autonomy is required. Without this, the management of people, finance and service provision becomes fraught with problems. In order to establish autonomy and stability, it is necessary to establish procedures which are likely to be affected minimally by changes in policy, and which will respond to the now much-vaunted twin objectives of public sector management, efficiency and cost-effectiveness. A thorough analysis of policy and the policy-making process is also required in order to determine the most effective ways and means of influencing policy, or at least being able to convey the organizational problems associated with policy implementation.

Policy is determined and influenced by a variety of sources about which the public sector manager needs to be aware. It is important to understand not only the impact of policy on the department or organization in which he or she is working, but on other departments as well. As J. J. Richardson and A. G. Jordan (1979, p. 25) have observed, policies 'are the outcome of departmental conflict within government as well as the result of pressures on the government from outside'. The political tensions within government undoubtedly affect policy formulation and they are often less easy to manage than those originating from rival interest groups. There are established procedures for dealing with interest groups whose reactions to policy are predictable. They can be dismissed as 'sectional' and frequently indifferent about the so-called 'public interest'. It is possible to anticipate how far interest groups and political parties will respond to policies. Historical factors are likely to be important as well as an analysis of the current social, economic and political climate. In this way, allowances may be built into the decisions and calculations of managers. Departmental conflict poses more intractable problems. As politicians compete for resources or challenge the decisions of colleagues, the manager may have to sit it out until the final battles have been won or lost in Cabinet. There is always an element of 'wait and see' in public sector management, which is where the incremental approach comes into its own.

Whatever the policy, managers will be expected to respond in a variety of ways to satisfy the goals of politicians on the one hand and maintain organizational stability on the other. While these dual objectives may at times conflict, they need not. The perceived success of policy is in the interests of managers and politicians alike. They depend upon each other although their tasks are different. Managers will respond in different ways to policy in accordance with where they are in the managerial hierarchy, what their experience is and the nature of the organization. The reaction of managers to policy may well depend upon how far the bureaucracy rather than the politicians is likely to control its content and passage. In all cases, managerial tasks are likely to be facilitated or illuminated by knowledge of the content, objectives and impact of policy.

Every government has priorities. Some take the form of responses to day-to-day problems while others may be manifesto objectives. A government that has staked its reputation on lowering unemployment levels, or reducing taxation and inflation may stand or fall on the perceived success of its policies. However, priorities may change. Governments may face implementational problems for a variety of reasons. Generally speaking, governments are publicly cautious about what they might achieve and circumspect about revealing too much information to the public. They may have contingency plans to modify policy and justify deviations from stated goals. If priorities change, so do objectives. Agreeing objectives is an important function in public sector management yet one of the most difficult. What is politically acceptable if policy fails to achieve objectives, is often uncertain. Sometimes, policies have little relevance to the problems they are expected to solve, or they simply generate new ones.

Policy implementation raises a wide variety of questions concerning organization, resources and techniques. At the implemenation stage, a knowledge of priorities will be particularly useful as resources are invariably scarce and inadequate. Here, departmental allocation procedures will be put to the test. Depending on the policy, flexibility or rigidity may be called for, in response to the uncertainty and changing circumstances. The importance of implementation arises because policies are modified through the subjective interpretation of objectives and the discretion afforded departmental officials. Some policies require an immediate response from departments, in which case, governments may request information or seek advice at short notice. At these times, managers will be consulted more than at others. Often, however, there is less urgency and greater continuity, with implementation smoother and requiring only minor adjustments.

In order to appreciate the impact of public policy on the public sector and by implication on both strategic and operational management, it is necessary to consider the changing role of the public sector as well as recent developments in public policy.

The changing role of the public sector

The nature and scope of the public sector in the late twentieth century and assumptions about the role of the state are being challenged and have been for a decade. However, just as public services and the organizations that run and operate them took centuries to evolve in some cases, so the functions of those organizations will take a long time to change, even though the organizations themselves may no longer remain in the public sector. Few policies are irreversible, so that a weakened public sector may eventually be strengthened, in some cases in a relatively short time. In view of the many and often rapid and radical changes that have been taking place since the election of the first Thatcher government of 1979, it is worth recalling how and why the public sector developed in the first place.

The development of the public sector since the mid-nineteenth century owes much to the impact of political economic and social theory, as well as to the response of political parties, public officials, professional interest groups, trade unions, enlightened members of middle class and the interests of the capitalist and land-owning classes to the social and economic problems created by the industrial revolution and the largely unplanned urbanization of Britain. The development of a liberal–democratic political system during the nineteenth century in which parliamentary representation was extended to the adult male population was instrumental in the growth of the state. The key to this growth lay in legislation which secured a permanent role for the state in the areas of public health, education, regulation of employment and working conditions, the provision of poor relief and law and order, in addition to defence and public finance. Once a new function for the state had been identified, fought for and established, public expectation and bureaucratic self-perpetuation ensured that its growth would be difficult to reverse. The extension of state activity during the twentieth century to include responsibility for all social policy areas, unemployment and health insurance, as well as key industries and services, owes a great deal to the nineteenth century and in particular to the development of municipal government and administration on the one hand and collectivist political social and economic theory on the other. Nineteenth-century social and political theory focused more on the idea of societal or social rights than natural rights, which had hitherto characterized social and political theory and identified man as naturally self-interested, competitive and acquisitive, and the role of government in society as essentially negative. So long as the citizen's property was protected and the state defended, the intervention of government in the economy in particular was to be minimal. Early nineteenth-century utilitarian theory marked the boundary between classical laissez-faire liberalism and collectivist liberalism, which inspired social legislation, the great liberal reforms of 1906–11 and ultimately the welfare state and managed economy of the post Second World War period. Although the utilitarian theory of Jeremy Bentham and James Mill supported the laissez-faire doctrine of political economists such as Adam Smith and David Ricardo, it advocated a more positive role for government to remove obstacles to the ultimate end of society, the greatest happiness of the greatest number. The utilitarian view that each individual knew his or her interests and was rational and capable of exercising choice, was promoted by the enlightened industrialists and urban middle class who wanted increased representation of the industrial centres in Parliament and limited extension of the franchise. The great Reform Act of 1832 and the Poor Law Amendment Act 1834 (a turning point in state poor-relief provision), owed much to the utilitarian school.

Further extensions of the franchise in 1867 and 1884, and the concern of political thinkers like John Stuart Mill about the quality of education and employment (which ultimately determined human happiness), led to greater demands for social provision and expanded the functions of government at central and local level. Late nineteenth-century collectivist liberals argued for greater social (collective) provision in order to enhance the development of individual consciousness and morality. The influence of Fabian socialism and the growth of municipal government ensured that by the early twentieth century the role of the state had been extended from protecting and removing obstacles to freedom to its promotion through state (public) service provision.

Both the left and right in British politics could claim adherence to collectivism, although for different reasons. The differences between the collectivism of the Liberal party of the late nineteenth century and that of the socialist organizations that eventually formed the Labour party were more fundamental than is sometimes suggested. Democratic socialism, particularly in its Fabian form, favoured public ownership and provision over private, and viewed the state as a central force in controlling the economy. The use of the state was a first rather than a last resort. The extension of the franchise to the urban and rural working class in 1867 and 1884 respectively, the threat of socialism, industrial competition from Germany and the USA and the disaster of the Boer War, which highlighted the physical inadequacy of those enlisted to defend the British Empire, all contributed to the social imperialism of the Conservative party during the 1890s. The defence of empire, protection of domestic industries and the extension of state provision to improve the living conditions of the working class, became Conservative objectives also.

By the 1920s collectivism in its various guises had established itself in the ideologies of the mass political parties in Britain. That is not to say that individualism was dead, rather that social, economic and political developments during the nineteenth century necessitated a more positive response from governments. This response can be seen in the Liberal reforms of 1906–11, the central planning of production during the First World War, the public housing programme of the interwar years, and the general, though means-tested extension of social provision during the 1930s in the face of mass unemployment. The Second World War was a catalyst in the development of the collectivist state. The Beveridge Report of 1942 recommended the establishment of a unified system of national insurance, a national health service and family allowances. The proposals were implemented by the Labour government of 1945–50. Labour's nationalization measures established an extended role for the state in owning and running a number of vital industries and services, notably coal, steel, the railways and public utilities. The impact of the economic theory of John Maynard Keynes was considerable, particularly during the Second World War, and it contributed to the development of a postwar economic consensus about state intervention in and management of the economy.

In spite of an element of consensus in postwar British politics, the basic division between the two major parties about the level of state intervention in the economy and society was never far from the surface. These differences have re-emerged with the coming to power of neo-liberal Conservative governments in Britain since 1979. Echoes of Adam Smith and the nineteenth-century anti-state thinker, Herbert Spencer, can be detected in the speeches and policies of leading Conservative politicians, notably the Prime Minister. However, in spite of de-nationalization measures and a monetarist economic strategy, several bastions of the collectivist state remain although they are under pressure to compete with the private sector and are increasingly starved of resources. If the collectivist state of the postwar era owes much to William Beveridge, then the revival of laissez-faire owes a great deal to F. A. Hayek, who until recently could have been regarded with some justification as a minor if not discredited thinker. Like most of his contemporaries, Beveridge argued that unemployment was the primary cause of the many social problems that restricted individual freedom, so that it was the direct duty of the state to help create and maintain full employment: 'Full employment cannot be won and held without a great extension of the responsibilities and powers of the state exercised through organs of the central government' (1944, p. 36). If these words are ironical in today's context, those of Hayek are certainly reflected in the policies of the present government: 'Freedom to order our own conduct in the sphere where material circumstances force a choice upon us, and responsibility for the arrangement of our own life according to our own conscience, is the air in which alone moral sense grows and in which moral values are daily created in the free decision of the individual' (1944, p. 157).

The extent of change during the last decade has been funda-mental. The aim of Conservative governments since 1979 to replace the 'welfare culture' associated with the Beveridge Report and democratic socialism with a new 'enterprise culture' founded on neo-liberal principles of the free market and individual choice has transformed many key areas of the public sector. Its impact on public sector management goes much further than merely adopting new techniques, being more efficient and giving value for money. The collectivist role of the state itself is being challenged. The fundamental aims of the Thatcher governments to replace the collectively consumed tax-funded and publicly subsidized services with a range of private or market-based alternatives, has not only presented a major challenge to public sector managers to transform their procedures, but has taken many public employees out of the public sector altogether. The principle of public service has been challenged. The trend away from local political control, illustrated by the abolition of the Greater London Council and Metropolitan County Councils, the proliferation of non-departmental public bodies, the tight control and proposed reform of local government finance, the prospect of schools 'opting out' of local authority control and a variety of local services being put out to competitive tendering, amount to a fundamental change in the role of local authorities which may be difficult to reverse. The same may be said of industries and services that have been privatized. At the present time it seems unlikely that a future Labour government would re-nationalize the public utilities as a matter of course given the party's new emphasis on consumerism. While there are many who disagree with privatization on the grounds that public monopolies under parliamentary control are preferable to private monopolies accountable to shareholders, the privatization of British Telecom, British Airways, gas and many others has not generated significant public protest or effective trades union resistance. In this respect, relatively little has changed since the Second World War in terms of public attitudes. Opinion polls then as now showed that people were much more concerned about health, employment and education provision than with public ownership.

The major challenge to the welfare state concerns the issue of selectivity over universality by aiming welfare provision at selected targets and encouraging private alternatives to public services. Here the Conservative governments have met their greatest challenge. The collectivist, universalist principles upon which the NHS in particular was founded appear to be supported not only by the great majority of UK citizens but also by those working within those institutions who are committed to the idea of collective provision of public services. The policies of the Conservative governments to centralize, managerialize and reduce the influence of professionals employed in public services, in particular the NHS and education, are well illustrated by their impact on public sector unions. Legislation to reform union functions, high levels of unemployment, increased competition from the private sector, privatization, an increase in temporary and part-time employment, the encouragement of single-union agreements and the growth of a low-wage service industry sector have, according to William Brown brought about a 're-evaluation of labour utilisation that is without precedent' (1986, p. 166). This is particularly true in the public sector. The creation of pay review bodies for a number of occupational groups including nurses and civil servants and the removal of the rights of teachers' unions under the 1987 Teachers' Pay and Conditions Act to negotiate pay and conditions with their employers are important examples of ways in which traditional employer–employee relationships in the public sector have changed. Another feature has been lack of consultation between central government and public sector unions and professional associations over new policy initiatives and changes in the organization of government. Two examples include the failure to consult sufficiently with the teaching unions over the introduction of a core curriculum, the GCSE and the proposed 'opting-out' scheme, and with the civil service unions over plans to reform the civil service contained in the Efficiency Unit Report, *Improving Management in Government: The Next Steps* (1988). This shows the extent to which the role of professional advice and management has been devalued and according to the unions undermined. A reduction of the impact of professional management in favour of a more managerialist, operational and VFM approach is characterized by emphasis on more flexibility in public service provision, which reflects the desire for selectivity and partly explains the introduction of pay review bodies for most NHS employees. According to John Leopold and Phil Beaumont (1986, p. 34), now that health authority members are appointed by the Secretary of State, NHS employees are placed in a worse position than workers in other public sector spheres.

Whether or not changes in the structure of bargaining procedures will lead to improved or worsened conditions for public sector employees remains to be seen. A great deal depends upon public support for public services and public identification with the problems faced by particular groups of public employees, notably teachers, doctors and nurses. It is interesting to note that the policies of the present Conservative government reflect the view of the OECD Secretary General, Emil von Leniep, who argued that there were three main tasks for government in addressing structural changes and policy towards the labour market in order to limit costs and modernize methods of delivering public services: to ensure flexibility in private and public sectors; make sure that structural changes were regarded as opportunities rather than threats; to maintain open world markets (1983, p. 11). It is possible in the case of the UK at least, that in trying to limit costs and introduce structural changes, too much centralization may destroy the possibility of flexibility, in view of the fact that many public employees see the centralist trend as a threat rather than an opportunity.

Centralization has a tendency to heighten regional differences and identification. If coupled with marked economic and social differences between regions as is the case with the so-called north–south divide, it exaggerates problems endemic to regions like Northern Ireland or Scotland, with their own departmental structures and different political complexions, creating tensions with central government. The Westminster–Whitehall approach becomes more difficult to identify with and, increasingly, more difficult to apply, leading to a resurgence in demand for an increased degree of control over public services from within the regions. This creates pressure on the Scottish, Welsh and Northern Ireland offices to convince central government of the uniqueness of their regions, variation of problems and issues and demand a less uniform approach to policy from the Treasury and central government departments. For example, David J. Hunter and Gerald Wistow have concluded that in community care policy variation in both means and ends of the policy spectrum was required, thus testing the notion of public uniformity (1987, p. 21).

The fiscal and political assault on local government, the privatization of nationalized industries, the challenge to trade unions, decline of manufacturing industry and cuts in public services and subsidies during the last ten years have weakened the role of a number of prominent interest groups in the process of government. Consequently, local authority associations, public sector unions, the Confederation of British Industry, professional organizations such as the British Medical Association and the National Farmers' Union have had less influence on government policy than was the case during the 1960s and 1970s when decision-making was characterized by a 'corporate' relationship between government ministers, bureaucracies and representatives of organized interests. The decline of Parliament in the process of government and the continuation of 'consensus' politics made public policy both predictable and uniform, strengthening the role of the civil service and Whitehall lobby groups. Since 1979 the position has changed markedly not only for the TUC but for the CBI as well. The days of 'beer and sandwiches at No. 10' have long gone and the CBI has been ignored regularly when it has called for a modification in government policy. Although there may still be a corporate tendency in British government (Middlemas, 1979), this tends to manifest itself in the relationship between central government, non-governmental bodies and business interests in the locality rather than in Whitehall.

For all the changes that have taken place during the past ten years, the public sector remains strong. As Geoffrey K. Fry (1988) has pointed out, the non-industrial civil service has not so far been reduced significantly in size. The state retains overall responsibility for defence and foreign policy, the environment, public health and education, economic and fiscal planning, social security and a wide range of associated services. The extent to which any government can privatize state concerns, cut public expenditure, encourage competitive tendering and promote 'market' competition in service provision rests upon how far people depend upon or perceive that they depend upon the state. So far, 'rolling back the state' has not created a legitimation crisis for the state, in spite of the fact that in a number of key services, notably health and education, government does not appear to be 'delivering the goods'. So long as these shortcomings can be offset by satisfying the material interests that consumer credit, low inflation and tax cuts can provide, there is not likely to be such a crisis. There are several paradoxes associated with current policy about which students and practitioners of public sector management and public policy need to be aware. The paradox of regional divisions and unformity of policy is one; the extension of consumer choice and erosion of local democracy and accountability is another; the politicization of bureaucracies accountable to central government and the depoliticization of local government services is a third. The aim of rolling back the state while strengthening central government is perhaps the most obvious of all.

Many of the issues raised in this introduction are dealt with in more specific and applied form in the following chapters, which are concerned with the environment of the public sector, the institutional framework, strategic and operational management as well as management techniques and approaches in a number of different areas. All are concerned with recent trends and developments and many emphasize future uncertainties. If there is a common theme to be drawn from the various chapters it is that the public sector is concerned not only with processes and techniques but also with the wider environment. It has broad, strategic aspects as well as narrower, operational ones. The public sector manager in a changing, uncertain environment needs to be concerned not only with his or her day-to-day tasks but increasingly with evaluating the utilization of private sector values and techniques in the implementation of public policy.

References

Audit Commission (1983), *Improving Economy, Efficiency and Effectiveness in Local Government in England and Wales* (HMSO).

Beveridge, W. (1944), *Full Employment in a Free Society* (London: Allen & Unwin).

Bourne, John (1979), *Management in Central and Local Government* (London: Pitman).

Brech, E. F. L. (1972), *Managing for Revival* (London: BIM).

Brown, William (1986), 'The Changing Role of Trade Unions in the Management of Labour', *British Journal of Industrial Relations*, vol. 24, 2 July.

Chapman, Richard A. and Greenway, J. R. (1980), *The Dynamics of Administrative Reform* (London: Croom Helm).

Claycamp, H. J. (1985), 'Strategic Management Fundamentals', in H. Thomas and D. Gardner (eds), *Strategic Marketing and Management* (New York: John Wiley).

Drucker, Peter F. (1973), *Management: Tasks, Responsibilities* (London: Heinemann).

Drucker, Peter F. (1987), *The Frontiers of Management* (London: Heinemann).

Dunsire, A. (1978), *Implementation in a Bureaucracy* (Oxford: Martin Robertson).

Fry, Geoffrey K. (1988), 'The Thatcher Government, the Financial Management Initiative and the "New Civil Service"' *Public Administration*, vol. 66, no. 1, Spring.

Fulmer, R. M. (1978), *The New Management* (New York: MacMillan).

Fulton Report (1968), *The Civil Service: Report of the Committee*, Cmd 3638. (HMSO).

Hayek, F. A. (1944), *The Road to Serfdom* (London: Routledge & Kegan Paul).

Hodgkinson, Christopher (1978), *Towards a Philosophy of Administration* (Oxford: Blackwell).

Hosmer, La Rue T. (1982), *Strategic Management* (NJ: Prentice Hall).

Howe, W. Stewart (1986), *Corporate Strategy* (London: Macmillan).

Hunter, David J. and Wistow, Gerald (1987), 'The Paradox of Policy Diversity in a Unitary State: Community Care in Britain,' *Public Administration*, vol. 65, no. 1, Spring.

Keeling, Desmond (1972), *Management in Government* (London: Allen & Unwin).

Kotler, Philip (1975), *Marketing for Non-Profit Organisations* (NJ: Prentice Hall).

Leopold, John and Beaumont, Phil (1986), 'Pay Bargaining and Management Strategy in the NHS', *Industrial Relations Journal*, vol. 17, no. 1, Spring.

Leniep, E. von (1983), *Employment Growth and Structural Change* (Paris: OECD).

Lindblom, C. E. (1959), 'The Science of "Muddling Through"', *Public Administration Review*, vol. 19.

McFarland, Dalton, E. (1974), *Management: Principles and Practice* (New York: Macmillan).

McSweeney, Brendan (1988), 'Accounting for the Audit Commission', *The Political Quarterly*, vol. 59, no. 1.

Martin, Shan (1983), *Managing without Managers* (London: Sage Publications).

Middlemas, K. (1979), *Politics in Industrial Society* (London: Deutsch).

Nagel, T. (1978), 'Ruthlessness in Public Life' in S. Hampshrie (ed), *Public and Private Morality* (Cambridge: Cambridge University Press).

Newman, William H. (1958), *Administrative Action* (London: Pitman).

Perrin, John (1988), *Resource Management in the NHS* (London: Van Nostrand Reinhold).

Peters, Tom and Austin, Nancy (1985), *A Passion for Excellence* (London: Collins).

Peters, Thomas J. and Waterman, Robert H. (1982), *In Search of Excellence* (New York: Harper & Row).

Richardson, J. J. and Jordan, A. (1979), *Governing Under Pressure* (Oxford: Martin Robertson).

Rohr, J. A. (1978), *Ethics for Bureaucrats* (New York: Dekker).

Report of the Efficiency Unit (1988), *Improving Management in Government: The Next Steps* (HMSO).

Roll, Y. and Moran, S. (1984), 'Hospital Productivity Measurement: an Engineering Approach', *Omega*, vol. 12, no. 5.

Schroeder, Roger G. (1981), *Operations Management* (New York: McGraw-Hill).

Simon, Herbert A. (1945), *Administrative Behaviour* (New York: Collier Macmillan).

Taylor, F. W. (1911), *Scientific Management* (New York: Harper).

Thomas, Rosamund (1978), *The British Philosophy of Administration* (New York: Longman).

Wildavsky, A. (1980), *The Art and Craft of Policy Analysis* (London: Macmillan).

Wild, Ray (1980), *Operations Management: A Policy Framework* (Oxford: Pergamon).

Wilson, Woodrow (1887), 'The Study of Administration', *Political Science Quarterly*, vol. 2.

1 The public sector economy in the 1980s

MARTIN UPTON

'Public expenditure is at the heart of Britain's economic difficulties.' These were the first words in the Conservative government's White Paper on public spending in 1979 (Cmnd 7746). This interpretation of the public sector economy has underpinned policy on public expenditure since that date. It may be difficult to reconcile the statement with the perception of the public sector's activities and output since the provision of defence, policing, education, the health service, pensions, social services and major consumer services like water and electricity would seem to be facets of a civilized and prosperous society rather than the source of 'economic difficulties'. To understand this issue and to enable an evaluation of government policy towards the public sector in the 1980s it is first necessary to appreciate the composition of the public sector, the differences between the outputs of the public sector and private sector economies and the debate about the impact of public spending on the economy.

The public sector economy – its composition and growth

The White Paper on Public Expenditure, which has been published annually since 1969, represents the yearly culmination of the public sector planning process by the government and provides a financial summary of the public sector economy.[1] A summary of the annual planning process is provided in Table 1.1 indicating that the White Paper is usually published early in the year shortly before the Chancellor's Budget Statement. The table also indicates that the annual debate about public spending is about its composition as well as its total level.

Table 1.1   *The Public Expenditure Planning Process*

Period in financial year	
April, May, June	Government departments work up spending bids for future years.
July	Overall planning totals agreed in Cabinet.
July, August	Spending guidelines and initial Rate Support Grant totals for local government announced.
September, October	Bilateral negotiations between Treasury and spending departments. Use of 'Star Chamber' (a special committee established by the Cabinet) to resolve disputes on bids for resources.
November	Departmental totals agreed. Details given in Chancellor's 'Autumn Statement'.
December, January	Detailed estimates drawn up.
February	Public Expenditure White Paper published.
March, April	Budget Statement followed by Finance Bill and commencement of financial year incorporating the agreed plans.

The Public Expenditure White Paper gives out-turn details of public spending in the immediately preceding years, estimates of the out-turn spending in the current year and the plans for spending in the following three financial years. The details in the document enable the public sector economy to be divided between:

(a) service categories: defence, education, social security, etc.;
(b) the spending bodies: the central government departments, local government, the Welsh, Scottish and Northern Ireland offices;
(c) current and capital expenditure;
(d) those areas of the public sector whose output is 'marketed' (i.e. where goods are produced for sale – like coal and electricity) and those areas whose output is 'non-marketed' (e.g. the provision of social services).

Collectively the data show the total level of public spending and the changing composition of the public sector economy. For much of the last two decades the White Paper has catalogued an expansion in the total level of public spending.

A summary of public expenditure growth since 1960 is given in Table 1.2. Total expenditure is expressed at constant 1985 prices to depict the trend in 'real' spending and is also expressed as a percent-

Table 1.2 Public Spending since 1960 (UK: Summary), (£m cash prices, unless specified)

Year	Total spending	Total spending (1985 prices)	Goods and Services Current spending	Goods and Services Capital spending	Grants and subsidies current spending	Capital transfers, debt interest and net lending	Total spending as % of GDP[b]
1960	8,944	68,013	4,236	843	2,156	1,709	34
1965	13,324	84,979	6,011	1,493	3,344	2,476	37
1970	20,897	106,721	9,033	2,447	5,383	4,034	40
1975	51,470	142,469	23,131	4,986	14,286	9,067	49
1980	104,060	147,258	48,936	5,549	33,016	16,559	45
1985	157,532	157,532	74,012	7,156	57,199	19,165	45

Notes: [a] Net lending to public corporations, private sector and overseas and cash expenditure on company securities (net).
[b] Some published measures of public expenditure as a proportion of Gross Domestic Product (GDP) exclude debt interest and net lending in the totals of spending. Such an adjustment would reduce the percentages shown in the table by approximately 6 per cent in each year.

Source: *Economic Trends Annual Supplement*, 1987 ed (CSO), Table 153.

age of Gross Domestic Product to indicate the changing share of the economy accounted for by the public sector.

Three presentational factors relating to the data in Table 1.2 require clarification. First, spending levels are shown in *cash* terms, reflecting the government's practice since 1981 of planning public expenditure in terms of cash rather than 'volume'. The distinction is important – cash planning shows the cost of providing planned services at their estimated out-turn cash cost; volume planning shows the cost of future services using a constant price base, with the plans being subsequently updated to take account of inflation between the price base adopted and actual price levels. Reservations about volume planning had been held in the late 1960s,[2] but by 1980 with price inflation above 20 per cent the Conservative government decreed that volume planning was a recipe for an open-ended cash cost for public services. The switch to cash planning, with optimistic assumptions about future levels of inflation often being adopted within the planning process, became a vital tool in constraining the growth of public spending in the 1980s. Secondly, spending levels in Table 1.2 are divided between *current* and *capital* expenditure. Current expenditure relates to cash spent on wages, salaries and consumable goods and services. Transfer payments like pensions and unemployment benefit also count as current expenditure. Capital expenditure relates to spending on fixed capital formation – like roads, bridges, school buildings and housing – where the asset acquired is used over several years. In theory there are supposed to be financing differences between the two with current expenditure being funded by the government's tax and other income receipts and capital expenditure being funded through the issue of government debt. In recent years, however, and particularly during the 1970s, government borrowing has been greater than the level of capital spending implying that the government has been funding a proportion of its current spending by borrowing as opposed to raising taxes. Thirdly, it is the government's practice to net the proceeds from the sale of assets off the total spending level rather than to show such proceeds as an enhancement to income. During the period of intensive selling of public assets during the 1980s this accounting treatment deflated the level of public expenditure. In 1984/5, for example, asset sales realized £2.1 billion.

Once these presentational points are appreciated certain important observations about the public sector economy can be gleaned from Table 1.2. First, public spending has grown significantly in real terms and as a percentage of GDP since 1960. The growth has not been uninterrupted; in 1968 public expenditure cuts were made in the wake of the devaluation of the pound in November 1967 in an attempt to reduce the balance of payments deficit; in 1977 sharp public expenditure cuts were implemented following the sterling crisis of autumn 1976 and the infamous review of the economy by the International Monetary Fund (Holmes, 1985, ch. 5). The late 1970s and early 1980s nevertheless witnessed a renewed real growth in public spending levels despite the plans and protestations of the Conservative government. Secondly, Table 1.2 indicates a shift within total spending from capital to current expenditure. Since the early 1970s capital spending has fallen in real terms to levels below the size of the government's public sector borrowing requirement (PSBR). This phenomenon says much about the relative abilities of governments to control and cut different types of spending: capital spending may always be curtailed quite quickly by the issuing of directives to central government spending departments and local government on permitted expenditure and borrowing levels. There is also the tendency for capital spending plans to 'slip' (i.e. fall behind the planned timescale for completion) due to climatic, planning or technical problems. Current spending is less easy to cut with a large proportion of this expenditure being made of transfer payments (represented in Table 1.2 within the total for current spending on grants and subsidies). Transfer payments are a 'demand related' element of public spending, meaning that expenditure is dependent upon the number of people entitled to and claiming pension and social security payments. Unlike other areas of the public sector, expenditure on transfer payments is not amenable to 'cash limiting'. Elsewhere much of the total of current expenditure relates to the salaries of public sector employees; reducing expenditure in this area can only be achieved at the cost of higher unemployment and by reducing the manpower available for the provision of public services.

Table 1.3 provides a service breakdown of public expenditure, comparing the shares taken by each service category in 1978/9 and 1984/5 with the planned shares for 1988/9 indicated in the 1986 Public Expenditure White Paper. The statistics highlight the domination of total spending by social security and health and personal social services (PSS) which collectively account for over two-fifths of the total with the vast majority of these services being provided through the Department of Health and Social Security.[3] The plan for 1988/9 sees these services increasing their share of total spending over the 1984/5 levels – largely as a result of the growing demands placed on these services by the ageing trend in the distribution of the population. Defence and education are the other two high-spending

Table 1.3   *Public Spending by Function*

Service	1984/5 £bn	% of totals for the year		
		1978/9	1984/5	1988/9 (plan)
Employment/Training	3.1	1.6	2.3	2.7
Health and PSS	19.6	13.9	14.7	16.2
Law and Order	6.0	3.7	4.5	4.7
Defence	17.2	11.3	12.9	12.9
Agriculture, Fisheries, Food	2.4	1.5	1.8	1.8
Transport	5.5	4.9	4.1	4.0
Industry, Trade, Energy	5.8	5.1	4.3	1.0
Housing[a]	5.9	7.6	4.4	3.7
Education and Science	17.0	14.3	12.8	12.1
Social Security	39.3	25.6	29.5	32.3
Other	11.5	10.5	8.7	12.9
Total[b]	133.3	100.0	100.0	104.3

Notes: [a] Housing figures are gross of receipts.
      [b] Total figure for 1984/5 is gross of privatization proceeds and housing receipts.
Source: *The Government's Expenditure Plans 1986/7 to 1988/9*, Cmnd 9702 – I HM Treasury, 1986, p. 20; Cmnd 9702 – II HM Treasury, 1986, pp. 17.

services – and since these services are largely not demand related they have tended to bear the brunt of cuts in public spending when these have been made in the last two decades. The falling share of total spending accounted for by education relates to the declining numbers of school pupils and students following the reduction in the birth rate in the 1960s. The growing share for employment and training reflects the cost of training schemes, like YTS, introduced to combat the growing level of unemployment which increased from 1.4 million to 3.2 million between 1978 and 1986. Higher shares for law and order and defence expenditure reflect the policy priorities of the Conservative governments during the 1980s, while the decline in the share planned for industry, energy and trade relates to the aim to eliminate subsidies to the private sector and the reduction in the extent of public industry via privatization.

Table 1.4 provides a summary showing who is responsible for undertaking public spending. Central government is responsible for spending nearly three-quarters of total public expenditure while local government spends most of the rest. Approximately 70 per cent of central government spending is voted by Parliament through the annual supply estimates. The remainder consists

Table 1.4 *Expenditure by Spending Authority*

Authority	1984/5 out-turn £bn	% of total	1988/9 plan £bn	% of total
Central government	92.0	71.0	108.8	73.2
Local government:				
current	30.3	23.4	31.7	21.4
capital	4.5	3.5	3.9	2.6
Nationalized industries	3.8	2.9	0.0	0.0
Public corporations	1.1	0.8	1.0	0.7
Contingency reserve	0.0	0.0	8.0	5.4
Privatization proceeds	(2.1)	(1.6)	(4.7)	(3.2)
Total	129.6	100.0	148.7	100.1

Source: The Government's Expenditure Plans 1986/7 to 1988/9, Vol. II, p. 22.

mainly of social security payments from the National Insurance Fund.

Over 40 per cent of local government spending is on education, with the majority of the remainder being spent on law and order, housing and other environmental services, personal social services and transport with the responsibilities for these services being distributed between the county and district tier of local government.

The totals for nationalized industries and other public corporations are small and do not reflect their contribution and importance to the activities of the public sector economy. This is because the figures in Table 1.4 show the amounts required by nationalized industries to finance their activities after accounting for the earnings from the sale of their goods and services. These amounts are known as the external financing requirements and relate to the borrowing and leasing undertaken by the nationalized industries plus grants from the government. The figures show that the external finance requirements are expected to decline and be close to zero in net terms in the future as financial losses are reduced in some industries and the profitability of others is improved. The programme of privatization for the nationalized industries will also reduce the demands for external finance – although British Rail, British Coal and London Regional Transport are expected to remain recipients of external finance in the near future.

Table 1.5 identifies the content of public spending by economic category and confirms that a third of the total takes the form of cash

Table 1.5   *Public Spending by Economic Category*

Economic category	1984/5 £bn	1984/5 % of total	1986/7 plans £bn	1986/7 plans % of total
Transfers to the personal sector	45.5	33.7	50.2	35.1
Departmental running costs	12.0	8.9	13.3	9.3
Other public sector pay	34.6	25.6	36.3	25.4
Purchases of goods and services[a]	31.0	23.0	34.1	23.8
Transfers to the corporate sector	9.2	6.8	6.6	4.1
Payments overseas	2.7	2.0	2.5	1.7
Total[b]	134.9	100.0	143.0	99.4

Notes: [a]   Approximately two-thirds of these totals represent capital expenditure.
  [b]   The totals exclude the proceeds from privatization, allowances for the
  contingency reserve and running costs receipts.
Source: *The Government's Expenditure Plans 1986/7 to 1988/9*, Vol. I, p. 7 and
Vol. II, p. 13.

payments to the personal sector – mainly pensions and other social
security benefits. The other major form of spending is on public
sector pay which accounts for the majority of departmental running
costs in addition to the quarter of public spending absorbed by
'other public sector pay'.

The large proportion of public expenditure accounted for by the
pay bill is indicative of the labour intensiveness of the public sector
economy. Attempts to cut public spending must therefore
inevitably address the question of public sector manpower levels.
Consequently 'control totals' for running costs have been introduced as a mechanism for financial management within central
government departments. Manpower cost control is, however,
more difficult outside the central departments. Control of manpower in the armed forces is constrained by the United Kingdom's
wide-ranging defence commitments and is geared to the objectives
set out in the defence White Paper, 'The United Kingdom Defence
Programme: The Way Forward' (Cmnd 8288, 1981) – although
these commitments were latterly enhanced by the South Atlantic
manpower requirements that resulted from the 1982 Falklands War.
Within the National Health Service the Conservative government
encouraged the introduction of management initiatives in the 1980s
as a means to reduce manpower levels from their level of close to
one million. In local government, manpower accounts for about
three-quarters of current expenditure and although there was a

Table 1.6   *Public Sector Manpower 1978–84* ('000s)

Year	Central government Civil Service	Local government	Armed services	National Health Service	Nationalized industries and public corporations	Total[a]
1978/9	734	2,325	326	923	2,033	6,565
1980/1	697	2,343	336	963	1,976	6,551
1982/3	658	2,274	334	1,007	1,709	6,206
1984/5	621	2,275	336	995	1,563	6,011

Note: [a]   Totals include some employees not included within other categories.
Source: *The Government's Expenditure Plans 1986/7 to 1988/9*, Vol. II, pp. 28–9.

small reduction in numbers between 1979 and 1982 the number of employees since then has remained constant at around 2¼ million. The numbers employed by local government in education has fallen in recent years in parallel with the reduction in school rolls while those in the police have increased in accordance with the policy objectives of the Conservative governments since 1979.

The manpower statistics confirm that the greatest reduction in manpower in the public sector since 1978/9 has occurred in the nationalized industries as a result of sharp contractions in the capacity of certain state industries (e.g. British Steel) and the removal of certain firms from the public sector by privatization.

This review of the composition of the public sector economy highlights many important factors which have had a bearing on recent government policy towards public spending. First, at least three different types of goods and services provided by the public sector may be identified and the diversity in the nature of these outputs creates problems for all governments in determining the proper level for the supply of public services and the proper price (if any) to charge customers for the services. There are 'public goods' like the provision of defence, law and order, street lighting and roads, which are provided without any direct charges for the benefit of the country as a whole. In most cases with public goods it is not possible to determine who the consumers are or the extent of their consumption. In the case of defence it is arguable whether anything tangible is normally 'consumed' by the public. With 'public goods' there is little dissent between the political parties about the fact that their provision should be the responsibility of the government, with the costs being met through taxation and borrowing. There are also 'public services' like health care, education and social services for which the consumer is usually identifiable and for which a charge could be directly levied. Indeed the existence of private health and education services prove that market forces can apply to their provision. To help to ensure a healthy and educated work-force, governments since 1945 have, however, taken the responsibility for providing the vast majority of such services – usually without a direct charge to the consumers. Nevertheless even with the public sector provision of such services charges may be levied on the consumer – for example, prescription charges in the health service and tuition fees in certain sectors of higher education. Finally, there is the 'marketed output' of the public sector – chiefly the produce of the nationalized industries – which is offered to the consumer at a direct price. The determination of prices for these goods is based largely upon the interaction of the market forces of demand and supply. The importance to the economy of the output of the nationalized industries means, however, that some interference in price and supply levels has been brought to bear by most governments – particularly in the case of the fuel, power and transport industries – to ensure that social factors are accommodated in the provision of services. The continued operation of loss-making lines within the British Rail network is an example of the application of social factors in determining the supply of state industries. With such a diversity of services and goods being supplied by the public sector it is difficult for consistent and coherent policies for the sector to be applied by governments and this problem is exacerbated by the fact that the demand for some services cannot be measured accurately. It is thus hardly surprising that policy towards the public sector sometimes seems to be based upon little more than an 'ad hoc' view of what the economy can afford and what is politically expedient.

Secondly, the analysis of the public sector indicates that governments have unenviable decisions to make when reductions in public spending become necessary. People's expectations of the services to be provided by the government have been continually enhanced because the public sector economy has been growing steadily in real terms over the past 25 years and the proportion of the economy accounted by it has risen by over 10 per cent in that time. The demographic demands upon health and personal social services and upon social security payments requirements have meant that over 40 per cent of public spending is accounted for by these 'demand related' services – and any government wishing to shirk its responsibilities in these areas has to risk the potential electoral consequences. With the public sector's labour intensity extensive cuts in spending must inevitably increase unemployment. Further-more the central government only controls directly three-quarters of the public sector economy with the result that any attempts at fundamental shifts in policy towards the public sector can be under-mined by countervailing policies by local government and the nationalized industries. Certainly the last two decades have shown that the public sector economy works on a 'ratchet effect' with increases in its size being effected with ease in comparison with the difficulties in reducing its spending levels and share of the total economy.

The public sector economy – its impact on the macro-economy

In the ideal world the level of public spending would be determined solely by the need and demand for public services; in the real world, however, constraints have always existed on the total of public expenditure. The resources which are made available to the public sector are dictated by the wealth of the economy and the proportion of that wealth which is allocated, via fiscal and debt management policy, to the provision of public services. Both the composition and level of spending are determined by the prevailing political and economic wisdom about the desirability of public expenditure, an estimation of the most appropriate level for such spending and the view about which services should be provided by the government through the public sector. In these respects the control of the public sector is interrelated with the overall management of the economy. It is this complicated and much debated relationship between public spending and the macro-economy that has shaped the changing views in postwar Britain about the size and activities of the public sector.

To understand the relationship between public spending and the macro-economy it is necessary to identify the central objectives of economic management. These are a steady rate of economic growth (the annual increase in Gross National Product which indicates the rate of expansion of national wealth), a low rate of unemployment, the avoidance of inflation and the avoidance of a deficit on the balance of payments. As a demander of resources and a provider of services, the public sector has a large direct impact on all of these objectives: price and wage levels set in the public sector affect the inflation rate; around a third of the labour force is employed in the public sector; and parts of the public sector – particularly the nationalized industries – are engaged in foreign trade. Clearly the management of the size and activities of the public sector is inevitably central to the management of the macro-economy as a whole. Two major problems exist, however, for governments attempting to gear the management of the public sector to their strategy for macro-economic policy. First, there is much debate about how the objectives of economic management 'trade-off' against each other. Many economists have argued that there is a 'trade-off' between inflation and unemployment (Phillips, 1958) with low inflation being achieved only at the cost of higher unemployment. Fast economic growth may create inflationary pressures and a deficit on the balance of payments by boosting demand for imports of raw materials. Consequently the simultaneous attainment of a satisfactory level for all the objectives of economic management is generally deemed unlikely as a result of these 'trade-offs'. The upshot is that governments tend to aim at a mixture of differential achievement on these objectives – with some governments focusing on the elimination of inflation and others concentrating on lowering unemployment and stimulating growth. It is this debate about how the goals of economic management 'trade-off' against each other and the varying priorities adopted by governments in the pursuit of the goals that creates much uncertainty about how and towards what ends the public sector economy should be managed. A government wishing to cut unemployment may, for example, normally be more inclined to boost public spending than a government concentrating on the elimination of inflation. Secondly, there is considerable debate about exactly what effects public spending has on the rest of the economy. This debate has become very intense over the past decade and has been characterized as a confrontation between monetarism and Keynesianism. This debate which has always been tainted by social and political views about whether governments should be deeply involved in the economy or whether market forces should be allowed to predominate, has gone through two distinct phases since 1945.

The years of Keynesian consensus, 1945–70

The necessities of the Second World War radically increased government expenditure and control of the economy (Pollard, 1983, ch. 5). The war years acted as a catalyst for changes in attitudes towards the need for and ability of governments to manage the economy. The 1942 Beveridge Report (Cmd 6404), which laid the foundation stones for the postwar development of the welfare state, noted that the realization of the social objectives of eliminating want and poverty required the government to control the economy through the management of public spending:

> a satisfactory scheme of social insurance assumes the mainte-nance of employment and the prevention of mass unemploy-ment . . . unless such measures are prepared and can be effective much that might otherwise be gained through the plan for social security will be wasted. (Cmd 6404, pp. 163–5)

The same theme was taken up in the 1944 White Paper on Employ-ment (Cmd 6527) which articulated the philosophy that was to be adopted by postwar Britain of enhancing public spending to main-tain full employment.

> The Government accepts as one of their primary aims and responsibilities the maintenance of a high and stable level of employment . . . the first step in a policy of maintaining general employment must be to prevent total expenditure from falling away. (Cmd 6527, pp. 3–16)

Underpinning the sentiment in postwar Britain for expanding public services and for greater governmental regulation of the economy were the economic theories of John Maynard Keynes which provided the mechanisms for macro-economic manage-ment. At the heart of Keynesian theory is the notion of the multi-plier. Keynes stated that it is

> to the general principle of the multiplier to which we have to look for an explanation of how fluctuations in the amount of investment, which are a comparatively small proportion of the national income, are capable of generating fluctuations in aggregate employment and income so much greater in ampli-tude than themselves. (Keynes, 1936, p. 122)

Expressed simply, an injection of government spending into the economy will have a multiplier effect upon the overall level of spending as the money injected becomes 'recycled'. Government expenditure on, for example, the supply of materials for road building becomes the wages paid by the supplying firm to their work-force which in turn uses the money for shopping and so on. The injection of cash into the economy thus has an accentuated effect on the volume of economic activity. The potency of the multiplier will hinge upon how quickly money injected into the system 'leaks' out by individuals saving money instead of spending it, by people buying imports instead of domestically produced goods and by the money being paid back to the government through taxation. The higher these propensities to save, import and tax, the lower will be the multiplier and the more limited will be the effect of higher government spending on the economy.[4]

The multiplier thus provided the linchpin to Keynesian economic management; unemployment could be reduced by an increase in government spending and/or a cut in taxation. If the economy started to experience inflationary pressures demand could be reduced and inflation eased by reducing government spending and/or raising taxation. The multiplier implied that significant macro-economic change could be wielded by minor changes in public spending – although critics of Keynesian theory said that the real level and potential of the multiplier in Britain was limited because of the high rates of 'leakages' from the economy in the form of imports and taxation. Nevertheless, fuelled with a popular sanction for enlarged public services and government control of the macro-economy and confident that with Keynesian economic policies such management was feasible, postwar governments got down to the task of controlling the economy through the manipulation of public spending levels and taxation.

Between 1945 and 1970 the steady expansion of public spending facilitated by the resources generated by steady economic growth coincided with low inflation rates and full employment. Although there were periodic balance of payments crises, no apparent contradiction existed between an enlarged public sector and the economic and social well-being of the community. Despite these outward signs of success some weaknesses were detected in the Keynesian 'model'. The regulation of the economy through frequent changes in public spending created a 'stop–go' effect with economic activity being successively stimulated to enhance growth and constrained to reduce inflationary pressures. 'Stop–go' adversely affected long-term planning and investment by industry and the 1975 report by the House of Lords Select Committee on Overseas Trade confirmed that among the reasons for Britain's low investment rate were:

the lack of confidence which firms placed in the future . . . uncertainty as to changes in policy of successive governments, high capital taxation and the high cost of capital . . . . . (House of Lords, 1985, 238–41, pp. 22–5)

Table 1.7   *The PSBR in the 1960s*

Year	PSBR £m	PSBR as % of GDP
1964/5	980	2.9
1965/6	1,170	3.2
1966/7	949	2.5
1967/8	1,847	4.5
1968/9	1,253	2.8
1969/70	(534)	−1.1

Source: Economic Trends Annual Supplement, 1987 ed (CSO), Table 156.

By the 1960s the steady growth in public spending was leading to an expansion of the public sector borrowing requirement. The increase in wage and price inflation and the social security reforms introduced by the Labour governments in the mid-1960s helped to enlarge further the PSBR, casting doubts about the economic effects of higher public spending and resulting in the need for public expenditure cuts in 1968.

Further criticisms of Keynesian management hinged upon the feasibility of a government steering the economy towards the selected economic goals when time lags in obtaining information on the state of the economy and acting upon it were always likely to lead to a mismatch between policy and the prevailing needs of the economy. Furthermore, Keynesian policies seemed less adept at handling the balance of payments crises that dominated the economy in the 1960s than at controlling the level of employment.

Whatever the growing disillusionment in the 1960s about the Keynesian view on public expenditure, the growth of public spending in postwar Britain and the expansion of the public sector economy were central to the maintenance of low unemployment rates at a time when the labour force was expanding in size rapidly. It was therefore understandable that until the 1970s the prevailing wisdom of governments was that a buoyant public sector economy contributed to, rather than detracted from, the health of the overall economy.

The years of post-Keynesian debate, 1970–1986

In January 1970 the Conservative Shadow Cabinet met at Selsdon Park to shape their party's strategy for the next general election. The philosophy and policies that emerged marked a turning point in postwar attitudes towards the public sector economy. The 'Selsdon' view was that the high levels of government spending and the associated high tax rates were producing socialism in Britain through the back door of Keynesian policies. The Conservative party's strategy was to roll back the level of public expenditure thereby facilitating cuts in taxation and a reduction in the role of the government in the economy. Among the policies advocated was the reduction in aid to ailing industries and the abolition of statutory prices and incomes policies. The 'Selsdon' view was in clear contrast to the conventional wisdom of Keynesian economics; it was stressed that the health and expansion of the private sector was contingent upon reducing government spending and liberating market forces. The application of this philosophy proved difficult in practice after the Conservatives had won the June 1970 general election. After an eighteen-month flirtation with reduced governmental involvement in the economy a reversion to a Keynesian reflation with higher public spending and tax cuts occurred in 1973. This 'U-turn' on policy was a reaction to the upswing in unemployment – which rose above one million in 1972 – and the near collapse of leading firms including Rolls-Royce and Upper Clyde Shipbuilders.

The arguments for reducing the size of the public sector economy were not abandoned for long. After the sterling crisis of autumn 1976 and the subsequent financial support provided to Britain by the IMF, a cluster of economic theories emerged which exemplified the adverse effects that high public spending levels had on the economy. The New Cambridge School (Cripps and Godley, 1976) expounded a theory that the size of the balance of payments deficit was directly related to the PSBR – implying that an elimination of deficits on the external account required reduced government spending.

Of greater significance to future policy was the 'crowding out' theory (Bacon and Eltis, 1976; Brunner and Meltzer, 1976). Its basic theme was that, in the long term, an expansion of the public sector would not stimulate overall economic activity since an enlarged public sector could be achieved only at the expense of a reduction in activity in the private sector. Higher public spending would therefore only result in a shift in the balance of the economy between the public and private sectors – it would not generate greater economic wealth in total. The 'crowding out' theory has two strands: real resource crowding out and financial crowding out. Real resource crowding out relates to the shortages of skilled labour and materials that may be experienced by the private sector if public spending is increased and such resources are drawn into the public sector. Financial crowding out relates to the way the government finances higher public sector activity – either tax rates will be raised or interest rates will be forced up as the government funds the resultant increase in the PSBR through the issue of debt. Crowding out occurs here because the private sector, confronted by higher interest rates and taxation, has less retained income and is thus less able to undertake investment. Other refinements of the crowding out theories divided the economy between the marketed and the non-marketed sectors. The marketed sector includes the private sector plus the marketed parts of the public sector (i.e. the nationalized industries and most public corporations). The non-marketed sector incorporates those parts of the public sector whose goods and services are not sold to the public and whose 'outputs' or benefits to the community are sometimes immeasurable (e.g. defence). Any expansion of the non-marketed sector through higher public expenditure would be at the expense of the marketed sector which produces 'real' goods with the result that economic growth and material living standards may be reduced.

These explanations of low investment and poor economic growth in Britain which are offered by the crowding out theories have the virtues of simplicity and apparent voracity. There would appear to be little substance to the real resource strand of the theory. With unemployment rising dramatically between the 1960s and the 1980s there seems little logic in arguing that the expansion of the public sector was generating a labour shortage for the private sector. In any case the expansion of public sector employment was facilitated by the expansion of the labour force and the increased participation in the labour force by women and not by labour drawn from the private sector. While some parts of the private sector have experienced shortages of skilled labour this has not largely been the fault of the increase in numbers employed in the public sector. Financial crowding out is a more tenable argument although the relationships between the PSBR and the level of interest rates, and between interest and tax rates and the level of investment are complicated and uncertain. Certainly interest rates rose to historically high levels in the late 1970s (with minimum lending rate rising to 17 per cent in November 1979), but it is questionable whether periodic changes in interest rates have a marked impact upon the long-term plans of industry.

The re-emergence of monetarism (Friedman, 1968; Laidler, 1976) in the 1970s also provided a theoretical basis for linking a reduction in the size of the public sector to the elimination of inflation which by 1975 had reached 24 per cent. Monetarist theories attributed inflation to excess growth in the money supply with the cause of excess growth being excessive public spending – since this may be financed by expanding the stock of money or quasi-money in the economy.[5] Cutting inflation therefore required a reduction in public expenditure. Most of the leading monetarists in the 1970s also subscribed to the 'crowding out' thesis and to the view that market forces should not be inhibited by governmental regulation (Friedman and Friedman, 1980). As a consequence the package of policies adopted towards public spending by the Conservative governments of 1979 and 1983 have commonly become termed 'monetarist' despite the fact that the chief tenet of monetarism – tight control of the money supply – ceased to be central to the strategy of the Conservative government after 1984 (Nield, 1985).

By the end of the 1970s a collection of economic theories had emerged which explicitly or implicitly gave the cause of Britain's economic problems of inflation and slow growth as an oversized public sector and an excessive growth of governmental expenditure. These theories also laid greater stress on the 'supply side' of the economy, arguing that the supply of goods and services within the economy would not necessarily respond to increases in demand generated by higher public spending. These views were starkly in contrast to the interpretation offered by the Keynesian demand management theories which dominated government policy until the 1970s. Even during the latter stages of the Callaghan government between 1977 and 1979 greater control of money supply combined with public expenditure cuts was viewed by the Labour administration as a valid means of reducing inflationary pressure in the economy. The May 1979 general election saw a Conservative government elected which identified lower inflation and faster growth as the key goals of economic policy, found the 'crowding out' and monetarist theories of Britain's economic difficulties sound, found the policy prescriptions of these theories – chiefly reducing public spending and government controls on the private sector – ideologically attractive, and appointed advisers[6] on economic policy who subscribed to this approach to economic management. The years after 1979 thus saw radical changes in the composition of and policy towards the public sector economy.

Restructuring the public sector economy, 1979–1986

The reduction in public expenditure was axiomatic to the economic strategy of the Conservative government from May 1979. The objective proved highly difficult to realize. It has already been observed that the demands on social security expenditure from demographic trends and rising unemployment were putting upward pressure on public spending. In addition central government only directly controlled three-quarters of public spending, with local authorities and nationalized industries having their own inputs into the public expenditure total. Further problems, which were more specific to the economy in the late 1970s, threatened the Conservatives' plans for cutting spending. First, the Conservatives were committed to *increasing* public expenditure on certain services – principally defence and law and order (Cmnd 7841, 1980, part 1, p. 6). Additionally the decision to replace key defence systems (e.g. replacing Polaris with Trident), added to projected public spending in the 1980s. Cutting total spending while simultaneously boosting expenditure on selected major services was to prove an impractical equation. Secondly, the late 1970s saw an upswing in price inflation (which reached 21.5 per cent in 1980) largely as a result of higher oil prices. This further encouraged an increase in the rate of wage inflation on top of the acceleration in wage growth that resulted from the abandonment of pay controls, the pay settlements resulting from the 1978/9 'winter of discontent' and the Clegg Commission's comparability studies.[7] The effects on public spending levels were considerable given the labour intensiveness of the public sector. Thirdly, both the Conservative government of 1970–4 and the Labour government during the 1978/9 'winter of discontent' had experienced the potency of trade unions in the public sector in changing government policy. Introducing significant changes in the structure and size of the public sector was likely to invoke strong union resistance. The series of Acts introduced to regulate trade union activities after 1979 was thus a vital tool in the Conservatives' policy towards the public sector. Finally, many government public expenditure commitments are dictated by international laws or agreements which cannot be unilaterally ignored by the British government: defence expenditure levels are influenced by the commitment to NATO; EEC regulations have increasingly had an impact upon expenditure on social security, farming support and other public services as well as creating, through the annual contribution to the EEC budget, its own element of public expenditure.

Confronted with these problems the approach of the Conservative government was to apply fundamental structural changes to the public sector economy as well as adopting the more usual 'incrementalist' methods to attempt to change, to lower real levels, the volume of public spending. Tighter control over public expenditure planning, the encouragement of value for money (VFM) studies, the insistence upon greater competition in the provision of public services and the privatization of wide areas of the public sector economy were all features of the strategy. Underpinning these changes was a distinct move towards the greater centralization of control by the government over all areas of public spending.

Central government expenditure

The main platform for the planning of government spending from 1980 was the Medium Term Financial Strategy (MTFS) which attempted to co-ordinate and control the levels and growth of public spending, the PSBR and money supply over a four-year period. This approach to financial policy was intended to avoid the pitfalls of short-term economic planning (for example, stop-go) and gear policy towards the chief goal of the reduction of inflation. Reductions in public expenditure were viewed as paramount if the MTFS was to succeed in combating inflation – particularly because the Conservatives' promise in 1979 to cut personal taxation threatened an increase in the PSBR unless spending could be curtailed. Other important changes in the planning of government spending were adopted with cash planning replacing volume planning in 1981. This change, together with the continued application of cash limits on spending departments, produced an expenditure planning process that was less likely to be blown off course by changes in inflation rates. Much tighter control was exerted over the activities of the spending departments by the Treasury and the establishment of the 'Star Chamber' system (a special Cabinet committee) headed by Viscount Whitelaw for making decisions on the bids by government departments for additional resources, for resolving debates on spending and for determining the distribution of the public spending total.

The £150 million cut in grant aid distributed through the UGC to universities, which was announced in 1981, together with the £130 million cut in support for the BBC and other cuts in foreign aid, legal aid and in grants for the Arts Council, were examples of the 'fringe' areas of public expenditure which the government attempted to trim in the early 1980s. These cuts attracted major opposition even from within the Conservative party whilst doing little to reduce total government spending.

The theme of value for money was reflected in the establishment of the National Audit Office in 1983, the reorganization of the government's auditing service and the work of Sir Derek Rayner who was brought in from Marks and Spencer to identify areas for economies in the government departments. Modest savings were achieved through these initiatives and by the implementation of the plans in the 1980 White Paper on *Non-Departmental Public Bodies*. The Conservatives' election manifesto in 1983 was able to boast that 500 quangos had been eliminated during their period of office, helping to achieve a reduction in the number of civil servants.

It became increasingly clear that if major cuts in central government spending were to be made the largest spending departments, Defence and the DHSS, would have to make extensive economies. The 1981 Defence Review made several recommendations for cost cutting including a sharp reduction in the size of the Navy. Such reforms invoked fierce opposition from many Conservatives who saw the proposals as alien to the party's election pledge in 1979 to strengthen defence. The 1982 Falklands War, however, interrupted the plans for defence savings and undermined the proposals for a small Navy.

Difficult problems were also posed by the vast and rapidly expanding social security budget. Constraining benefits expenditure was made more difficult by the doubling of unemployment between 1979 and 1983. Some attempts to trim expenditure were made with the elimination of the earnings related supplement to unemployment benefit in 1982 and the greater clampdown on social security fraud. These marginal changes were deemed inadequate with the result that the Secretary of State for Social Services, Norman Fowler, developed and outlined in the 1985 White Paper, *Reform of Social Security: Programme for Action* (Cmnd 9691), the ill-fated proposals for the fundamental reform of the social security system. The White Paper's proposals included modifying the state earnings related pension scheme (SERPS) to reduce the growing costs to the Exchequer, encouraging the development of occupational and personal pension schemes and simplifying the housing benefit system. The plans aimed to reduce the costs of the social security system with the intention that £450 million would be cut from the cost of housing benefit. The opposition that the plans have invoked underlines the difficulties governments have had in making economies in the social security budget. Cuts in central government spending thus proved to be difficult and controversial even within the Conservative party. The one significant achievement was the reduction in the size of the civil service which fell by 113,000 between 1979 and 1985.

Local government expenditure

The difficulties in making local authorities of differing political persuasions to the Conservative government abide by the philosophy of a smaller public sector economy frequently came to light after 1979 in a series of hard-fought battles over legislation and the reform of local government.

The central planks of action were more extensive controls on local authority revenue and capital spending. Capital allocations, which give local authorities the power to borrow to finance capital spending, were reduced in real level. The use of capital receipts to finance capital spending was also limited by the application of percentage limits on their use to supplement borrowing allocations. This latter policy was rather ironic given that the majority of capital receipts obtained by local authorities were from the council house sales which followed the introduction of the 1980 Housing Act. These receipts provided local authorities with substantial amounts of capital cash which could be used to finance new capital spending or to reduce outstanding debt and their volume necessitated action by the government to prevent capital spending targets being breached.

The revenue constraints imposed on local government provoked even greater debate with the 1980s seeing a reduction in the percentage of total local government spending met by government grants. An increasingly higher proportion of spending had to be met from local rates, with the result that authorities that were anxious about the electoral implications of higher rates would be deterred from raising their spending levels. This manoeuvre also shifted the requirement to tax from central government, which finances grants to local authorities out of tax receipts, towards local government.

The increases in rate levels prompted by the reduction in government grant[8] were accentuated by the decision to add to the grant system a series of revenue spending targets for all local authorities in the 1980s. If these targets, that were based either upon previous years' spending levels or targets were exceeded, a penalty system by way of reductions in grant came into force for the overspending authorities. Once again the impact of reduced grant was higher rate levels, and the prospect of the adverse electoral response to higher

Table 1.8　*Rate of Grant Support to Local Government – Great Britain*
£m

Year	Local government current and capital spending	Local government spending relevant for Exchequer grant support[a] (planning totals)	Total Exchequer grants	Rate of grant support (%)
1978/79	17.7	12.5	7.6	61.0
1979/80	21.3	14.1	8.6	61.0
1980/81	24.7	15.7	9.6	61.0
1981/82	26.2	18.4	10.9	59.3
1982/83	28.7	20.5	11.5	56.1
1983/84	32.7	22.3	11.8	52.9
1984/85 (estimate)	34.4	22.9	11.9	52.0
1985/86 (estimate)	34.8	24.2	11.8	48.4

Note: [a]　Only certain categories of current expenditure are eligible for grant support.
Sources: *The Government's Expenditure Plans 1986/87 to 1988/89*, Vol. II, p. 339. Rate Support Grant 1980/81; 1981/82: Associations of Local Authorities. Local Government Finance (England and Wales): Rate Support Grant 1981/82; 1982/83; 1983/84; 1984/85; 1985/86 (Main Reports).

rates was intended to encourage authorities to cut spending rather than incur penalties. During the lifespan of the target system, between 1981/2 and 1985/6, the extent of the collective budgeted overspend against targets by local authorities was reduced – although it still stood at £771 million in 1983/84.

The target system was abandoned because the 1984 Rates Act had introduced 'rate-capping' as an alternative and more potent means of controlling local government spending. Under the terms of the Act the government could, either on a selective or universal basis, impose a maximum rate levy for local authorities. By simultaneously limiting grants and rate income through the rate levy limit, the government secured the means for total central control over local authority spending. Nineteen local authorities were selected for rate-capping in the first year of operation in 1985/6. To date rate-capping has only been applied on a selective basis, although reserve powers to apply it to all but the lowest spending local authorities exist within the Act.

The 1986 Green Paper on Local Government Finance presages still greater central government controls with non-domestic rates

Table 1.9 Sales of Public Sector Dwellings 1979/80 to 1984/85

Year	Local authority sales	Total public sector sales[b]	Capital receipts from sales[a]	
			annual (£m)	cumulative (£m)
1979/80	53,500	55,300	472	472
1980/81	68,200	71,800	603	1,075
1981/82	128,200	141,400	1,045	2,120
1982/83	181,200	204,600	1,877	3,997
1983/84	122,000	144,200	1,955	5,952
1984/85 (estimate)	91,600	105,400	1,784	7,736

Notes: [a] The totals for capital receipts include, but are not exclusively, the product of the sale of dwellings.
[b] Public sector sales also include those by Housing Associations and New Town Corporations.
Source: The Government's Expenditure Plans 1986/87 to 1988/89, Vol. II, pp. 140 and 146.

being fixed and collected by the government and shared out to local authorities on a per capita basis. The promise of domestic rates being superseded by a community charge on each adult in the near future indicates that still further radical changes to local authorities' fiscal powers are pending.

The encouragement of privatization and the requirement for greater competition were two further facets of government policy towards local authority services. One form of privatization, council house sales, has radically altered the social fabric of the housing market as well as reducing local authorities' direct role in housing provision and providing authorities with substantial capital receipts.

The 1980 Local Government Planning and Land Act made local authorities' direct labour organizations (DLOs) submit to a competitive tendering process when large contracts are let. DLOs are also expected to operate at a profit, with a 5 per cent return on capital, so that their services do not draw on authorities' rate income. Competition from the private sector for the provision of traditional local authority services – particularly cleaning services, refuse collection and the supply of school meals – has also been encouraged. The move to introduce competition on bus routes was taken by several local authorities before the 1985 Transport Act made competition obligatory for all areas from October 1986.

To encourage greater value for money the Audit Commission was established in 1983 to co-ordinate the operations of local authorities' external auditors and to encourage greater cost efficiency, economy and effectiveness in the provision of services.

Finally, an important structural change to local government came with the abolition of the six metropolitan county councils and the Greater London Council at the end of 1985/86, with these authorities' services being transferred to the district councils within each county or, in the case of fire, transport and police services, being transferred to a joint board covering the county area, or being phased out. The government's plan was to make economies by eliminating the duplication of services in the upper and lower tiers of local government in the counties. It seems unlikely, however, that significant real savings will be achieved through reorganization. Since the counties and the GLC were, at the time of their abolition, run by Labour groups who were vociferous opponents of the Conservative government's policy towards the public sector, it would seem that their abolition was an act of political rather than economic convenience.

With these extensions of government control over the activities and financial independence of local authorities, the balance of power in Britain between central and local government has been radically altered since 1979. The latitude for determining service levels and the rate levy to support service expenditure has been substantially curtailed with local authority spending being put at the forefront of the Conservative government's attempts to reduce the size of the public sector economy.

Nationalized industry and public corporation expenditure

The post-1979 strategy to reduce the level of public spending incurred in supporting the nationalized industries had three facets. First, external financing limits (EFLs) – were applied and attempts were made to reduce grant aid. This strategy was designed to encourage the industries to generate more income internally (through higher sales and higher prices) thereby reducing their need to borrow and eliminating their trading losses (or boosting their profits). This strategy ran into problems; some of the nationalized industries had been running at severe losses throughout the 1970s and the recessions which followed the surges in oil prices in 1973/74 and 1978/79 accentuated the problems of excess capacity and low productivity. Nevertheless by the early 1980s the external financing and grant aid requirements of the nationalized industries were very

Table 1.10   *State Industries: EFLs and Grant Aid 1979 to 1985 (£m)*

State industry	Out-turn external financing			Grant aid (capital and revenue)		
	1979/80	1981/2	1984/85[a]	1979/80	1981/2	1984/85[a]
British Coal	651	1,225	1,720	244	334	1,538
Electricity Council[b]	189	(221)	850	5	9	8
British Gas	(447)	39	(189)			
British Steel	579	766	523			
Post Office	240	(19)	(100)			
British Airways	171	149	(335)			
British Rail	714	960	1,045	687	881	923
Water Authorities[c]	n/a	n/a	286	n/a	n/a	
Total[d]	2,613	3, 254	3,827	1,087	1,391	2,715

Notes: [a]   The figures for 1984/85 were distorted by the effects of the miners'
strike between March 1984 and March 1985.

[b]   Figures are the totals for Electricity (England and Wales); North of
Scotland Hydro-Electric Board; and South of Scotland Electricity
Board.

[c]   Figures are for Water Authorities in England and Wales. EFLs were first
applied to the Regional Water Authorities in the 1983 Public Expenditure White Paper for application from 1982/83.

[d]   Totals include figures for state industries not shown separately in Table
1.12.

Source: *The Government's Expenditure Plans 1981/82 to 1983/84*, p. 172; ibid.,
1983/84 to 1985/86, Vol. II, p. 97; ibid., *1986/87 to 1988/89*, vol. II, pp. 347.

largely accounted for by just three of the state industries – British
Coal, British Steel and British Rail.

The tightening of financial controls and the drive to eliminate
losses in the state industries in the 1980s inevitably meant plant
closures, the streamlining of activities and substantial job losses.
These occurred when the private sector was also reducing output
and the combined effect of contraction in both public and private
industry largely explains the rapid rise in the jobless total in the
1980s. The reductions in capacity were most severe in the cases of
British Steel, British Coal and British Leyland (BL) and the geographical concentration of these industries meant that regional
inequalities were accentuated by the cuts. Substantial reductions in
the rail network foreshadowed by the 1982 Serpell Report were,
however, not implemented.

The policy of tighter financial controls and plant closures was not
without its 'U-turns'. In 1981 Sir Keith Joseph as the Secretary of
State for Industry presided over additional support of £990 million

Table 1.11   *State Industries: Profits and Losses 1980/81 to 1984/85* *(£m)*

Selected state industries	Current cost operating profit (loss)[a]				
	1980/81	1981/82	1982/83	1983/84	1984/85[b]
British Coal	(300)	(248)	(275)	(718)	(1,901)
Electricity Council (England and Wales)	303	475	868	901	(1,292)
British Gas	383	312	666	668	651
British Steel	(465)	(343)	(295)	(98)	(70)
British Airways	(148)	(132)	126	232	307
Post Office and National Girobank	21	87	148	135	146
British Rail	(707)	(1,001)	(942)	(873)	(1,286)[c]
Water Authorities (England and Wales)	n/a	n/a	308	268	291

Notes: [a]   Some industries use historic costs in their accounts. The figures in their accounts will therefore differ from these in Table 1.11.
    [b]   The figures for 1984/85 for British Coal, the Electricity Council, British Steel and British Rail, were adversely affected by the March 1984 to March 1985 miners' strike.
    [c]   Figure is for a fifteen-month period from January 1, 1984 to March 31, 1985.

Source: *The Government's Expenditure Plans 1982/83 to 1984/85* (Cmnd 8494 – II); ibid., *1983/84 to 1985/86* (Cmnd 8789 – II); ibid., *1984/85 to 1986/87* (Cmnd 9143 – II); ibid., *1985/86 to 1987/88* (Cmnd 9428 – II); ibid., *1986/87 to 1988/89* (Cmnd 9702 – II).

for BL to prevent the state firm from collapsing.[9] This was soon followed by a £6.6 billion support package for the British Steel Corporation which was then losing £2 million per day and which was on the verge of liquidation. The money was injected to support the plans of the chairman, Ian MacGregor, to streamline the industry. Despite the considerable social costs of the reduction in capacity and employment, the desired effect of reducing losses was achieved in some state industries – particularly British Steel and British Airways.

The second facet of the government's strategy was the exposure of state industries to greater competition. This was partly achieved through the enactment of the 1980 Competition Act. The Act extended controls over monopolies in the private sector to certain public sector bodies defining such bodies as those supplying goods and services whose members are appointed by a Minister under legislation, plus public bus services and water undertakings, certain agricultural boards and others. A principal objective was to provide a mechanism for enquiring into the efficiency of nationalized industries (Cable, 1984, p. 217)

It had long been held within sections of the Conservative party that the losses incurred by some state industries were the result of inefficiency induced by their monopoly position. It was argued that greater competition would force the industries to cut costs and become more profitable or else lose market shares to private sector competitors.

The competition policy has proved difficult to apply. Some of the state industries are already open to competition – albeit mainly from overseas producers. This is particularly the case with Rover Group (formerly BL), British Steel and British Coal. There is the problem of how to enable true competition between private firms and state industries when the latter have already undertaken the substantial capital investments needed to meet their production requirements. The notion of competition also cuts against one of the chief reasons for the establishment of nationalized firms – namely that economies of scale and the need for national co-ordination in the supply of such basic services as transport and fuel demand the existence of a large single supplier instead of several smaller suppliers. The potential problems of encouraging competition have been demonstrated by the experiences after the deregulation of local bus services from October 1986. Many areas found that deregulation merely meant the disappearance of certain bus routes and over-congestion on other profitable routes.

Privatization was the third facet of the government's strategy with selected state industries being returned to the private sector usually through a share issue and through government holdings in certain firms' shares being reduced.

Besides the long-term and – assuming no renationalization – permanent reduction in the size of the public sector, privatization had the immediate benefit to the government of cutting the PSBR with the proceeds counting as a credit against public expenditure.

Among the problems posed by privatization was the price at which shares in the state industries should be issued to ensure that the assets of the industries were being properly valued and that sufficient investors were attracted. Some commentators observed, however, that state industries should not be sold to the public on the grounds that, through nationalization, they were already in public ownership.

Privatization has met with differing degrees of success. Some share issues fell flat – most notably the 1982 issue for Britoil where the sale was overshadowed by fears about lower oil prices. Other share issues, in particular those for Amersham International and Associated British Ports, were massively oversubscribed leading to criticisms that the government had offered the shares at unnecessarily high discounts. Some industries earmarked for privatization had their plans temporarily shelved; the privatization plans for the water industry were suspended in autumn 1986 and the plans to sell the commercial vehicles division of BL were withdrawn in spring 1986 after a last minute change of heart by the government. Table 1.12 summarizes the major privatizations between 1979 and 1986. At the end of 1985/86 the proceeds to the Treasury from privatizations had amounted to £7.6 billion.

Future policy towards the nationalized industries will be related to the plans for privatization since much of the Conservative government's strategy for state firms has been geared towards preparing them for sale. The future for privatization itself is contingent upon the continuation in office of a Conservative government. Even then the pace of privatization should slacken since many of the industries which have not been privatized to date are ostensibly less attractive to purchasers than those which have been sold, due to their records of financial losses and management problems. The privatization achieved during the mid-1980s – most notably that of British Telecom and British Gas – was fuelled by the public's growing desire for share ownership. At some point the growing participation in share ownership may be sated, particularly if a falling stock market reduces the share value of the earlier privatized companies. Nevertheless the plans for the privatization of the water industry, the electricity industry and British Steel seem likely to keep the process of selling off state industries going in the short term. Additionally there are possibilities for the sale of certain public corporations: the 1986 Peacock Report, while failing to deliver to the Conservative government the hoped-for recommendations for introducing large-scale private funding (particularly through advertising) for the BBC, did suggest the privatization of Radio 1 and Radio 2.

Finally it is important to stress that the ability of the Conservative government to cut the size of the PSBR (relative to GNP)[10] has been aided by the receipts earned from privatization. When the possibilities for selling state industries are exhausted, net public expendi-

Table 1.12 *Privatization 1979–1986*[a]

State firm	Date(s) of privatization	Process of privatization	Earnings to the Exchequer £m
British Petroleum	Nov. 1979; Sept. 1983	Share offer	551
British Aerospace	Feb. 1981; May 1985	Share offer	43
Cable and Wireless	Nov. 1981; Dec. 1983; Dec. 1985	Share offer	445
National Carriers	Feb. 1982	Management buy-out	5
Amersham International	Feb. 1982	Share offer	64
Britoil	Nov. 1982; Aug. 1985	Share offer	627
Associated British Ports	Feb. 1983; Apr. 1984	Share offer	97
Enterprise Oil	July 1984	Share offer	386
Jaguar	Aug. 1984	Share offer	297
British Telecom	Dec. 1984	Share offer	1,357
Vickers Shipyard	1986	Management buy-out	n/a
British Gas	Nov. 1986	Share offer	5,602[b]
British Airways	Feb. 1987	Share offer	900[c]

Notes: [a] Major privatization schemes only are shown.
[b] Received in three calls: Dec. 1986; June 1987; April 1988.
[c] Received in two calls: Feb. 1987; August 1987.

Sources: Investors Chronicle, 17 October 1986, p. 12. *The Government's Expenditure Plans 1986/87 to 1988/89,* Vol. II, p. 29.

ture and the PSBR seem likely to increase. The economic consequences of such an increase could include higher taxation and interest rates.

Conclusions and the future

The future for the public sector economy will continue to be determined by the relationship between economic theory and public spending, the political characteristics of governments and the financial and demographic demands for and constraints upon public services.

The last two decades have witnessed a trend towards greater centralization in the control of the public sector economy. This trend, which is favoured by the Treasury and many leading politicians, seems set to continue.

The likelihood of a worsening balance of payments in the 1990s in the wake of the falling earnings from North Sea oil presage a continuation of very tight control over public spending – whatever the view taken by future governments about the merits of the 'crowding out' theories. Reduced public spending may be needed within the package of deflationary measures to deal with the likely balance of payments crises. Yet such cuts in expenditure would be at odds with the heightened demands for public spending arising from the higher number of pensioners and the need to improve education services to meet the demands of the twenty-first century. The consequent imbalance between the demand and the supply of services from the public sector may have to be resolved through privatizing further parts of the public economy. But if services like health care become extensively offered through the private sector, the public sector service (i.e. the NHS) would be likely to assume the position of a second-class service for the poor and this would act to increase social polarization within the community.

Whatever the nature of future governments a public sector economy of some size will exist, will be distinct from the private sector in its determination of output levels and its sources of finance, and parts will still be administered – if not controlled – by non-central government bodies. One of the great challenges facing future governments will be to reconcile the expectations of the community for good public services with the inevitable financial constraints upon their provision.

Notes

1   Other important data on the public sector economy can be obtained from the *'The Blue Book': National Income and Expenditure* (CSO, London), which is published annually. Further details on the public expenditure planning process may be obtained from 'Making a Budget – 1: the Decisions', *Economic Progress Report: The Treasury*, no. 133 (January 1983) and 'The Management of Public Expenditure', *Phillips & Drew Public Authorities Review*, no. 16 (November 1986), pp. 2–6.

2   In the late 1960s the Labour government adopted the 'relative price effect' in the expenditure plans. This was designed to build into the process of volume planning the differential impact of inflation on the private and public sectors.

3   Expenditure on health services is largely administered in England by the Regional and District Health Authorities who receive virtually all their funds from the DHSS. In Scotland and Wales health services are administered by the Scottish and Welsh Offices.

4   The Keynesian multiplier equation may be expressed as follows:

$$\Delta Y \quad \Delta E \quad = \Delta G \times \frac{1}{(t+s+m)}$$

where Δ = change in the level of
         E = national expenditure
         Y = national income
         G = government expenditure
         t, s, m = marginal propensities to tax, save, import.

5   This point is succinctly explained in Cairncross, F. and Keeley, P., *The Guardian Guide to the Economy* (Methuen: London, 1981), p. 15. when the public sector borrows it can raise cash from two main sources. First, it can tap savings. It may do this by selling gilt-edged securities . . . If it does that – if it borrows real savings – it is generally held not to be increasing the supply of money. But if the government borrows by selling government debt to the banks, it is usually seen as increasing the money supply. The reason is that the gilt-edged securities increase the assets on the bank's balance sheet. Broadly speaking, an increase in assets allows a bank to increase its liabilities. So a bank can accept extra deposits and lend more money. Thus the money supply increases.

6   Principally the appointments of Professor Alan Walters as the Prime Minister's economic policy adviser and Professor Terry Burns as chief economic adviser to the Treasury.

7   The Conservative party had pledged at the time of the 1979 general election to respect the public sector pay awards recommended by the Clegg Commission – with the result that pay awards for many public sector employees amounted to between 20 per cent and 30 per cent increases in 1980, adding millions to public expenditure.

8   The White Paper, *Rates: Proposals for Rate Limitation and Reform of the Rating System* (London: HMSO, August 1983) states (paragraph 1.22) that 'between April 1979 and April 1983 domestic rates in England increased on average by 91 per cent while the RPI rose by only 55 per cent'.

9   The injection of money into BL was announced in January 1981 and followed BL's £181.5 million loss in the first half of 1980. The government's aid was not supported by all sectors of the Conservative party – but was justified on the basis of the support needed to ensure the success of the chairman's (Sir Michael Edwardes) restructuring plan for the ailing car and vehicles group.

10 The most recent government plans, following the Chancellor of the Exchequer's Autumn Economic Statement on 6 November 1986, envisage that the PSBR will be 1¾ per cent of GDP in 1986/87 compared with 3½ per cent of GDP in 1979/80.

References

Bacon, R. and Eltis, W. (1976), *Britain's Economic Problem: Too Few Producers* (London: Macmillan).

Beveridge, W. H. (1942), '*Social Insurance and Allied Services*', Cmd 6404 (London: HMSO).

Brunner, K. and Meltzer, A. H. (1976), 'Government, the Private Sector and "Crowding Out"', *The Banker*, July.

Cable, J. (1984), 'Industry', in Prest and Coppock, *The UK Economy*.

Cripps, F. and Godley, W. (1976), 'A Formal Analysis of the Cambridge Economic Policy Group Model', *Economica*, November.

Friedman, M. (1968), 'The Role of the Monetary Policy', *American Economic Review*, March.

Friedman, M. and Friedman, R. (1980), *Free to Choose* (New York: Harcourt Brace Jovanich).

HMSO (1944), *Employment Policy*, Cmd 6527 (London).

HMSO (1980), *The Government's Expenditure Plans 1980/1 to 1983/4*, Vols I and II, Cmnd 7841 – I/II, March (London).

HMSO (1985), *Reform of Social Security: Programme for Action*, Cmnd 9691 (London).

HMSO (1986), *The Government's Expenditure Plans 1986/7 to 1988/9*, Vols I and II, Cmnd 9702 – I/II, January (London).

Holmes, M. (1985), *The Labour Government 1974–79: Political Aims and Economic Reality* (London: Macmillan).

House of Lords (1985), *Report from the Select Committee on Overseas Trade*, Vol. I, Hol. 238–1 (London: HMSO).

Keynes, J. M. (1936), *The General Theory of Employment, Interest and Money* (New York: Harcourt Brace); reprinted in *The Collected Writings of John Maynard Keynes*, vol. 24 (London: Macmillan, 1973).

Laidler, D. E. W. (1976), 'Inflation in Britain: a Monetarist Perspective', *American Economic Review*, September.

Nield, P. (1985), 'The Death of Monetarism', in *Phillips & Drew Market Review*, May.

Phillips, A. W. H. (1958), 'The Relation between Unemployment and the Rate of Change of Money Wage Rates in the UK 1861–1957', *Economica*, November.

Pollard, S. (1983), *The Development of the British Economy, Third Edition 1914–1980* (London: Edward Arnold).

Prest, A. R. and Coppock, D. J. (eds) (1984), *The UK Economy: A Manual of Applied Economics*, 10th edn (London: Weidenfeld and Nicolson).

2 Financial management in the public sector

TONY BOVAIRD and
SANDRA NUTLEY

Introduction

Financial management in the public sector has undergone rapid changes in recent years. The traditional stereotypes of the public sector accountant – cost cutting, looking no further ahead than the annual budget cycle, rigid in the control of spending within and between budget heads, in general disposition the 'Abominable No-man' – have largely been replaced or at the very least complemented by a new image. This portrays the Director of Finance setting up big finance deals with major City institutions, negotiating grants with the DOE and the European Community, setting up private companies to encourage local economic development, encouraging decentralization to give more control and accountability to budget holders, and practising innovative (perhaps even risky) 'creative accountancy'.

While it is probably true that both these stereotypes can indeed be found in public sector organizations, neither gives a fair and representative picture of best-practice in the profession. However, there certainly have been major changes in the finance function as public spending has been subjected to cuts, new finance sources have had to be explored, and 'value for money' has become the watchword of all public expenditure programmes. In this chapter we aim to illustrate the key concerns of modern financial managers in public sector bodies and highlight the challenges which have still to be met successfully.

The chapter begins with the financing of public expenditure and resources planning in public agencies. It then considers the 'mechanics' of financial management – approaches to budgeting, capital investment appraisal, cost benefit analysis, financial control and 'value for money'. It ends with a look at the most exciting emerging issues in financial management in the public sector – ways of improving performance through performance measurement, through decentralization of budget holding and performance reporting in the organization.

Resource planning

Public sector expenditure is financed from a variety of sources:

* central government taxes;
* local authority and water authority rates;
* charges for goods and services;
* sales of surplus assets;
* borrowing on the private capital or money markets.

The size and distribution of public expenditure is planned via the *Public Expenditure Survey* (an annual survey of public expenditure) which projects forward the existing levels of approved expenditure. The results of this survey are circulated to ministers and the Chancellor of the Exchequer puts forward his own proposals for levels of public expenditure in relation to his judgement of the prospects for the economy. The theory is that a collective ministerial decision is taken about the scale and distribution of public expenditure. The reality is that ministers find themselves competing for scarce resources, with bilateral discussions between the Treasury and the spending ministers, ending in a meeting of the 'Star Chamber' (a special committee of the Cabinet set up to arbitrate when agreement cannot be reached by collective or bilateral discussions) to settle the final allocations. The results are published in January/February each year in the Public Expenditure White Paper, which sets out the government's expenditure plans for the coming three years.

A feature of the resource planning process in central government in recent years has been the move to a *cash limits* system. In 1987/88 about 40 per cent of public expenditure is subject to cash limits (HM Treasury, 1987, p. 11). The move to a cash limits system has been an important element in the present government's strategy for limiting the growth of public expenditure. There have been criticisms, however, that a cash limits system of planning leads to a covert underfunding, due to the unrealistic assumptions about pay and price increases in future years (Pliatzky, 1982; Likierman, 1984). In limiting recorded public expenditure, the sale of assets has been an important source of revenue in recent years. Income from such sales is treated as negative expenditure, and thus can be used to massage the public sector borrowing requirement (PSBR). Since the transfer of ownership does not in itself alter the underlying economic flows, this is an example of financial management by symbolic gesture.

Two important areas where the spending authorities are not central government, are the services provided by the National Health Service and local government, each with its own distinctive resource planning process.

The majority of funding for health authorities is provided by central government. The overall level of National Health Service expenditure is considered in the Public Expenditure Survey process. The DHSS is responsible for allocating the National Health Service 'cake' to the Regional Health Authorities. In the 1960s and early 1970s there was concern about the inequitable distribution of these funds between health authority areas, and 'equal access to health care' was one of the objectives of the 1974 reorganization. The *Resource Allocation Working Party* (RAWP) was established, and it reported in 1976 with new proposals for allocating funds within the NHS. The aims of the new allocation system were to provide objectivity in decision-making and equal provision of services according to need. The allocation process was based on a formula which for seven service categories produced a 'weighted population' estimate of need. The criteria used to produce this estimate include population (size and structure), standard mortality ratios (as a surrogate measure of morbidity) and cross-boundary flows of patients. Targets were established for each region and district – they represent an estimate of the funding needed if the population in all regions of the funding used resources at the same rate as the national average. Actual revenue allocations to each region are calculated from the previous year's approved expenditure – plus a percentage growth/ decrease determined by relative under/over funding against RAWP targets; minus a deduction of 'efficiency savings' deemed to be possible from 'good' management. The allocations are then uplifted by the government's estimate of pay and prices inflation in the forthcoming year.

Since the introduction of the RAWP formula there has been a convergence of regional funding towards RAWP targets. However, despite this there have been criticisms of the process. These include:

- the doubtful relationship between mortality and morbidity. The formula may even provide a perverse incentive to perform badly – if lower deaths are achieved then under the formula there is less money;

- the formula contains no consideration of the level of related services in estimating need (e.g. family practitioner services, housing, social services, etc.);
- the cross-boundary flow calculations are considered inappropriate (particularly at district levels) and at present only relate to in-patients and not out-patients;
- inadequate weighting is given to the costs of treating different conditions.

(For further discussion of the RAWP formula see Jones and Prowle, 1987.)

Local government is partly funded by central government (via rate support grant and specific grants) and partly by revenue raised locally (rates and charges). At present controversy surrounds both areas of funding. The present system of central government funding is based on the 1980 Planning and Land Act which was supplemented with additional legislation in 1982 and 1984 to allow central government greater controls.

The *rate support grant* is based on an assessment of the needs of an area (using primarily demographic data as indicators of need), together with an assessment of the ability of the area to raise its own resources (based on rateable values). Prior to 1980 these 'needs' and 'resources' elements were separately funded; the 1980 Act combined them into a unitary grant – the block grant.

The criticisms of the system of allocation prior to 1980 were that it was complex and inequitable in its treatment of local authorities. The assessment of the need to spend was in part determined by past expenditure patterns, so high spenders got more. There was also criticism of the inequity of the process by which local revenue was raised – a tax on property (the rates).

A major review of local government finance, the Layfield Report (1976), set out the following criteria for evaluating local government finance options:

- accountability
- fairness between individuals
- fairness between areas
- balance between consumption and investment efficiency
- stability
- flexibility
- comprehensibility.

The block grant system was introduced to overcome some of the above criticisms of the present system. The objectives were to

- provide a simpler system;
- deal with overspenders;
- promote equity;
- provide greater objectivity;
- reinforce local accountability and
- reduce central intervention.

Unfortunately many of these objectives have not been realized. The present system is complex and a moving target, as the criteria for assessing need vary from year to year. Resource planning in local government is characterized by uncertainty due to the lack of knowledge about the financial support which can be expected from central government in the medium term. The Audit Commission has criticized this 'stop–go' nature of resource planning because of the inefficiencies it promotes, and it has been very critical of the role of the block grant in reducing the cost-effectiveness of local authorities (Audit Commission, 1984).

In an attempt to deal with 'overspenders' the government has introduced new concepts of holdback and penalties into the rate support grant system. The rate-capping legislation (of 1984) heralded a new departure with central government taking powers to control the level of funds raised locally. This has led to more, not less, central government intervention, so one of the objectives of the block grant legislation has not been achieved. With greater central government intervention there is blurred accountability – who should be held responsible for any failures in services, central or local government? There has been local resistance to the increasing intervention by central government. Local authorities have searched hard, and often successfully, for loopholes in the new legislation, and a new breed of accountancy techniques (creative accountancy) has emerged to get around some of the effects of central government controls. There are fears that such techniques are 'ransoming' the future of local government for short-term gains. Now, more than ever, the focus in local government is on short-term resource planning (Parkinson, 1986).

Central government controls of local government expenditure relate to capital as well as revenue expenditure. Capital expenditure is controlled via the capital allocations process and the limitations on the proportion of sale proceeds that can be used in any one year to finance expenditure and supplement allocations. In this way local government is restricted in using the sale of its assets to subsidize expenditure, while central government is happy to spend all the proceeds from its own (much larger) asset sales.

Another imminent change with the stated aim of improving local accountability in local government is the introduction of the 'community charge' to replace the present system of domestic rates. This is a flat rate for all adult residents with low income housholds supported from social security, but obliged to pay the first 20 per cent of the charge. The new charge has been criticized because of its likely inflationary effects on house prices, its regressiveness as a tax, and the administrative difficulties associated with its collection (Whitehead, 1987; Foster, 1986).

In summary, containing and where possible reducing public expenditure has been a key government concern for the last decade or so. There have been a variety of mechanisms introduced to this end which have had the effect of increasing central control of local agency spending.

Approaches to budgeting

The results of the detailed resource planning process are encapsulated in an organization's budget statements. A budget can be defined as the process by which plans are operationalized – short- to medium-term plans which are expressed in financial terms. The budget fulfils three main purposes:

(a) the forward planning of activities;
(b) the co-ordination of activities;
(c) the provision of the basis for ensuring that expenditure is in line with plans (budgetary control).

The issue of financial control is considered later in this chapter. This section concentrates on the various approaches to budgetary planning.

The key building block in the budget process is the definition of the units for budgeting – the cost centres to be used. There are a variety of approaches. The most common are the definition of cost centres according to function (e.g. catering or medical staff services) or physical location (e.g. an area office or a ward). Other possibilities include the definition of cost centres according to programmes of care or client groups (e.g. the elderly or the unemployed). In the health service in particular there has been some attempt to try to establish cost centres around the generators of costs – the clinicians. There have been a number of experiments in Clinical Accountability Service Planning and Evaluation (CASPE) under the aegis of the King Edward's Hospital Fund. Interestingly, Jones and Prowle (1987) shed doubt on this emphasis on clinicians as generators of costs.

There has been a general trend in recent years to *localize* budgetary cost centres, and push budget responsibilities down to the lowest levels possible. The decentralization of budgets is considered at the end of this chapter.

The monetary basis on which budgets are planned has also shifted in recent years, away from a fixed price (volume) approach towards a cash planning basis. Where budgets are planned on a volume basis any pay awards and price increases occurring during the year are funded by the provision of additional monies. Cash based budgets include estimates for future pay and price increases and any additional monies required, due to underestimation, have to be found from within the existing budgets. As such, cash based budgets aid cost restriction and financial control.

The traditional approach to budgeting in the public sector has been *incremental*, a moving forward of last year's budget:

last year's   +   incremental inflation   +   other variations
revised   (pay and prices)   (including growth/
estimate   reductions)

There have been many criticisms of incremental budgeting. These include:

- Once an item is incorporatd into the budget its future inclusion is taken for granted.
- There is a tendency to spend up to the limit of allocation, because to underspend may affect next year's allocation.
- The emphasis is on monetary inputs rather than on the objectives those inputs might achieve.
- It does not encourage a systematic review of expenditures in terms of their efficiency and effectiveness.

However, there have been defenders (e.g. Lindblom, 1959) of the incremental approach. One of the arguments used in favour of incrementalism is that much of public sector expenditure is either mandatory or so fundamental that it is sensible to concentrate on marginal growth in the decision-making process. There is also the defence that change in small steps avoids serious mistakes, and that it is the only process that is politically and organizationally acceptable (Wildavsky, 1974).

Dissatisfaction with incrementalism has led to the development of alternative budgetary approaches, although the practicality of some of these alternatives has to be suspect, given their limited application to date. The two main alternatives which have been suggested have been *Planned Programme Budgeting Systems* (PPBS) and *Zero Based Budgeting* (ZBB), both of which were first applied in the United States in the 1960s.

PPBS is concerned with the identification of programmes of activity, e.g. care for the elderly, regardless of departmental boundaries. As such PPBS cuts across the normal hierachical organizational structure in order that appropriate inputs can be drawn together. PPBS is concerned with identifying different ways of achieving objectives and analysing the costs and benefits of these. In Britain there have been some experiments with a similar 'output budgeting' process in the health service, education and the police force (Culyer, 1980). The advantages of PPBS are that it concentrates on long-term planning and the likely effects of these plans. In so doing it exposes overlapping or contradictory programmes of expenditure. The choices under PPBS should be made on the basis of the benefit/cost relationship. Stated in this way PPBS sounds an ideal system, but there have been problems; technically PPBS has proved time-consuming and demands information which is not readily available. It has also been accused of ignoring the political realities of organizations. The problems have led Wildavsky (1974, p. 205) to comment that:

> PPBS has failed everywhere and at all times. Nowhere has PPBS been established and influenced governmental decisions according to its own principles.

ZBB, in its purest form, starts each year from a zero base. It is a bottom-up approach where the onus is on the 'unit' manager to justify the expenditure he is seeking. It can be seen as a three-stage process:

(a) The identification of decision units (the units within the hierarchy for which a budget is to be prepared). Each unit should have a manager who is clearly responsible for its operation and well-defined series of objectives.
(b) The development of decision packages which indicate alternative methods of carrying out activities, the costs and benefits of these, and the consequences of non-approval.
(c) Reviewing and ranking the decision packages – so that the

ranking list of packages can be used to establish a cut-off point once the level of funding has been established.

The advantages of ZBB are that it specifies objectives and looks at the cost effectiveness of different ways of achieving them. Decision packages should be prepared at the lowest appropriate level, so there is greater involvement of all managers in the budgetary process. The resulting budget should reflect current and not past priorities (as is the case with incremental budgeting). There are, however, disadvantages and the biggest one of these is the time consuming nature of ZBB. It is a bottom-up approach with managers' decision packages being referred upwards, combined with other decision units and then reviewed and ranked. Anthony (1977) in discussing ZBB in the state of Georgia refers to the unmanageable nature of the process. The problems of time consumption have led to a 'bounded rationality' approach to ZBB, where perhaps only 30 per cent of the budget is subject to rigorous scrutiny. While this may restrict the preparation time required, the resulting budget bears little relation to the principles of ZBB. There have been several hybrid approaches which have tried to cope with restricted growth and budget cuts in a more rational way than incrementalism, for example, priority-based budgeting.

Capital investment appraisal

Budgets are produced for capital as well as revenue expenditure. However, capital expenditure is an *investment* for the future, and as such requires specific consideration. An investment can be defined as 'any activity for which the required outlays and benefits are not expected to be concurrent' (Carsberg, 1974). The process of appraising investments is one 'by which information is gathered and presented in an objective fashion to decision makers, to assist them to reach an informed and rational choice between alternative courses of action (Sullivan, 1984). Traditionally, public sector organizations have given insufficient consideration to their investment decisions.

Surveys of the use of investment appraisal in the National Health Service and the Property Services Agency suggest that although it is seen as an important process, the practice falls far short of the principles. A study of selected central government projects in 1982 found that only 30 per cent by value had been subjected to full appraisal (Comptroller and Auditor-General's report to the Committee of Public Accounts, 1982). The project appraisal systems were particularly weak on option generation, treatment of intangibles and project monitoring. Similar results have recently been found in a survey of investment appraisal in 76 local authorities (Nutley, Bovaird and Thomas, 1987). Only 29 authorities said that they used appraisal and, of these, 12 used 'informal' systems in which there was not a consistent use of criteria.

The literature on investment appraisal tends to focus on the techniques of appraisal, rather than the process or system by which it is incorporated into the operation of an organization. There are two critical questions here – who should carry out the appraisal and when should appraisal occur?

HM Treasury (1983) recommends that responsibilities should be clearly defined and that line managers should generally be responsible for appraisal, drawing on expert advice where appropriate. This approach is echoed by the Property Services Agency, which suggested to the Public Accounts Committee that 'the important factor in an investment project was the quality of the underlying assumptions and that these were essentially clearer in the minds of line managers who, in the case of the PSA were professional and technical people' (Committee of Public Accounts, 1982). However, the Comptroller and Auditor-General in his report to the Public Accounts Committee (1982) placed greater emphasis on the importance of finance staff. He commented that there was greater accuracy and quality of appraisal where financially trained staff were involved.

On the question of when the appraisal should be conducted, there is more agreement. HM Treasury (1983) comments that appraisal should be carried out early in the expenditure approval process, before options are closed off and, if necessary, be reviewed at later stages. A similar point is made by the Comptroller and Auditor-General:

> Once a project is in a capital programme it is often difficult to dislodge, therefore projects should normally be appraised before they go into the programme, to help ensure that the most cost-effective projects are considered and that any underestimation to gain a place in the programme is detected. (Committee of Public Accounts, 1982)

An ideal model of the investment appraisal process would incorporate the following features (Nutley, Bovaird and Thomas, 1987):

- All projects should be appraised except where non-appraisal can be explicitly justified;
- a corporate group should be responsible for appraisal, rather than a particular profession;
- projects should be appraised before entry into the capital programme;
- post-hoc evaluation should inform future appraisal techniques and assumptions;
- an 'audit type' function should ensure that appropriate appraisal has been undertaken.

Investment appraisal should be part of the *evaluation* process. It therefore depends upon proper undertaking of the previous stages of a rational management cycle. Guidelines provided by HM Treasury (1984) outline the following basic steps in this process:

- define the objectives;
- consider the options;
- identify the costs, benefits, timing and uncertainties of each option;
- discount those costs and benefits which can be valued in money terms;
- weigh up the uncertainties;
- assess other factors;
- present the results.

The controversial subject of measurement of costs and benefits will be considered in the next section. The other problematic area of investment appraisal is the treatment of the time flow costs and benefits. Clearly costs which occur later have less influence on an investment decision than costs which occur at the start of a project; by the same token, benefits which occur later are less useful than benefits which occur early. The extent to which we place a lower value on cash flows in the future is known as the *rate of discount*.

The determination of the proper rate of discount for an investment appraisal is always a matter of some debate. HM Treasury provides a guideline for the public sector – the 'required rate of return' on new investment. This is currently set at 5 per cent in real terms and is intended to reflect the rate of return of investments in the private sector which have been 'crowded out' by the public sector investment. However, a single discount rate of this nature should always be qualified by consideration of the risks involved in specific investments and, through sensitivity analysis, the effects of different discount rates should always be explored in making a decision.

Other decision criteria are often used to deal with the time profile of costs and benefits. The *payback* method calculates the number of years within which the investment is likely to be able to pay for itself. This can grossly distort investment decisions in which major cash flows are expected to occur in later years, and is often inapplicable as a method in public services, where income flows are often negligible. The *First Year Rate of Return* method (often used in the property industry and by transportation planners) uses only the benefits likely to arise in the first full year of operation of the investment – once again this will distort investment decisions against projects whose major net benefits occur later in the life of the project. Fears that such approaches may lead to over-concentration on short-term investments have lead to an emphasis in recent years on *Whole Life Cycle Costing*, where all costs and benefits for the estimated life of the project are included. Yet this is still only a crude approximation of the results which will emerge from a full discounted cash flow (DCF). Now that microcomputing packages have taken most of the pain out of DCF calculations, there is little excuse for accepting inadequate substitutes.

Sullivan (1984) reports that one of the arguments used against investment appraisal techniques is that, in the public sector, decisions are political rather than rational. Political decision-making is a reality in public sector organizations, however, and these decisions must be informed and perhaps modified by the presentation of rational analysis.

Cost benefit analysis

Cost benefit analysis (CBA) is the most general approach to resource allocation planning in the public sector. It can be used for decisions on current expenditure as well as for capital investment appraisal.

The key features of CBA are:

- it includes all benefits and costs in the analysis;
- all costs are benefits foregone (the *Opportunity Cost Principle*);
- all benefits should be quantified and given monetary valuations where possible;
- the monetary value of benefits is the willingness to pay for that benefit on behalf of individuals concerned;

- a framework is adopted which highlights the non–monetary and non–quantified costs and benefits;
- the social rate of discount is used to bring all cash flows to their present value;
- a social welfare function is specified to provide the rules for aggregating net benefits across individuals.

While CBA has obvious parallels with financial appraisal in the private sector, it is much broader in that it aims to cover all non–traded implications of projects and plans. It also uses values for benefits and costs and the rate of discount which reflect their resource value rather than their unadjusted market value.

The monetary valuation of the benefits of public expenditures is usually regarded as the most problematic area for CBA. There are three main ways in which the individual valuations can be ascertained:

(a) Clients can be fully *involved* in the planning and management of services so that their valuations are incorporated in the decisions made about the service. This, however, is not possible in relation to the indirect beneficiaries of expenditure. The process is also liable to be unduly influenced by 'activists' among the direct clients, whose views may not be representative of the clients as a whole.

(b) Attitude surveys can be used to establish *willingness to pay* for benefits (or to avoid costs). There are, of course, problems of bias in formulating and interpreting survey questions. These can, however, be reduced by appropriate piloting of the questionnaire. A good example of this approach is by Flowerdew and Rodriguez (1978), in which residents of an urban renewal scheme were asked whether they would still have felt better off as a result of the scheme if their rents had gone up by specific amounts at the same time.

(c) The behaviour of those affected by a plan or project can be analysed to *infer* their valuations of the net benefits. This method is not biased by inclusion of purely speculative estimates of benefit; however, it is often extremely difficult to set up or to discover real life situations in which the behaviour in question will be exhibited, with a sufficiently small number of extraneous variables that their effects can be separated out in the analysis.

Cost benefit analysis has been carried out in most public services, although often more as an academic experiment than as a major tool for informing decisions. Application of CBA has been most advanced in transportation planning, where the Department of Transport has for twenty years required local authorities to carry out a computerized cost benefit analysis (COBA) of major new capital schemes before submitting schemes for approval or funding. The main features of CBA are well illustrated in the COBA computer package.

One of the principal benefits of transportation projects is travel time savings. These are valued in COBA by the application of a money value of time which has been derived from research into the trade-off made by travellers between quick, expensive modes of travel and slow, cheap modes of travel. This research on the value of time implied by actual behaviour has shown that the valuation of time varies over the country and is strongly correlated with travellers' wage rates. The corollary might be expected to be that more transportation schemes would be undertaken in higher income areas of the country. However, this is deliberately ruled out by the Department of Transport through the use in COBA of an 'equity value of time' – essentially a national average value of time (in pounds sterling per hour) which is used for all schemes, wherever they are located. It is, of course, open to any transportation authority to use a different value of time in its ranking of projects for internal purposes. The social welfare function embodied in the 'equity value of time' which successive central governments have used is that there should be a lower weighting on the willingness to pay of higher income groups – everyone's pound is *not* equal.

In transportation planning we can also see the operation of the opportunity cost principle, although not consistently. The resource costs of land used up in schemes has to be entered into the calculation, even when the land is already owned by the transportation authority and appears to involve no further financial cost. This resource cost consists of the valuation of the land in its 'next best use' – perhaps for housing, industry or social infrastructure. However, the COBA package does not allow the same proper distinction between resource costs and financial costs to be made in the case of labour costs. Even if much of the labour involved in a scheme were likely to have been otherwise unemployed and to have experienced little utility from this leisure, it has to be accounted for in terms of its *financial* cost to the transportation authority. This is because the Treasury is reluctant to move generally to a recognition that labour unemployment justifies more public (and private) projects than would be suggested on purely market criteria. While it must be recognized that there are indeed difficult technical issues in the calculation of a 'shadow wage' for labour (a wage which reflects the *resources* lost through employing the labour, rather than the financial transfer actually made to the workers), it seems both inconsistent and potentially highly inefficient not to make any adjustment at all to raw wage costs.

This example suggests that there is still progress to be made in the application of CBA, even in the transportation field where it is relatively well developed. Other fields where significant CBA analyses are frequently carried out include the water industry, energy, and agricultural policy. There are interesting case studies in social policy fields such as housing, health, personal social services and education but these are still very much 'one-off' studies rather than an integral analytical process within the planning for these services.

Financial control and 'value for money'

Financial control can be defined in a number of different but complementary ways. First, it can relate to keeping expenditure within the limits of plans and resource availability. Secondly, it can be used to refer to controls which ensure that the money which is spent is expended on the priorities and areas identified in the budget. Finally, it might be used to refer to the checks and controls made to ensure that no more money is spent than is necessary to achieve the desired result (the ubiquitous area of 'value for money').

The primary means of financial control operated in many public sector organizations is *budgetary control*. The budget process sets up procedures (financial regulations) for authorizing expenditure and the headings under which money can be expended. The accounting system provides information on the levels of actual expenditure against budgeted expenditure, and should highlight the differences between these two (variance accounting). Year-end variance accounting is common but this alone is insufficient to ensure adequate financial control. Monitoring information needs to be provided throughout the financial year, and is more useful if the expenditure to date can be matched against an estimate of how much should have been expended by that date. This necessitates the creation of spending profiles so that cumulative expenditure can be compared with estimates of what proportion of the budget should have been expended at certain points in time (Lewis, 1987). Monitoring information should be timely and reliable, and ideally it should provide information on commitments as well as actual expenditure.

Budgetary control procedures are needed, not only to gain an early warning of possible overspend, but also to identify areas of underspend. Resources are limited and areas of underspend should be identified early so that money can be vired to other areas of need. This is particularly important in monitoring capital budgets, where project slippage frequently leads to underspending against allocations. An important aspect of a budgetary control system is the means by which it encourages good performance and how it deals with overspenders. As Flynn (1987) points out, some penalties such as deducting the overspend from next year's budget may end up penalizing the clients rather than the managers. Performance incentives are considered in the next section.

Traditionally, budgetary control procedures and accounting systems have been concerned with ensuring the regularity of financial transactions. As such they focus on financial *inputs* and frequently give little consideration to the *level of outputs* achieved from a given amount of expenditure. There have been attempts to associate budgetary control statements with some measures of performance; however, as demonstrated in the next section, performance measurement is not always easy in the public sector. Ramanathan (1985) discusses possible ways of improving management control information, by a wider consideration of costs and benefits. A project management information system (PRISM), developed at Aston University, provides an innovative attempt at enabling local authorities and development agencies to monitor on a continuous basis the resources and manpower inputs to individual projects and the outputs or benefits these provide.

The quest for 'value for money' in the public sector has focused attention on the so-called 'three Es' – Economy, Efficiency and Effectiveness. These are conventionally defined as follows:

Economy entails buying all inputs of a given quality specification at the lowest possible cost.
Efficiency entails achieving the maximum possible output from a given level of input.
Effectiveness entails achieving the top level goals of the organization (which should essentially mean achieving maximum impact on community welfare).

'Value for money' is not a new concept, but it has gained currency under the present Conservative government, and thus for many people it is associated with public expenditure cuts. The way in which some 'efficiency' savings have been imposed (for example in the NHS) would seem to confirm this opinion, although a value for money approach need not be related to reductions in expenditure.

The ultimate responsibility for ensuring value for money lies jointly with service managers and elected members. However, internal accountants and external auditors also have an important role to play. At the end of the financial year public expenditure is subject to external checks and controls by auditors. Traditionally the role of the auditor has been to:

- provide assurance as to the *regularity* and lawfulness of published accounts;
- provide an assessment of any loss due to the lack of *economy and efficiency*.

Since the 1982 Local Government Finance Act, the audit of local government expenditure has also been concerned with the *effectiveness* of expenditure. The Comptroller and Auditor-General is moving in the same direction, although effectiveness is not formally specified in his remit. 'Value for money audits' are now charged with the responsibility in the public sector for ensuring that the three Es are being achieved and the appropriate management arrangements have been made to secure them. However, there is still much controversy and uncertainty surrounding the measurement of effectiveness in the public sector, so that auditors have so far tended to continue to restrict their activities to the more traditional fields of economy and efficiency (Tomkins, 1986). Auditors are not meant to question the appropriateness of the actual policies, but instead ensure that proper arrangements have been made to secure the effective use of resources – that is, it should be an audit of systems and not of policies.

Judgements on the efficiency and effectiveness of public expenditure require information which frequently is not readily available. The approach in central government, following the Rayner value for money scrutinies (Metcalf and Richards 1984) has been to establish a system of in-house scrutinies – selecting particular services and units for detailed consideration. The same approach has been adopted by the Audit Commission, who have investigated selected local government services and developed models of good practice.

Potential improvements in efficiency can be aided by a systematic consideration of the nature of the *costs* incurred. Efficiency measurement tends to be based largely on unit cost information, with insufficient consideration given to other costing approaches; for

Efficiency Indicators
Level of outputs/products
Level of activities
Productivity ratios
  (Output per member of staff)
Unit costs
  (Cost per unit of output)
Speed of service delivery
Achievement of specified service standards

Effectiveness Indicators
Throughput of clients
Client satisfaction
Changes in client welfare or client state
Client willingness to pay/rate of return of resources employed
Leverage of public or private investment
Changes in asset values

Figure 2.1   *Categories of performance indicators.*

example, marginal costing, which can indicate how productivity could be maximized at the margins (without increasing fixed costs). Similarly, a standard costing approach would enable some movement away from the fixed input budget approach, towards a system of flexible budgets where cash inputs are adjusted according to the outputs achieved. Public expenditure restrictions have entailed a closer consideration of costs and the development of cost reduction approaches (see Hallows, 1977), but the public sector in general can still learn from the management accounting and costing approaches used in the private sector.

Measuring performance – the use of performance indicators

Most public sector agencies have now accepted the need to measure and report their performance in a systematic manner. Such performance measures typically appear in the annual reports of local authorities and nationalized industries. Of late, Public Expenditure White Papers have increasingly included measures of output of central government departments and this tendency should be reinforced by the recent decision to produce annual reports for all government departments (as has been done for some years for selected government programmes, such as the Urban Programme).

In Figure 2.1 the most common categories of performance indicators for efficiency and effectiveness are listed. Efficiency indicators such as units costs and productivity ratios depend on a satisfactory unit of output/product/activity and this can be difficult to establish in the public sector. However, the difficulties can often be overcome by defining several possible outputs and doing the calculation of productivity and unit costs on each basis, so that an overall view can be arrived at.

Effectiveness indicators have traditionally focused on counts of client throughput and on the level of complaints from clients or from the general public. There is now a realization that both these dimensions of effectiveness can be handled much better in performance assessment. Client throughput figures can and should distinguish the priority client groups from the rest of service users; and *indirect clients* (such as firms helped by the multiplier effect of economic development activities) should be included.

While *complaints* have a high political profile, it is essential that they be judged within an overall understanding of the level of satisfaction of clients and the general public with the agency's services. The role of market research in providing this wider framework is discussed below.

Two areas where some progress has been made in extending performance measurement beyond its previous confines are in relation to *quality of service measures* and the measurement of *customer satisfaction*. The specification of quality of service requires an understanding of the different dimensions which are important to users of a service. Figure 2.2 illustrates some of the key dimensions (adapted from the National Consumer Council booklet, *Measuring Up*). A high quality service should be perceived as scoring high on all of these dimensions. While this provides a useful checklist against which to monitor progress, many of these dimensions are only capable of being subjectively assessed. Performance management has had to come to terms with the need to incorporate 'soft' information in its monitoring systems in order to cope adequately with the richness and variety of real world concerns with service quality.

Taking account of customer satisfaction has long been a weak area of public sector management. Analysis of complaints has often been used to alert decision-makers to situations in which inadequate services were being provided. However, this is a wholly negative approach which ignores *positive* feedback from consumers and is

Choice of service options
Information on costs and benefits of service options
Clarity of eligibility
Availability – easy access
              – suitable opening hours
              – clarity
Reliability
Consistency of decisions/treatment – over time
                                    – between people
Flexibility
Speed of response
'Comfortable and easy to use'
Clear, accessible and fair appeals/complaints procedure
Friendly and informed 'front line' staff

Figure 2.2   *Quality of service process.*

biased in any case by the poor mechanisms available in most
services for complaints to be made. There is also the problem that
those individuals who are most likely to make a complaint when
they have a grievance are likely to be unrepresentative. Consequently there is now a much greater appreciation in the public
sector of the need for systematic market research into customer
satisfaction levels. These responses have been used to provide
powerful feedback on the effectiveness of government programmes, as seen by the clients (e.g. PSMRU, 1985). Many local
authorities are commissioning local opinion polls, along similar
lines, to provide measures of satisfaction with services (Furze,
1986). The most systematic and long-running example is the annual
Social Survey which has been conducted since 1975 by Cleveland
County Council. This has provided a detailed data base from which
consumer reaction to changing council policies can be monitored
and partially evaluated over an adequate time period (Vamplew and
Gallant, 1983).

These approaches also fit well into current concerns in public and
private sectors to enhance and assure *quality* of services. While
quality assurance, in the traditional sense of measuring the proportion of defective products or services provided, is inherently quantifiable, the other key dimensions of quality can only be assessed
subjectively – *fitness for purpose* and *value for money to consumers*.
Consumer satisfaction surveys must therefore be central to service
design in the public sector. This is, however, a hope for the future
rather than a description of current practice.

In some services, such as social services and education, performance indicators have been developed to measure the changing
welfare state of the client (Bovaird and Mallinson, 1988). These
approaches tend to focus on indices compiled from professional
assessments of different dimensions of the client's welfare, with the
possibility of independent verification. The extension of such
approaches to other services may offer the possibility at some future
stage for more realistic comparison of the relative effectiveness of
different types of public expenditure.

There is also a set of economics-derived performance measures
of effectiveness which are used in those public services which are
traded in the market, especially the nationalized industries. These
hinge on the willingness of consumers to pay for the service and
the consequent rate of return on resources employed. The higher
the rate of return, the higher will be the asset values in the
services concerned; this latter is an interesting performance
measure in that it also includes the effect of appropriate asset
maintenance policies.

Finally, increased attention is being given to the performance of
the public sector as a *catalyst* in bringing about higher investment in
the private sector or by other public sector bodies. This *leverage*
does not measure the impact of the public services but it does
indicate the level of confidence which has been inspired in other
service providers as a result of the programme concerned.

The performance indicators discussed above are clearly partial
and incomplete. However, taken together they may give a much
clearer picture of the efficiency of the public sector than has been
available in the past. This offers the opportunity for performance
assessment to become much more integral to good management
practice in the public sector.

Improving performance in public sector organizations

Accountability for performance is central to management. Yet
systems for measuring and reporting performance, whether it be
performance at corporate level, at departmental or unit level, or the
performance of individuals, are still often regarded as difficult and
controversial.

The attitude to performance management is part of the culture of
an organization. 'The overall message is that culture reflects action.
People will take a new set of ideas if they are in tune with the
genuine wishes of those they hold [to be] in authority, but if they

are not getting messages to do that, their response to wider social pressures will be muted' (Richards, 1987).

While every manager is theoretically accountable for his/her performance, the real position in many organizations is that priority is given to 'fire-fighting' tasks and the need to report performance is not sufficiently pressing to make it worthwhile to set up appropriate systems. Even when top management gives the signal that performance assessment is required, there are major barriers of professional antipathy to conquer. In most professions there is a strong code, written or unwritten, that the judgements of a professional can only legitimately be questioned by another, similarly qualified peer. Since few professional groups have written down explicitly the criteria by which they judge each other's decisions, independent external assessment is thereby ruled out. Proper performance assessment therefore requires both a technical framework which encapsulates adequately the qualitative and quantitative dimensions which are believed to be important in a service and also a set of procedures which involves the relevant professionals in a way which they perceive to be appropriate. This latter requirement necessitates both incentives to bring their willing co-operation and sanctions so that poor performance, or an unwillingness to reveal performance, is seen as unacceptable within the organization.

Performance incentives

The role of *incentives* to increase performance in the public sector has been problematic in the past. It has largely been confined to work study-related incentive bonus schemes for the manual work-force. While they have often been introduced for laudable reasons, it has been the normal experience that these schemes have deteriorated over time into a constant and expected element of the payment system so that they cease to have any effect on performance. The deterioration has been most rapid during periods of national income restraint policies, when the schemes were often simply a way of evading the restraints; this misuse of incentive bonus schemes has destroyed many of the good schemes and given all of them a poor reputation.

The most recent approach to introducing pay incentives has tried to learn some lessons from these unsatisfactory antecedents. It also focuses on the professional and technical rather than the manual staff. 'Performance-related pay' schemes have been introduced in the civil service, government agencies and local government. Generally this has been on an experimental basis involving only a selected group of staff, although some organizations, like the Scottish Development Agency, now operate performance-related pay for most of their professional staff. In some agencies a more limited approach has been adopted, offering short- or medium-term contracts to top management at higher pay levels than previously. Here there is the option to renew the contract when it becomes due, if performance is judged to be satisfactory.

A more positive approach to incentives consists of allowing departments or units which perform well to benefit through a larger budget provision than would otherwise occur. For example, a proportion of any efficiency savings made during a year is often allowed to be retained by a department for developing the service (typically 33 per cent or 50 per cent). The rationale for this approach, deriving from studies of management motivation, is that top management is driven more by status and prestige than by money and that these pay-offs are generally associated in the public sector with the amount of budget growth and perceived quality of service which the manager is able to achieve.

Privatization and contracting-out

In the last few years a further sanction has become important in encouraging improved organizational performance – *privatization and contracting-out*. This essentially threatens that, unless a level of performance comparable to that of the private sector is achieved, some or all of the service will be contracted out or hived off completely to the private sector. In recent years it has been necessary for the Direct Labour Organization of local authorities to tender for larger contracts against the private sector and this practice is now spreading widely to refuse collection, office cleaning, etc. Central government has indicated strongly that it will make competitive tendering nearly universal throughout the public sector.

Privatization and contracting-out offer a number of putative benefits to public agencies:

(a) the opportunity for the public sector to concentrate on *policy* formulation within a strategic framework, leaving implementation to other agencies;
(b) the opportunity to concentrate service delivery on those areas in which the agency has a comparative advantage, buying in services from other agencies which have a corresponding competitive advantage in those services;

(c) the possibility of arranging for greater consumer choice, by contracting out to several competing organizations;

(d) the possibility of finding cheaper alternative sources of provision at equivalent quality, through the stimulus which competition will give (in-house and in the competing organizations);

(e) the possibility of stimulating innovation in service delivery by removing service design and implementation issues from the over-detailed examination of political decision-making (the 'dead costs of public accountability').

At the same time, it must be recognized that there are major concerns that these potential benefits will be lost if the process involves simply the transfer of monopolies from the public to the private sector, the sanctioning of cheaper but lower quality services and the removal of proper public accountability for value for money in designing and implementing public services. It must be expected that the balance of these arguments will alter from time to time and will differ from place to place. The arrangements made for service provision in the newly privatized or contracted-out services will need value for money monitoring and review just as much as those services remaining wholly within the public sector.

Budget decentralization

To enhance accountability, there has been a fast growing movement towards the establishment of accountability centres. In the private sector the comparable concept is 'profit centres' but in the more restricted fields of most public agencies this translates as 'cost centres', 'budget centres' or, more rarely, as 'performance centres'. These increase incentives, through offering the higher status of budget holder to good managers and they enhance control by giving responsibility for budgetary control to the person responsible for making the expenditure decision (Flynn, 1986). However, many organizations have found it difficult to reconcile these laudable aims with the simultaneous control of policy direction, since increased autonomy in local expenditure decisions has often allowed significant 'bending' of policy priorities to occur in practice.

The desire to decentralize some aspects of control and to delegate budget holding is evident in changing central government attitudes to financial management. Most central government departments have now specified budget centres under the Financial Management Initiative. Furthermore, greater decentralization has been imposed by central government on some public services in recent years – the move to unit management in the National Health Service and the proposals for local management of schools in the Education Reform Bill. This latter 'carries with it the requirements for an LEA to set objectives for its schools, to allocate resources to them and then, by means of monitoring their performance, to ask schools to account for their achievements and their use of resources' (Coopers and Lybrand, 1988, in a report to the Department of Education and Science). Yet it remains to be seen whether the increased diverstiy of practice which is likely to result from decentralization will prove more acceptable to a government which has attacked elected local authorities for the range of service delivery mechanisms which are currently being used.

Summary

The move towards performance management rests centrally upon a good information system which includes financial information alongside and in contrast to effectiveness information. Public sector financial information systems have become much more capable of serving the financial management needs of their agencies. However, financial management must now be integrated more successfully into performance management. It remains to be seen if the technical advances which have made this possible in respect of performance measurement and reporting will be matched by those major cultural changes which will be needed if organizations are to accept a performance–orientation in their political and managerial decision-making.

References

Anthony, R. N. (1977), 'ZZB – a Useful Fraud?', *Government Accountants Journal*, Summer.

Audit Commission (1984), *The Impact on Local Authorities' Economy, Efficiency and Effectiveness of the Block Grant Distribution System* (HMSO).

Bovaird, T. and Mallinson, I. (1988). 'Setting Objectives and Measuring Achievement in Social Care', *British Journal of Social Work*, vol. 18, no. 3.

Carsberg, B. (1974), *Analysis for Investment Decisions* (Haymarket Publishing).

Committee of Public Accounts (1982), 'The Use of Investment Appraisal in Straightforward Spending Decisions by Government Departments', *28th Report, Session 1981–82* (HMSO).

86 *An Introduction to Public Sector Management*

Coopers and Lybrand (1988), *Local Management of Schools: a Report to the Department of Education and Science* (HMSO).

Culyer, A. J. (1980), *The Political Economy of Social Policy* (Martin Robertson).

Department of the Environment (1972), *Getting the Best Roads for our Money: the COBA Method of Appraisal* (HMSO).

Flowerdew, A. J. and Rodriguez, (1978), 'Benefits for Residents from Urban Renewal: Management, Estimations and Results', *Scottish Journal of Political Economy*, vol. 25, November.

Flynn, N. (1987), 'Delegating Financial Responsibility and Policy-Making with Social Services Departments', *Public Money*, vol. 6, no. 4, March.

Foster, C. (1986), 'Reforming Local Government Finance', *Public Money*, vol. 6, no. 2, September.

Furze, A. (1986), 'What the Opinion Surveys say about Local Government', *Local Government Policy-making* (Longman), September.

Hallows, D. A. (1977), *Cost Reduction* (INLOGOV, University of Birmingham).

HM Treasury (1983), *Investment Appraisal in the Public Sector: A Management Guide for Government Departments* (HMSO).

HM Treasury (1984), *Investment Appraisal in the Public Sector: A Technical Guide for Government Departments* (HMSO).

HM Treasury (1987), *The Government's Expenditure Plans 1987–88 to 1989–90*, Vol. II (HMSO).

Jones, T. and Prowle, M. (1987), *Health Service Finance: An Introduction* (Certified Accountants Education Trust).

Layfield Report (1976), *Report of the Enquiry into Local Government Finance* (HMSO).

Lewis, C. (1987), 'Spreadsheet Graphics for Monitoring Spending', *Public Finance and Accountancy*, 7 August.

Likierman, A. (1984), 'Planning and Control – Developments in Central Government' in A. Hopwood and C. Tomkins (eds), *Issues in Public Sector Accounting* (Philip Allan).

Lindblom, C. E. (1959), 'The Science of "Muddling Through"', *Public Administrative Review*, vol. 19.

National Consumer Council (1986), *Measuring Up: Consumer Assessment of Local Authority Services – a Guideline Study* (National Consumer Council).

Nutley, S., Bovaird, T. and Thomas, C. (1987), *Can Local Authorities Improve their Investment Decisions?*, Aston University Public Sector Management Research Unit Working Paper no. 12.

Parkinson, M. (1986), 'Creative Accounting and Financial Ingenuity in Local Government: the Case of Liverpool', *Public Money*, vol. 5, no. 4, March.

Pliatzky, L. (1982), 'Cash Limits and Pay Policy', *Political Quarterly*, vol. 53, no. 1.

PSMRU (1985), *Five Year Review of Birmingham Inner City Partnership*, Public Sector Management Research Unit, Aston University (HMSO).

Ramanathan, K. V. (1985), 'A Proposed Framework for Designing

Management Control Systems in Not-for-Profit Organizations', *Financial Accountability and Management*, vol. 1, no. 1, Summer.

Richards, S. (1987), 'Cultural Change in the Civil Service', paper presented to P.A.C. Annual Conference, University of York, 7–9 September.

Sullivan, C. (1984), 'Project Appraisal', *Public Finance and Accountancy*, March.

Tomkins, C. (1986), 'Local Authority Audit under the Audit Commission and what it means to one Private Sector Professional Firm', *Financial Accountability and Management*, vol. 2, no. 1.

Vamplew, C. and Gallant, V. (1983), 'The Cleveland Case', *Local Government Policy-making* (Longman), November.

Whitehead, C. (1987), 'Housing Taxes and Prices', *Public Money*, vol. 6, no. 4.

Wildavsky, A. (1974), *The Politics of the Budgetary Process* (Little Brown & Co., Boston).

3 Financial objectives and control in the management of Britain's nationalized industries

ROGER BUCKLAND

Introduction – the privatization phenomenon

With the rapid progress of privatization since 1979 – sale of council houses, private contracting in local government and health, the sale of nationalized businesses – our perspective upon the state-owned and operated sector is changing. The years between 1945 and 1976, when most state businesses were acquired or established and when there existed an uneasy political consensus about the legitimacy of state enterprise, might now look like an aberration from the norm, a deviation from a predominantly private sector world. State control of transport, energy, aerospace, shipbuilding, steel and telecommunications appears to have been a transient stage of Britain's economy and society. Received wisdom in Westminster and Whitehall is now that the state runs businesses very badly: it interferes frequently and perversely in organizations which lack incentives, are immune to penalties and are isolated from competition.

That is an oversimplification, of course. Some activities have been state-owned for generations – the Post Office, the BBC, the Royal Ordnance Factories. Others are so venerable that they still hardly draw mention – crown activities such as the Customs and Excise, the Inland Revenue, the Armed Forces. At a different level, local and municipal enterprise, in forms such as water supply, sewerage, sea and air ports, libraries, public transport, policing and housing, have been a part of the British economic scenery for a century or more.

Yet the extension of this list remains a short-term, post-1945 phenomenon. In the late 1940s Britain's coal, gas, electricity, railways, steel, hospital and air transport industries were nationalized, extending the economic activity of the state deeper into the economy. Despite ideological opposition from Conservative administrations in the 1950s and 1970s expressed in the denationalization of the Iron and Steel Corporation during the 1950s, the public sector continued to grow – shipbuilding, aerospace, electronics, Rolls-Royce. Even Conservative governments viewed nationalization as a variable, if distasteful option when faced with intractable problems in private sector industry.

In this context the pronounced shift to privatization after 1979 expresses more than merely the ideological attitude of an incoming Conservative government. In this chapter we shall see that the shift reflects an important change in how the objectives and mechanisms of control of public sector businesses are conceived and viewed. This shift is one stage in the emergence of formal analysis of business control over these years, from casual and often anodyne directives in the early post-1945 years, through the positivist theory of the 1960s to the current dominance of principal and agent models, drawing on comparative institutional theory. The chapter will link the emergence of these models of financial control to public policy on state ownership and will question the correspondence of structures of control with public policy.

Privatization is quintessentially about management: about how the context of business and its control mechanisms motivate managers to meet the business objectives. History is presenting us with two contrasting norms: the Morrisonian Public Corporation, with its quasi-autonomous policy board and its reporting relationship to a sponsoring department of the state; and the independent public limited company, with any public obligations imposed by a regulatory structure responsible to Parliament.

Control in the Morrisonian public corporation

When the nationalized industry sector was expanded during the Attlee administration of 1945 to 1951, the architect of the new structures was Herbert Morrison MP (later Lord Morrison of Lambeth). His concept of the Public Corporation closely followed the models of municipal enterprise, with a commercially oriented business overlain by a supervisory, management board. The board itself was to be separated from direct political control, but subjected to it. Board members would be appointed by ministers and ministers would be accountable to Parliament for the corporation's activities.

This structure can fairly be described as ad hoc. It insisted upon a mixed economy, managed solution – as opposed to alternatives of co-operative, worker-controlled or other mainstream socialist organization. The compromise solution of the Public Corporation enabled government to be flexible in the application of power and patronage during appointment, boards of corporations to be flexible in the construction placed upon tensions between commercial logic and national interest and, lastly, allowed Parliament to be flexible in the terms and extent of its oversight of the nationalized sector.

The Public Corporation, which remains the hallmark of the nationalized industries (NIs) within the public sector, marked off public sector businesses from other areas of public goods and services. For these latter a bureaucratic solution was installed, where government departments took direct responsibility for the provision and delivery of services, either nationally (the Post Office, the National Health Service, the Armed Forces, the Civil Aviation Authority, for example), or devolved to local authorities as with education or housing. The model for the privatization of such bureaucracies has become that of contracting-out: narrowing the scope of public sector managerial control to decisions about levels of service, planning and monitoring of outcomes, rather than the mechanics of operations management (see Le Grand and Robinson, 1984, or Hartley and Huby, 1985, for reviews of the contracting process in public services).

In extending the public sector to industrial concerns the post-1945 corporations sought to fulfil quite separate objectives, which dictated the structures of their control. Here the driving forces towards nationalization were, first, that of controlling natural monopoly: in energy supply with electricity and gas, in the activity of the central bank, in water supply or rail transport. Secondly, the failures of private sector solutions to the interwar recessions suggested that some public direction of key industries could lead to different industrial strategies: that industries could work coherently and supportively if controlled under the aegis of some 'national interest'.

In so far as nationalization had any overtly socialist content, that lay in the equitable aims of limiting monopoly abuse and of the collective ambitions of industrial concerns operating in some national interest rather than in sectional owners' interests. The

impetus towards state control developed out of the pre-1939 dissatisfaction with the conduct of industry in Britain: the absence of
strategic planning and the impotance of private sector responses to
recession and unemployment. During the war years of 1939 to
1945, government had gained wide experience of detailed industrial
control and intervention, moving decisively towards the state's
assumption of responsibility for full employment and industrial
growth.

Otherwise the device of the Public Corporation presents the state
as owner and as beneficiary. The outcome of the Attlee government's nationalization programme fell far short of the prewar 'com-
manding heights' philosophy; and excluded the centrepiece of a
central state planning authority. The state is acting as the people's
agent, not promoting their involvement as a principal. The state
may be more kindly disposed to workers, but is not any more
obligated to operate in their interests or to their benefit.
Undoubtedly, this side-step from socialist goals is one reason why
Conservative administrations were not more hostile to the NIs in
the 1950s and 1970s.

In common with the bureaucratized public sector services, nationalization vested control over businesses with departments of state.
The corporations were accountable to Parliament, but sponsored by
a responsible minister, being grouped under the departments of
transport (airlines, railways, road freight), energy (the coal, gas, oil
and electricity boards) and industry (steel, shipbuilding, aerospace,
motor vehicles and telecommunications). The accretion of power
over these sectors formed one part of the post-1945 expansion of
intervention and the increasing influence of ministers from the
Board of Trade and the Ministry of Power. The NIs form one
strand of the emergence of the power of industry and trade posts
within the British Cabinet, countervailing the long-established
dominance of Exchequer and administrative functions.

In the Morrisonian Public Corporation the mechanisms and application of control were carried over from the municipal enterprises.
The public interest was to be secured by divorcing the corporation
from sectional interests rather than by providing it with positive
goals. Indeed, the definition or description of the statutory relationship between the corporations and their political sponsors was vague
and imprecise. Central or integrative planning mechanisms or goals
were absent; Morrison himself would go no further than to write:
'The Public Corporation must be no mere capitalist business . . . its
Board and its officers must regard themselves as the high custodians
of the public interest' (Morrison, 1933, pp. 156–7).

As a moral sentiment this may be unexceptionable, but by the mid-1960s the absence of core direction to the corporations was leaving them well behind: 'Ministerial control is something that has grown up in a somewhat haphazard way. It has been distorted by the troubles of individual industries and has not been planned with foresight, prescribed with clarity or applied with consistency. It is the product and not the master of its environment' (Select Committee, 1968, para. 50). The core problems of control lay in, first, determining a valid yardstick of the 'national interest' which corporations were to aim for; and, second, to control effectively the corporations' efforts to advance towards such goals while maintaining some level of commercial autonomy.

In a historical perspective, the initial format of oversight, with the interposition of a supervisory board separated from the sponsor and the operation of the business, could be expected to provide some answers to those problems. Owners' control over business in general was itself rudimentary, based largely upon survival, financial strength and accounting measures of performance. However, as scientific management advanced and the appraisal of activity became more orderly the financial control of owners over their businesses advanced also. Not only was information more widely and rapidly available, but it was better codified, more reliable and more comparable between businesses. Objective-setting and objective-monitoring became feasible control tools.

When this emergence of scientific financial management[1] is set alongside the experience of the novel Public Corporations in action through the late 1940s and 1950s, the pressure for closer articulation of control can be readily understood. Occasional reports upon specific industries during the 1950s, such as that of the Herbert Committee (1956), laid increasing stress upon commercial criteria and concrete guidelines and objectives, but the basis of controls in the founding charters of the corporations remained one of a medium-term break-even criterion. Initially, indeed, this financial objective was both ambiguous and ill-defined. Corporations were to meet the demand for their products – whatever that might be – but otherwise were obliged 'that their revenues should, on an average of good and bad years [or some similar phrase], be not less than sufficient to meet all items properly charged to revenue' (Cmnd 1337, 1961, para. 5). Thus the NIs were given a minimum performance hurdle rather than positive targets or efficiency and effectiveness criteria.

Throughout the 1950s, then, the new nationalized undertakings were operated in order that properly charged costs be covered and that output be generated where demanded. Under such circumstances the national interest is served in so much that any profit or value added by the industries' operations is gleaned by their customers. In other words, the monopoly powers of, say, electricity boards were curbed indirectly by the expectation that the state would not seek to maximize revenues, but only to cover costs.

On the other hand, such vague and rudimentary controls do little to encourage effectiveness and efficiency, they may stultify investment and growth and they can be frustrated by the special circumstances of the industry. There is, for example, no mechanism for controlling costs, so that the abuse of monopoly can be expressed in high costs rather than high profits. With such lax controls it may be that suppliers and/or employees gain from nationalization rather than the national interest, however that might be defined. Throughout the 1950s the Corporations, even where they broke even, failed to provide sufficient finance to fund their own investment programmes; and for several NIs breaking even could only be interpreted by excluding statutory items such as provision for reserves, capital redemption or depreciation.

In the face of such lax financial control, the full burden of regulating the activity and performance of the NIs fell upon the activities of their boards and the relationship with individual ministers. The Select Committee on Nationalized Industries, in their report upon ministerial control, put it this way: 'it was inevitable that Ministers and the industries have been forced to arrive at informal arrangements and understandings (or – all too often – misunderstandings) about the duties of the industries' (Select Committe, 1968, para. 49).

1960–1970: The development of positivist controls

The NIs were not only seen as vital elements within the economy (see, for example, Webb's comments in his survey of 1973), but they were also test beds for the application of the emergent, positivist models of financial control developed by economists during the 1940s and 1950s. Drawing directly upon the neoclassical framework of general equilibrium theory, with elegant diagrammatic or algebraic solutions to pricing and output problems, economists proposed that the marginalist solutions of theory could be used as a basis for decision-making in the public sector. On pricing, since welfare would increase as long as the marginal social cost of delivery did not exceed the marginal social benefits of consumption, then marginal cost pricing should determine the price and output decisions of the public sector. On investment, value would be maximized by application of discounted cash flow (DCF) models to measure and compare the marginal merits of investment proposals (Curwen, 1986; Heald, 1980).

The influence of these rationalist and prescriptive theories of control underlay the crucial steps in the evolution of policy towards NIs. The White Paper of 1961 attempted to draw together the haphazard histories of control into some more coherent picture. Some definition was given to the break-even period, by requiring corporations to achieve it over any five-year period (Cmnd 1337, 1961, para. 19(a)). Break even itself was codified as inclusive of the building of reserves, both for capital developments and for contingencies (ibid., para. 19(b)). Corporations were to agree upon financing plans (ibid., para. 24) and there would be a financial target set, determined by pricing, investment and any social obligations; breach of the targets agreed would necessitate new negotiation with the sponsoring department.

While the 1961 White Paper established some goals, it still left matters imprecise. In 1967 a second White Paper built upon this philosophy and sought to regulate NIs by a set of ideal precepts. The paper was clear that it was theory-led: 'Discounted Cash Flow techniques are recommended for all major projects . . . these techniques enable proper comparison to be made between alternative projects' (Cmnd 3437, 1967, para. 8); and 'pricing policies should be devised with reference to the costs of the particular goods and services demanded' (ibid., para. 18). The 1967 White Paper set out a framework whereby a nationalized industry sought to establish what it was in the national interest to do, working on the basis of optimal resource allocation through marginal cost pricing. Based upon such projections and any special circumstances of social, technological or national interest factors it would then be set a financial target, probably as a return to be made on capital employed. This target would be the result projected on the basis of optimal policies and hence breaches of the target would signal some sub-optimal behaviour which would need to be explained and justified in renegotiation with the sponsoring department.

The increasing confidence of the neoclassical economists can be seen in the progression from the 1961 White Paper – with its reliance upon an imprecise break-even criterion, over a rolling five-year horizon – to the detailed prescriptive contents of the 1967 paper. Webb sees the 1967 White Paper as providing 'criteria for pricing and investment decisions that would promote a more efficient allocation of resources' (Webb, 1980, p. 120). In proposing the common use of a single, public-sector 'Test Discount Rate' and in its espousal of marginal cost pricing the government adopted the principles of the neoclassical school.

However, NIs found chronic and increasing difficulties in implementing the 1967 White Paper guidelines. Three distinct problems can be identified. First, the NIs discovered that the investment and pricing rules were difficult to interpret and impossible to implement. Even where forecast cash returns could be obtained, one essential characteristic of public sector business is that there exist some significant, material national or public interest connotations to activity; hence social costs and benefits are central to the calculation of discounted 'cash' flows. The quantification of national interests was acknowledged to be 'in its infancy' (Select Committee, 1968, para. 726) and yet ministers were to be encouraged 'instead of scrutinising programmes and projects in detail ... [to] concern themselves with ensuring that the proper criteria and techniques of appraisal are used and [to] then approve without further detailed scrutiny' (ibid., par. 574).

It is not surprising that such injunctions, to abandon the responsibilities of sponsoring departments to the vagaries of a largely untested academic technique, were rejected by ministers and their officials. In fact, to follow a second and parallel line of problems, this prescriptive approach failed completely to comprehend the contextual limitations of policy. Drawn from the neoclassical tradition, the 1967 White Paper's pricing and investment criteria were to operate as if in a black box. There was to be no intrinsic difficulty in finding agreement upon definitions and measures of marginal social costs and benefits, nor any conflict of organizational or regulatory cultures in using such measures as the tools of policy. When the realities of problem-solving are addressed, as in the British Steel Corporation case of the following section, it becomes clear that the intellectualization of the neoclassical economists' rules of behaviour were no match, nor any substitute for the dominant managerial cultures.

Thirdly, the emergence of the marginalist model in financial control was already being undermined by powerful academic challenges. These stemmed both from within and from outside the neoclassical paradigm, from radical economists in behavioural, Marxian and Austrian schools of thought. From within, it was already recognized that the marginal cost pricing rules required sophisticated modification to cope with circumstances under which their application might lead to chronic losses, over-provision and misallocation. The most obvious of such circumstances was that of diminishing marginal costs. Here, average costs lie above marginal costs and a marginalist pricing rule would always imply a price below average cost and hence perpetual losses for the business. It was also recognized that, if other competing businesses were not themselves acting optimally, then it might not be optimal for the NI itself to adopt optimal rules of behaviour. Such a 'first-best' solution might – and in general would – be inferior to a 'second-best' outcome, distant from any marginal solution (Lipsey and Lancaster, 1957).

The seminal insider critique of marginal cost rules appeared as early as 1957, in Wiseman's shrewd observation of public utility pricing theory as 'An Empty Box' (Wiseman, 1957). Articulation of criticism from outside the neoclassical paradigm came much later. In a caustic review of the failures of nationalized industry controls, Nove argues that 'politicians' confusions on how nationalized industries should be run are a result of the advice of conventional micro-economists' (Nove, 1973, p. 7). From across the spectrum of political economy, in the Austrian school, Littlechild pins down the neoclassical approach's shortcomings more precisely: 'The intellectual task facing the nationalised industries was misunderstood, and the rules derived from static welfare economics were inappropriate to the real world of uncertainty' (Littlechild, 1981, p. 54).

Neoclassicists themselves would still maintain that their nostrums have 'failed' only by not being applied. As Webb introduces his 1980 critical appraisal: 'it [microeconomics] was never given a proper chance to show what it could achieve because government policy in the early 1970s was dominated by macroeconomic considerations' (Webb, 1980, p. 120).

Certainly the period between the establishment of positive control, in the 1967 White Paper, and the 1980s abandonment of nationalization as a means to controlled, public interest solutions, is a key factor in understanding the shift towards privatization itself. In 1978 a third White Paper sought to re-define and to re-establish financial controls over the NIs. On investment, it stated that 'the Test Discount Rate system has not lived up to expectations. In practice only a limited proportion of investment has been appraised in this way . . . so far the TDR has neither provided nor stimulated the development of an adequate way of relating the cost of capital to the industries' financial objectives' (Cmnd 7131, 1978, para. 59). On marginal cost pricing the White Paper was equally blunt: 'for the most part they [the NIs] have been unable to follow this principle, not only because of price restraint and adverse market conditions but also because of serious difficulties of interpreting its practical application in particular cases' (ibid., para. 66). This reflected the conclusions of the National Economic Development Office (NEDO) study in 1976: 'none of the four nationalised industries currently base their pricing policies on long-run or short-run marginal cost' (NEDO, 1976, p. 100).[2]

The 1978 White Paper shifted attention away from rigorous application of microeconomics, with a consequently determined financial target, to issues of supervision, control and monitoring. The new 'required rate of return' (RRR) to replace the defunct TDR could be manipulated and cross-subsidized by the NIs. 'It will no longer specify a general TDR to be used for all appraisals' and 'for management reasons they [the NIs] might choose to appraise revenue earning investments at a [different] rate' (Cmnd 7131, 1978, para. 64). As Webb concludes, 'the 1978 White Paper, unlike the 1967 White Paper, did not stress the need for adoption of consistent pricing and investment policies by the nationalised industries' (Webb, 1980, p. 136).

In effect, the 1978 White Paper recognized that the NIs could not, would not or should not apply consistent marginalist rules to determine a consequential financial target. The target had to be derived separately, even independently of the allocative decisions taken by the industry. In 1978 emphasis shifted decisively towards the counter-inflation policy; and social and sectoral objectives (Cmnd 7131, 1978, para. 73).

At the same time government was introducing the system of cash limits for public sector activity, to tighten budgetary discipline and planning (Cmnd 6440, 1976); and this additional tool of financial control, which developed into the system of External Financing Limits (EFLs), remains the prime financial discipline upon the remaining NIs. While it was still conceivable to view industries' EFLs as a product of their rational application of optimal internal financial controls, it was in practice clear that after 1978 government recognized that the target and the EFL were to be the determining constraint upon public sector activity, given the overwhelming evidence that the NIs had been unable, unwilling or prevented from applying optimal internal controls.

Not only was this a crucial defeat for the NIs – particularly for the independence and influence of their boards and chairmen – but it represented also a retreat from influence for the sponsoring departments and ministers. From their connections to the activity, investment and operations of the NIs these departments derived much of their influence within the economy and also within government.

Under the present cash limit system, the departments' role is reduced to little more than one of policing the financing framework established by the Treasury, which has reassumed a dominant position in the management of the economy.

A Case in point: Controls in the British Steel Corporation

NEDO's general conclusion that optimal controls were not operated successfully within the British Steel Corporation (BSC) have already been noted. Within this section some further aspects of BSC's case will be examined to shed light upon why the clear prescriptions of the 1967 pricing and investment rules could not be operated and how this reflects upon the development of financial control and the pressures for privatization of the NIs.

First it is plain that BSC simply could not operate by the 1967 rules of the game. Its investment decisions are complex, interrelated and very long term in nature. In order to deliver a particular specification of steel, both metallurgically defect and dimension specified, it is necessary to exert sophisticated control over iron and coke feedstocks, iron-making, steel-making and alloying, casting, rolling/forging and finishing processes. The level of sophistication required to conduct useful DCF appraisals of investments is technically conceivable, but is never in practice achieved, either in BSC or elsewhere. The models are quite simply too demanding of forecast information to produce any determinate, 'optimal' result.

In addition to the technical complexities of modelling interdependent or alternative options, programming their possible variation, abandonment, links with developing or novel technologies, susceptibility to scenarios of forecast levels of world, UK and BSC market share of demand, BSC had also the requirement to build in the evaluation of its national interest and social obligations. It was planning not merely for its own financial results, but for the improvement of conditions for its customers, its fellow private sector UK steel producers, its employees and the communities within which its plants were located. In other words the 1967 White Paper asked BSC, like other NIs, not only to operationalize optimal controls at a level which was not even approached by the private sector, but also to apply them to intangibles and unknowns which would never impinge upon such private sector business.

Inevitably BSC's modelling of investment and price became drastically simplified, sometimes in damaging areas. Rowley has reviewed the implausibility of pricing policy in steel (Rowley, 1971) and the control of investment has been critically reviewed by academics (Bryer, Brignall and Maunders, 1982, for example) and by Parliament (Select Committee, 1978). There is ample evidence to show that decisions taken 'scientifically' have been taken in error, with the principles of DCF appraisal adapted and bent in order to achieve some, or any, quantification of an essentially fuzzy evaluation.

Such studies document BSC's failures in investment control: its wrong choices, its over-investment in steel-making and under-investment in finishing, its resulting financial distress through the decade of 1975 to 1985. However, one should not ascribe these only to technical failures, with an unimplementable policy of financial control. Also, BSC could not sensibly apply the 1967 rules because its own financial structure prevented the proper linkage between control and financial performance. In common with other NIs, BSC is deemed to be financed by a combination of borrowing through the National Loans Fund and by Public Dividend Capital from the Treasury. Although not disciplined by bankruptcy, BSC found itself financially crippled by the very absence of a bankruptcy option. Where a private sector business would inevitably have been financially reconstructed in the early 1970s, BSC instead found itself progressively weakened by an accumulation of losses and of the interest burden upon those losses. The tardiness of its sponsoring department in recognizing distress by the writing off of past investment was joined by a reluctance of managers, undisciplined by technical bankruptcy or insolvency rules, to take hard decisons on abandoning projects and reappraising strategy.

It is also crucial to recognize that BSC not only could not, but would not implement optimal controls. One central reason for this is that such controls rely upon a scientific management culture which is alien to the internal structures of the NIs themselves. Just as the theory of controls can be described as an empty box, so it assumes that it can supplant any existing system of decision-making and control, without strain or dissonance.

In ignoring the complex political and organizational problems of decision both within NIs and between NIs and their sponsoring departments, the policies of the 1960s and 1970s evaded the central issues of control. BSC's planners found themselves used not as a resource for generating decisons, but as a weapon within decision-making. This is seen particularly clearly within decisions with uncertain and fuzzy outcomes, such as that over-investment in 1975 in innovative iron-making plant at Hunterston in Scotland. The benefits of such speculative investment in a new technology are indefinable in terms of DCF modelling: rather they form elements of game-playing and of defensive strategies amongst competitor firms. In this particular case, a route to iron feedstocks, independent of coal deliveries, was seized upon as a counter to militant action in the coal industry. The new technology itself was a key element in BSC's self-image as a leading innovator, not as a financially valuable project. Not least, the investment project contained its own dynamic, with the negotiators driven by goals of short-term success in contracting rather than by any long-term viability of the project to some distant 'national interest'.[3]

Given such complexities of environment and of decision process, one is close to linking 'would not' with 'should not': the deterministic models of the White Papers in the 1960s should be supplanted by more useful models of control. In concluding our discussion of BSC, however, there are other very cogent reasons why these models should not have been used to control BSC's decisions. Intellectually, the case for strict marginalist procedures falls when others, particularly competitors, are not behaving under the same rules of the game. What could be optimal behaviour in a first-best world of general equilibrium[4] cannot be regarded prima facie as optimal if other economic units are themselves not behaving optimally. This was demonstrably true of competing private sector UK steelmakers, true of the heavy cross-subsidization in the Japanese bulk steel sector, true of direct and indirect state subsidization in the European steel sector businesses: true also of aid-financed competitors in Third World areas.

Even had first-best conditions prevailed, BSC operated within an environment where it was statutorily prevented from adopting the criteria of the 1960s control regime. It was strictly subjected to domestic prices and incomes legislation, which precluded marginal cost pricing; it was increasingly subjected to discretionary intervention in its investment policies, for unquantified and uncompensated regional and local employment considerations; its output was stringently controlled under the quota regimes of the European Coal and Steel Community plans for a radically lower EEC steel-making capacity.

Since BSC did not have available to it the levers by which it could implement financial controls, it is extraordinary that it was expected to translate those abstract principles into a concrete financial outcome. Given that its decision processes were also alien to the analysis behind those abstract principles, it is unsurprising that BSC's financial outcomes were at variance with the targets based on

them. Throughout the 1970s BSC, in common with other NIs, was effectively out of formal control and operating instead under whatever informal regulation was developed between itself and its sponsoring department. Into this vacuum stepped the reformists arguing for a privatization solution and, in the interim, exerting control within a crude framework of short-term cash limits on the public sector.

The emergent theory of control in principal and agent relationships

The public sector has never, in practice, been managed according to the prescriptive rules articulated in the 1960s. Underlying the official concern with TDRs and marginal costing, with social cost benefit analysis and the determinacy of financial targets there has always been an undercurrent of concern with some alternative scheme of ministerial control. Even within the White Papers of the 1960s it is obvious that, with pricing control, investment control and, in addition, financial targets, the system was technically over-determined: any two of those controls would determine the third. In the reports of parliamentary committees there are clear signs that ministerial control was consistently intended to interpose itself between outcomes and corporation boards' interpretation of controls. In its major study of the 1967/8 session, the Select Committee on Nationalized Industries sought to draw this together in its report, *Ministerial Control of the Nationalised Industries* (Select Committee, 1968): 'the Committee, noting the concern that previous Committees had reported regarding the operation of Ministerial control, decided that the time had come for an independent attempt to study and learn some of the lessons' (ibid., para. 5).

This Select Committee report gives details of practice and of criticism, but it lacks the central organizing ideas of why ministerial control is needed and what makes it problematic. It is this relationship between a business and its owners or sponsors which forms the nub of control policy and which is so signally evaded by the financial controls of the 1960s and early 1970s. The theory of these relationships is now commonly articulated as principal and agent theory, where managers (agents) are contracted by interest groups (principals) to carry out activity which benefits the principals. By concentrating attention upon these transactions and contracts, principal and agent theory transforms notions of control from 'what rules are optimal to generate behaviour?' into questions of 'what

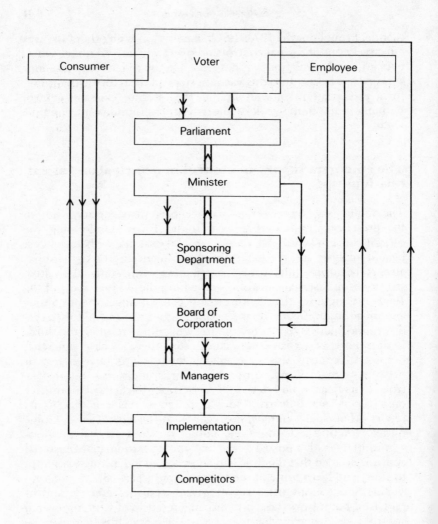

Key: ───────► Impact
     ──►──► Authority
     ══════► Responsibility

Figure 3.1 *Control networks in Public Corporations.*

rules will effectively encourage agents to act in principals' best interests?'

This section will not explore the fundamentals of principal and agent theory (for which, see Arrow, 1986; Rees, 1985; Williamson, 1986). Rather it will use a principal and agent framework to uncover the problems of control which have resulted in privatization and explain why this programme has gained a firm hold as a form of public sector control. This section will also explore alternative routes towards an improvement in public sector accountability and performance. First, let us see, schematically, what the nature of the control problems are.

In the representation within Figure 3.1 of impact on, authority over and responsibility to, the complexities and scope for control loss can be seen. For a Public Corporation, control over implementation is several stages removed from the interested principals (voters, consumers and employees). The consumer has the standard recourse to direct influence through product markets; and traditionally has some delegated representation in policy review through user committees and departmental lobbying. Employees of Public Corporations have few avenues of influence other than through their intersection with voters (where, of course, they may be out-voted by non-employees). However, their practical influence over the managers in collective bargaining may be enhanced by any institutionalized presence on boards and through any corollary impact of monopolization and their increased leverage in any disputes.

Any public interests of voters must be articulated and exercised through a series of contractual relationships. First, the voter must elect or lobby parliamentary representatives, to whom sponsoring ministers are responsible and through whose committees corporations' boards must explain their activity and outcomes. The boards are held responsible only to the sponsoring department, however. Clearly, much of the critical stance on the control of NIs relates to the definition and enforcement of contracts of performance as between boards and departments, departments and their ministers, ministers and Parliament. The financial control regime devised in the 1960s impinges only upon managers, in an attempt to ensure that principal and agent problems elsewhere would be marginal, if optimal rules were enforced at the point of implementation. We have seen with the example of BSC that this could never have been the case, even if defects in the linkages elsewhere had not themselves interfered with the implementation.

The system of control over the Public Corporation depicted in the figure has the patent disadvantage of several disputed transfers of control, where some subjective and contentious public interest (whose? what? how much? when?) needs to be conveyed and enforced. Over the thirty years from 1948 to 1978 successive Parliaments, governments, ministers and boards wrestled with these problems and achieved some measure of compromise. Their efforts were not aided by the notions of optimal financial controls. Indeed, such notions distract from the intractable nature of contracting difficulties by abstracting from their existence: nationalization came to be judged by its failure to attain ideal goals, not by any success in its achievements in behaving in the public interest (see Redwood's seminal critique, 1981; or Pryke's examination of the shortcomings of NIs. 1981). Appraisal of the underlying contractual difficulties is now taking place, as for example in the work of Ashford (1981), Peacock (1984) and particularly Perotin and Estrin (1986); but public policy can be seen to have shifted decisively towards another polar solution, privatization, rather than to a reappraisal of effective control.

As Williamson insistently argues, the first principle of an economic analysis of organizational behaviour is that it be treated in a comparative institutional manner (Williamson, 1986). Instead of comparing an imperfect reality with an unattainable ideal, one must compare the virtues and vices of differing institutional alternatives. In Figure 3.2, analogous to Figure 3.1 above, the dominant institutional model of contemporary privatization is presented. The Public Corporation is shifted into the private sector domain by restructuring it as a financially strong public limited company (PLC). Its objectives become those of all PLCs: to operate in the interests of its shareholder owners, who have sole legal title to its residual assets, profits and wealth. The equity of this PLC is then sold by the state to private sector bidders, who become its shareholders. Its links to departments, ministers and hence to Parliament are severed, to be replaced by some variation on a licence agreement with an independent, regulatory authority. This authority is set up to control any abuse of private monopoly and to enforce any remaining public interest requirements. Otherwise, government and voters can affect the PLC only by the purchase of compliance (with, for example, subsidy payments for operation on specific bus routes; subsidy of employment in specific areas or of training schemes).

Figure 3.2 shows the salient changes in control and accountability. Employees, always marginalized in the Public Corporation structures, are now sidelined, except in so far as they take up any equity and hence voting interest in the business. Since these priva-

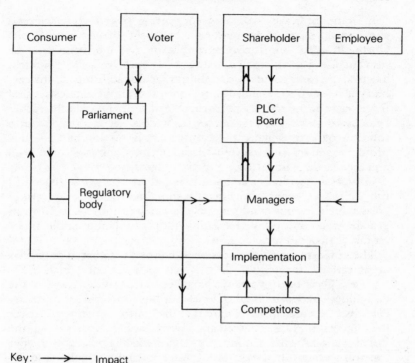

Key: ———→—— Impact
      ——→→—— Authority
      ═══→══ Responsibility

Figure 3.2 *Control networks in regulated PLCs.*

tized PLCs are typically giant firms, such an ownership stake offers no effective influence over the PLC's activities, but only a financial interest in that activity producing a financial surplus. Voters are disenfranchised from influence over the PLC, except in so far as Parliament can set the agenda of the regulatory body. These bodies (for example, Oftel in the telecommunications field, Ofgas in the natural gas industry) are responsible to Parliament, but operate independently under their founding statutes. Thus any perceptions of public interest aspects of the PLC's actual or potential activity are incapable of being translated into control. Only by purchasing compliance can the state introduce public interest elements. Consumers similarly have been distanced from influence, appearing only in product markets or as instigators of the concern of the regulatory body.

In comparing the two, now contrasting, frameworks, several considerations can be brought out. First, the change from Public Corporation to PLC is forcing public interest intervention to be measured and compensated, rather than perceived and enjoined. There are advantages here, of visibility, accountability and enforceability. However, it is unclear whether the public interest is any more quantifiable and any more capable of compensation than it has been since 1948. On the face of it, it does seem strange that a solution of externalizing the transaction is now proposed to a problem where, over several decades, internalization has been regarded as the – imperfect – practical necessity.

In working within clear boundaries, then, the privatized PLCs run the risk of being incapable of responding to public concern in areas which are not conducive to market solutions. This form of privatization constitutes a retreat from the problem of public interest rather than a resolution of it.

The PLC structure also begs the question of whether its particular organizational form is any less flawed than the one which it has replaced. Over thirty years we have become painfully aware of the difficulties between Public Corporations and their sponsors. However, we are equally aware that the control of principles over their agents in PLCs is flawed and uncertain, particularly when the PLC is very large in relation to any shareholder. Direct shareholder control, through their election of directors and directors' enforcement of shareholders' interests, is an unsupportable fiction. Information is asymmetrically distributed and understood, the formation of controlling blocks is haphazard and the personal cost of shareholders' oversight is prohibitive. The private sector has devised palliative schemes of profit-related bonus pay, or of executive s. are option schemes, to alleviate these quite intractable issues of control loss in modern corporations; but these manipulations of agents' contracts only serve to highlight the difficulties.

One benefit of the private sector solution is that there are alternative disciplines on agents/managers, which may induce them to operate in their principals' interests. By severing the links between the industry and public sector financing, it might be thought that the business is no longer protected from bankruptcy. When leaders or shareholders perceive this they will begin to assess their exposure to the business's risk before continuing to lend to or invest in the new PLC. This financial discipline might be thought to enforce rigorous financial appraisal in ways which the White Paper's procedural rules could never achieve.

The divorce from government sponsorship should also open the field for more equality of status with competitors. While this is hardly apposite for the privatized natural monopolies, it is relevant for the industrial and transport sectors. By redressing the balance of competitors' impact upon implementation, the scope for agents to act in their principals' interests to the detriment of others should be attenuated. On the other hand, of course, this merely proposes a possible solution to a problem which hardly impinges upon the Public Corporation. Since the latter's principals are the state in general and since competitive exploitation is either controlled or was a central reason for the initial nationalization, competitive forces may well be weaker in the PLC solution than regulated behaviour was within nationalization. It is worrying, also, that the privatized PLCs have been constructed in such a way as to exclude competition, rather than promote it (Steel and Heald, 1984; Kay and Silberston, 1984; Vickers and Yarrow, 1985).

A further boon from privatization is that dissatisfied principals can take direct action to disengage from the business. Since the principals' interest is reduced to a financial advantage, they may sell their share in the PLC to another – perhaps even in the context of a takeover or a build-up of control which can exert explicit pressure on the board and on managers. We must be extremely careful about this 'benefit', however. While it is true that the shareholders can transfer their pecuniary benefit, they cannot, of course, transact in any public interest served by the activity of the privatized PLC (Stein, 1976).[5] Indeed, it is difficult to see the merits of principals' tradability in relation to the business's public interest dimension (assuming that one exists, of course). Not only would it be illogical for any individual to be trading in a collectivity, but it is clearly worse, from the public interest standpoint, for the privatized PLC to be pressurized solely by reason of the pecuniary advantage of its own owners.

Summary and conclusions

This chapter has examined the emergence of a theory of business control, alongside the efforts to establish a control regime within the UK nationalized industries. These efforts mirror the emerging debate upon the internal behaviour of business. During the 1960s and 1970s control over nationalized industries was informed by the prescriptions of neoclassical microeconomics. It was suggested that, if pricing was guided by marginal cost criteria and if investment was conducted through discounted cash flow analysis of the alternatives, then the industries' behaviour would be optimal and control over them would be unproblematic.

Within the chapter it has been seen that this system of control was inappropriate, incorrect and unimplementable. The nationalized industries increasingly operated as extensions of the political power of their sponsoring government departments, augmenting the influence of the non-Treasury departments of state during the post-1945 period. Thus while the formal controls – of objective guidelines and criteria – appeared to bolster the primacy of the Treasury and of the decisions of the public expenditure round, the inevitable overlay of ad hoc lobbying and piecemeal control served the interests of the devolved power of the more junior ministries.

In the face of the inevitable failure of neoclassical controls, it has become fashionable to regard nationalized industries as uncontrollable and to replace them by a new model of a privatized, but regulated public limited company. By confronting this debate with the theory of business control as the relationship between principal and agent, the reality of the difficulties of control has been highlighted. In the process, it has been found that the new alternative does not face up to these control problems, but in fact constitutes a retreat, into a private sector model which is arguably at least as deficient in terms of control and where there is little prospect of its serving the national interest. If there is a remaining notion of collective interests which are affected by the activity of major industries, the regulated PLC is singularly ill-fitted to respond. Its owners, were they to be able to exert effective control, have no conceivable concern with a collective interest. The regulatory bodies are both untried and are handicapped by the absence of discretion in their exerci of limited controls. Since the original imperatives toward public intervention remain, it seems likely that government will need to devise further means of intervening and exerting control in the future. With the benefit of the development of principal and agent theory, it is to be hoped that any such mechanisms of control will be drawn up by consideration of the possible and the alternatives, not by reference to Utopian ideals of optimality.

Notes

1 That is, application of explicit models in decision-making and behaviour: for example, in the development of time and motion study of operations, standard costing in management accounting, survey

methods in marketing, discounted cash flow analysis in investment appraisal.

2 The NEDO study examined policy implementation in steel, gas, railways, and telecommunications.

3 The reader will find wider discussion of this particular case in Bryer *et al.* (1982).

4 The economics of such a world are set out in the writings of Kenneth Arrow, Gerard Debreu and Frank Hahn. See Arrow and Hahn, 1971, for a (severe) introduction.

5 An issue thoroughly discussed in Perotin and Estrin's 1986 paper, distinguishing between the interests of the 'collectivity' in public ownership and the fundamentally separate 'distributive' ownership of a private firm.

References

Arrow, K. J. (1986), 'Agency and the Market', in K. J. Arrow and M. Intrilligator (eds), *Handbook of Mathematical Economics*, vol. 3 (Amsterdam: North Holland).

Arrow, K. J. and Hahn, F. H. (1971), *General Competitive Analysis* (San Francisco, Calif.: Holden-Day Inc.).

Ashford, D. E. (1981), *Policy and Politics in Britain. The Limits of Consensus* (Oxford: Blackwell).

Bryer, R. A., Brignall, T. J. and Maunders, A. R. (1982), *Accounting for British Steel* (London: Gower).

Curwen, P. (1986), *Public Enterprise* (Brighton: Wheatsheaf).

Hartley, K. and Huby, M. (1985), 'Contracting Out on Health and Local Authorities: Prospects, Progress and Pitfalls', *Public Money*, vol. 5, no. 2, pp. 23–6.

Heald, D. (1980), 'The Economic and Financial Control of UK Nationalized Industries', *Economic Journal*, vol. 90, June, pp. 243–65.

HMSO (1961), *The Financial and Economic Obligations of the Nationalised Industries*, Cmnd 1337 (London).

HMSO (1967), *Nationalised Industries: A Review of Economic and Financial Objectives*, Cmnd 3437 (London).

HMSO (1976), *Cash Limits on Public Expenditure*, Cmnd 6440 (London).

HMSO (1978), *The Nationalised Industries*, Cmnd 7131 (London).

Kay, J. A. and Silberston, Z. A. (1984), 'The New Industrial Policy – Privatization and Competition', *Midland Bank Review*, Spring, pp. 8–16.

Le Grand, J. and Robinson, R. (1984), *Privatization and the Welfare State* (London: Allen & Unwin).

Lipsey, R. G. and Lancaster, K. (1957), 'The General Theory of Second Best', *Review of Economic Studies*, vol. 24, no. 63, pp. 11–32.

Littlechild, S. C. (1981), 'Ten Steps to Denationalisation', *Economic Affairs*, vol. 2, no. 1, pp. 11–18.

Morrison, H. (1933), *Socialization and Transport* (London: Constable).

NEDO (1976), *A Study of UK Nationalised Industries* (London: HMSO).

Nove, A. (1973), *Efficiency Criteria for Nationalised Industries* (London: Allen & Unwin).

Peacock, H. (1984), 'Privatization in Perspective', *Three Banks Review*, no. 144, pp. 3–25.

Perotin, V. and Estrin, S. (1986), 'Does Ownership Matter?', paper given at annual conference of the European Economic Association, August.

Pryke, R. (1981), *The Nationalized Industries: Policies and Performance since 1968* (London: Martin Robertson).

Redwood, J. (1981), *Public Enterprise in Crisis* (Oxford: Blackwell).

Rees, R. (1985), 'The Theory of Principal and Agent', *Bulletin of Economic Research*, vol. 37, nos. 1 and 2, pp. 3–25, 75–95.

Rowley, C. K. (1971), *Steel and Public Policy* (London: McGraw-Hill).

Select Committee (1968), *Ministerial Control of the Nationalised Industries: First Report from the Select Committee on Nationalised Industries 1967/8*, HC 371–I (London: HMSO).

Select Committee (1978), *The British Steel Corporation: First Report from the Select Committee on Nationalised Industries 1977/8*, HC 26–II (London: HMSO).

Steel, D. and Heald, D. (eds) (1984), *Privatizing Public Enterprises: Options and Dilemmas* (London: Royal Institute of Public Administration).

Stein, B. A. (1976), 'Collective Ownership. Property Rights and Control of the Corporation', *Journal of Economic Issues*, vol. 10, pp. 298–313.

Vickers, J. and Yarrow, G. (1985), *Privatization and the Natural Monopolies* (London: Public Policy Centre).

Webb, M. (1973), *The Economics of Nationalised Industries* (London: Nelson).

Webb, M. (1980), 'A Critical Appraisal of United Kingdom Policy for the Nationalized Industries', in B. M. Mitchell and P. R. Kleindorfer (eds), *Regulated Industries and Public Enterprises* (Lexington, Mass.: Lexington Books).

Williamson, O. E. (1986), *Economic Organization: Firms, Markets and Policy Control* (Brighton: Wheatsheaf).

Wiseman, J. (1957), 'The Theory of Public Utility Price – An Empty Box', *Oxford Economic Papers*, vol. 9, pp. 56–74.

4 Civil Service management

MARTIN GROCOTT

To the student of this subject, one can envisage the above chapter heading meaning everything and nothing. At least three questions are likely to spring to his or her mind. First, perhaps, what exactly is to be included in a definition of the civil service? Secondly, why does the issue of management concern us? Thirdly, what precisely is the meaning of management in this context? We will attempt to answer these queries from the outset.

For the purposes of this chapter the civil service refers to the non-industrial civil service, which is composed of those 'white collar' or office staff who work for the government in Whitehall, or in regional and local offices around the country, as well as overseas. As at 1 January 1987 there were approximately 507,000 civil servants so defined. This compares with the high mark of over 570,000 reached before the Conservative party came into office in 1979 (HMSO, 1987). These include all manner of 'ordinary' office staff of many ranks and salary levels, including typists, messengers and others in such organizations as the science group and the professional and technology group. Over half of the total is engaged in more or less routine tasks at or below the rank of clerical officer. Almost half are women who are concentrated in the lower ranks. Three-quarters of clerical staff are women. About one-third of the total are aged below thirty. The headquarters bureaucrats in Whitehall constitute no more than 5 per cent of the total and 75 per cent work in centres outside London.

Turning to the second question, it is now perhaps commonplace to assert that the hitherto rather unexciting and specialized topic of the civil service has become, in recent years, a political issue. Undervaluing civil servants and even blaming them for all manner of social and economic ills is nothing new, but there is now an extra edge to criticisms honed by the experiences of harder times. Unemployment and belt-tightening are easily contrasted with the allegedly secure and privileged world of the higher or administra-

tive civil servant. Since 1979, governments have been elected partly
on the promise to 'roll back the frontiers of the state', to reduce the
public payroll, and force the disciplines of business on the 'inefficient' bureaucracy of the state.

The newsworthiness of some of the more sensational consequences of an abrasive, confrontational style of government, new
styles of industrial relations, the bitter acrimony over the banning
of unions at GCHQ, court trials following 'leaks' by civil servants,
wrangling over their conduct and loyalties, make it easy to see how
managing the state bureaucracy has attracted attention.

The third question, the meaning of management in this context,
is of particular importance in view of the developments that have
taken place since 1979. To provide a straightforward answer is by
no means easy. The vastness and complexity of managerial problems in central government are often not appreciated. Now that
'management' is being accepted, reluctantly by many as just as
worthy as 'policy work', the more glamorous activities at the top
must be seen as simply part of the whole picture.

It is convenient to sub-divide this management dimension into
operational management, or management *in* the civil service, which
is mainly the concern of the lower levels in the hierarchy, and the
management of the strategic aspects, or management *of* the civil
service dominated by the higher echelons.

First the 'lower' level activity is concerned with actual operations,
often carried out at regional or local level, or through agencies
mainly concerned with financial and manpower resource allocation.
Though there are significant differences between management
problems in the private and public sectors, it is at this 'micro' level
of operational efficiency that many problems are similar. In many
cases, techniques or methods from the private sector can be utilized
to good effect. There is no doubt that this cross-transfer has taken
place over a very long period and become part of the accepted
orthodoxy of Conservative governments. This is not to say,
however, that there have been no innovations or initiatives from
within Whitehall itself.

As a general principle, what is required at this level is the development of an appropriate personnel policy; with proper financial
control, budgets, audit and costing; better organization and
methods; the imposition of standards in the general sense; the
acquisition and management of adequate office accommodation and
other property; the employment of the latest technology and
mathematical and associated techniques. All these and others are
needed to cope with non-strategic management issues. Here the

problem is to 'oil the wheels' of government, to strive for efficiency and economy; to search for acceptable ways of making democracy efficient. However, 'efficiency' is not as readily disentangled from political ideology as management scientists and indeed many politicians, particularly of the new right, are so ready to assert.

Secondly, and perhaps more importantly, there is that 'higher' realm where administration inevitably embraces government and must cope with the less comfortable world of politics and its different values. Politics and politicians have been perceived by many civil servants as a nuisance or embarrassment, but are inevitably the essence of much of their work. As J. D. Stewart (1974, p. 137) never tired of reminding us in the local government sphere, 'the function of management thought in government should be to assist the political process not to assist a retreat from politics'. This message can be adapted for Whitehall. Indeed, this is what Mrs Thatcher in more strident terms has advocated for the civil service since she came to power. Too often civil service managers have used their expertise and guile to mitigate the effects of 'inefficiency' thrust on them by the political process.[1] In any model, politicians should not be an irritant to management, but should be its inspiration. The democratic ethos requires no less. Also it is at this level that change has to be accommodated if democratic government is to remain vibrant. The whole bureaucratic apparatus needs to be responsive though not wholly compliant; innovative if not radical; political but never ideological; enthusiastic but not dogmatic. There are changes brought about by political chance and sometimes electoral factors, but others are generated by new problems of the environment, higher general expectations and a more critical public awareness. Somehow the permanent civil service as a prime actor in the drama of government must accommodate these realities.

This chapter is designed to survey both these dimensions of the management of the central bureaucracy but with an emphasis on the 'macro' level and the more prominent philosophies, events, initiatives and experiments of recent times.

'... still fundamentally a product of ... the Northcote–Trevelyan Report' (Fulton, 1968, Vol, 1, p. 9, para. 1)

Like most things British, the civil service and its management style have been the subject of evolutionary change over long periods of time. There have been watersheds like Northcote–Trevelyan 1853/4 (reprinted in Fulton, 1968, Vol. 1, pp. 108–18) and Fulton (1968) and much talk in recent years of 'revolutions', but the reality has rarely lived up to the plans or the rhetoric.

It is usual to seek the roots of our modern system of government in the nineteenth century. For local government, the Municipal Corporations Act 1835 is the common starting-point. With central administration it is the Northcote–Trevelyan Report, *'On the Organization of the Permanent Civil Service'*, that is usually chosen. The early civil service was quite small: 16,000 or so in 1797, 21,000 in 1832, and around 39,000 by 1851 (and this included the already quite large Post Office staff and the Irish Departments' staff). Though small in present day terms it was considered a 'drain' on the public purse that alarmed many, and the whole issue became a matter for debate and attention. Problems of efficiency, competence, organization and pay moved up the political agenda.

What emerged from this new interest was a realization of the poor state of the system. An inquiry of 1836 into 'The Fees and Emoluments of Public Offices' found that the corrupt vestiges of an ancient tradition, allowing remuneration by the retention of taxes or fees, still remained. In 1848 a committee exposed the anarchy in administration and pay within the 'service'. For the first time, mostly owing to the evidence of Sir Charles Trevelyan, patronage in appointments and the purchase of sinecure posts was publicly criticized by an official body. The 'system' was exposed as a muddle of ad hoc arrangements varying between departments, which were largely the personal instruments of their head officers.

Into this mire the shining light of Northcote–Trevelyan was directed. The report itself is almost a piece of political theory, a blueprint of how a model civil service ought to be if the pressures on government to tackle the problems of contemporary life and respond to the growing influence of the democratic ethic and the demands of hitherto subordinated class interests were to be accommodated. Specifically, the report condemned nepotism, the rudimentary training, inefficiency in terms of 'delays, evasions of difficulties, official reluctance to improvement', the fragmentary character of the service and failure to recruit suitable personnel. It urged 'a supply of good men', to be carefully nurtured; 'young men', to be selected and retained for a lifetime career, 'who should be employed from the first upon work suited to their capacities and their education'. They should be made 'constantly to feel that their promotion and future prospects depend entirely on the industry and ability with which they discharge their duties'. There should be

instituted 'A proper system of examination before appointment
... followed ... by a short period of probation', the examinations being supervised and conducted by a 'Central Board' of
'men holding an independent position'. The examination was to
be 'in all cases a competing literary examination' plus 'careful
previous inquiry into the age, health, and moral fitness of the
candidates'. The report nevertheless recognized that some specialist jobs would have to be filled by appropriate examinations,
adapted to particular needs. The last paragraph of the report
anticipated that reform would not succeed without a struggle.
Vested interests and political hostility ensured that the proposals
took time to implement, even though eventually, much was
achieved.

To quote Fulton, reviewing in 1968 the evolution of the
service, 'In our view the structure and practices of the services
have not kept up with the changing tasks. The defects we have
found can nearly all be attributed to this. We have found no
instance where reform has run ahead too rapidly. So, today, the
service is in need of fundamental change' (Fulton, 1968, Vol. 1,
p. 11, para. 14).

By the time Fulton reported it was the conventional view that
management had become complacent. Merely reacting in an ad
hoc manner to the problems of an industrial society, was not by
itself adquate to cope with the ever-increasing demands of a
wider electorate, or to the functions of more interventionist
governments.

His indictment of the service expressed a common view of the
nature of the service and its management in the late 1960s. Fulton
found the service inadequate in six main respects: first, the cult of
the 'amateur', the 'generalist' or the 'all-rounder' was obsolete;
secondly, the rigid class compartmentalism of the administrative,
executive and clerical classes circumscribed career prospects;
thirdly, scientists, engineers and other professionals were
excluded from most top management posts, the exact opposite of
the position existing in local government; fourthly, too few civil
servants were skilled managers and lacked adequate management
training; fifthly, the service was professionally and, at the 'top' at
least, socially isolated from the 'rest of the community'; finally
personnel management was seriously deficient and promotion
depended too much on seniority (Fulton, 1968, Vol. 1, pp. 11, 12
and 13). Lord Simey, a member of the Fulton Committee, took
exception to much of this and recorded his dissent in the report.

1960–1979: Revolutions and plans

By the 1960s there emerged a vision of Britain's 'national plight' which partly focused attention on administrative methods and the quality of civil servants. It was alleged that civil servants were complacent and that their selection and training were outdated. Management and modern technology were matters which they appeared to scorn. It seemed that a 'new world' needed new personnel to cope with it. The Treasury was perceived as the main culprit. As criticisms increased, the pressure for action became difficult to resist. This was first recognized officially in the Plowden Report (1961) which confirmed the deficiencies exposed by the Commons Estimates Committee in its report of 1958. The civil service, especially the Treasury, was criticized for its lack of planning capacity and management culture, particularly the absence of cost consciousness. Some reorganization of the Treasury followed, designed to facilitate planning and better management. Following the election of the Labour government of 1964, a new Department of Economic Affairs was established primarily to provide for the long-term economic planning the Treasury neglected, together with a Ministry of Technology.

Although encouraging, such changes were not sufficient. Consequently the Fulton Committee was set up in February 1966. Its terms of reference were to 'examine the structure, recruitment and management, including training, of the Home Civil Service and to make recommendations' (Fulton, 1968, Vol. 1, p. 2).

Fulton's diagnosis has been outlined above. The proposed remedies were extensive and broad in scope, comprising over 150 proposals. The main recommendations for our purpose were as follows: to establish a new 'management department', to be named the Civil Service Department, the head of which would be 'Head of the Home Civil Service', changed with co-ordinating modernizing efforts and 'with wider functions than those of the "Pay and Management" group of the Treasury, which it should take over. The new Department should absorb the Civil Service Commission.' Furthermore, it should develop greater professionalism and provide more training in management, partly through a new Civil Service College with important research functions, open to outsiders from public sector organizations and private industrial and commercial firms. This was in keeping with Fulton's wish to open-up Whitehall, encouraging a 'cross-fertilization' of ideas through the college, expanded late entry, temporary appointments for fixed terms, short-term interchanges of staff and freer movement in and out of the service. In addition the Civil Service Department was to bring to bear the whole range of personnel management techniques, expand 'O and M', develop Management Services Units for all major departments, and encourage modern management techniques wherever they could be used to advantage. It was to change the orientation to efficiency by applying the principles of accountable management, establishing budget centres with defined objectives. In higher administration 'management by objectives' was to be encouraged.

To break away from the stranglehold of short-term problem solving, small departmental planning units should be established, supported by a senior policy adviser (SPA) and, where appropriate, a chief scientist or other senior specialist. The SPA was to head the planning unit, and have direct access to the minister as his or her main adviser on long-term policy. In addition a unified (classless) grading structure, embracing eventually all non-industrial civil servants, was recommended.

Fulton thought that hiving off some work of central government was feasible, that the SPA might be an outsider and that ministers should be able to employ on a temporary basis such small numbers of experts as he or she personally considered necessary (Fulton, 1968, Vol. 1). The report, partially accepted by the then government, established a blueprint for reform and criteria of achievement for the future. The Prime Minister, Harold Wilson, set in train moves towards most of the recommended reforms, but later 'progress reports' had an air of disappointment, sometimes exasperation, about them. It is fair to say that much was achieved but more was left unfinished.[2]

The new Civil Service Department's Permanent Secretary, Sir William Armstrong, had previously headed the much maligned finance and expenditure side of the Treasury. The fate of Wilson's so-called 'white hot' technological revolution was sealed by relying on changes in form to bring about changes in culture, leaving its implementation substantially in the hands of those who had prospered under the old system. The rhetoric outstripped the actuality of change; predictably not all agreed that this was a bad thing. Indicative of the failure of the 'revolution' was the demise of the Department of Economic Affairs and the Ministry of Technology.

The coming to power of a Conservative government under Edward Heath, in 1970, saw a leader of the Conservative party determined to pursue the issue of civil service management and to outplay Wilson at his own game. The tactic was a 'quiet revolution', less ostentatious but more profound. The Heath government's White Paper (1970), *The Reorganization of Central Government*, emphasized better planning and more 'rational' organization. The essence was encapsulated in three main developments: the acceptance of the 'big is beautiful' thesis, in the form of an extension of the 'giant department' experiment begun under Wilson; the establishment of Policy Analysis and Review (PAR) as a complement to the post-Plowden Public Expenditure Survey Committee system (PESC); and the establishment of the Central Policy Review Staff (CPRS) soon to be referred to as the 'Think Tank', attached to the Cabinet.

In part these innovations orginated with the Prime Minister's advisers from the world of business. However, even by 1974 the PAR reports in particular seemed to have lost their way: they asked the 'wrong' questions, and they became less and less action-oriented. Often the reports read like essays – albeit excellent ones – a sure sign that the traditional civil service approach had neutralized another challenge to its dominance.

To see this period in terms of revolutions and grand strategic plans only would be misleading. Such experiments as PAR and CPRS were in terms of numbers involved and budgets designated rather peripheral; glosses on the dull bureaucratic machine. Nevertheless, these initiatives attracted great attention, especially that of outside observers, and were often presented by insiders as if they were genuine means for more effective government.

The CPRS in particular appeared to hold out great hopes, at least during Heath's time. As Simon James (1986, pp. 424–5) observes, '... the insiders ... rediscovered in a brief stint of licensed free-thinking a creativity stifled by their civil service upbringing ... its weekly "no holds barred" meetings excited surprise and some jealousy in Whitehall and generated confidence and high morale which sustained the CPRS in lean times'. Many regretted at the time, and some still do, that this potential was not fully developed. Jealousy, lack of ministerial commitment and the post-1974 political and economic difficulties, plus the collapse of the postwar consensus, eventually conspired to kill off perhaps the most radical attempt to revitalize the management of government before it really got started.

The mid-1960s and early 1970s were, however, periods when some senior civil servants with little or no previous managerial training, became acquainted with such terminology as discounted cash flow and cost benefit analysis and voluntarily attended courses in economics at Regent Street Polytechnic, with a view to career advancement (Delafons, 1982, p. 261). It was also an era of inquiries and Royal Commissions, with the bureaucratic establishment displaying a propensity for diluting or ridiculing ideas with potential.

The Thatcher era: government as business

As we have seen, the 1960s and 1970s had witnessed an emphasis on recruiting and training better managers, on improving the analytical potential of the policy process, of eroding the 'amateur' ethos, of breaking out of the straight-jacket of short-term expediency. The social elitism of the upper reaches of the service was also attacked and ridiculed. This pre-Thatcher era also witnessed the skills of the established civil service in avoiding change which it did not support. Much energy was channelled into reformulating political initiatives so that there was no great threat to the independence of the bureaucracy itself.

With the arrival of Thatcher came a greater determination to do what was 'necessary' to rescue Great Britain from the perceived national decline for which the civil service was partly to blame. Reducing public expenditure, eliminating waste, rolling back the frontiers of the state, lifting the dead hand of bureaucracy, cutting the public payroll were the objectives of a crusade given authority by a clear electoral victory and leadership of a peculiarly visionary and dogmatic kind.

This new vigour manifested itself in terms of often heated polemics directed at the consensus-oriented 'chameleons' who had allegedly led us to the very brink of ruin. This new style Conservative leader, unlike some of her predecessors, was not the slave of classical ideas in organizational matters. She soon showed an instinctive contempt for mere tampering which, in her opinion, had produced only the appearance, never the reality, of change. What mattered to her was whether people had the 'right' attitude, whether he or she was 'one of us' and not where one appeared on the organization chart. Nevertheless, in the early 1980s the CPRS and the Civil Service Department were abolished and a Management and Personnel Office, dealing with aspects of the civil service, was set up in the Cabinet Office.

The government's agenda was mainly concerned with the perceived ills of the economy. In particular, it asserted a determination to conquer inflation and improve productivity and output. Whitehall was to be geared to this greater need and not merely reorganized. Individual ministers and their departments became main targets of this strategy. Rooting out waste was the first objective and the departments were expected to co-operate in every way possible in reducing expenditure. To this end the government mobilized a dormant parsimonious sub-culture within Whitehall, providing it with leadership, at least in the short term, from outside. Mrs Thatcher selected Derek Rayner, joint managing director of Marks & Spencer, reputedly both sensitive and determined, for the task. 'Raynerism' was born as a direct successor to PAR and by the end of 1981 Rayner scrutinies had identified annual savings of £300 million and £34 million capital.

Impressive as this seems, Rayner wished for something more substantial: the establishment of new procedures and systems based on the new philosophy. In Rayner's own terms 'lasting reforms' proved the most difficult. He set in motion moves towards cost awareness, charging for resources consumed by departments (stationery, energy, telephones, etc.); securing accountable management procedures generally; streamlining administrative procedures and rooting out bad practice; modernizing the office environment; motivating via merit pay and promotion; developing or recruiting the necessary personnel and upgrading professional expertise; calling for a review of career development ensuring that those who were known to have capacity were promoted to top positions, rather than those whose claim to fame was seniority (Rayner, 1983).

The political 'clout' was backed by managerial 'clout' but it had to be brought in from outside. As Sir Peter Carey, until 1983 Permanent Secretary to the Department of Industry, put it, 'I personally regretted that it was necessary to bring in Lord Rayner to help us do what we should have done for ourselves; but necessary it was. Of course, we had already instituted a lot of reforms and brushed up our professionalism immensely. But we lacked the sense of urgency which Lord Rayner's arrival injected' (Carey, 1984, p. 83).

A parallel development which received a great deal of publicity was the establishment of a management information system for ministers known as MINIS, developed in the Department of the Environment under Michael Heseltine, a prime advocate of the view of minister as manager. The ideas were initiated following a Rayner scrutiny in that department in 1979. It is fair to say that the MINIS was really only a label for a system which had its origins in Heseltine's earlier ideas formulated during his business and ministerial experience (1970–4). Heseltine took the idea with him when assigned to the Ministry of Defence and tailored it to suit the requirements of a very different department.

The system was essentially developed to enable ministers to obtain a clearer picture of the highly fragmented activities taking place in a large department. The assumption was that without such information ministers could not properly control the department or make sound decisions on organizational, staffing or other managerial matters. In particular MINIS provided a suitable instrument for 'rational' management cuts.

The Prime Minister urged all ministers to introduce similar systems into their own departments. It seemed for a while that MINIS would achieve an ascendancy over the simpler Rayner scrutinies. With the departure of Rayner in 1982 the issue of institutionalizing the new financial disciplines arose; however, for various reasons the future development of such ideas proceeded under a new banner – the Financial Management Initiative (FMI).

The FMI got under way in May 1982, outlined in the White Paper, *Efficiency and Effectiveness in the Civil Service*, being a response to the Treasury and Civil Service Committee's Third Report of the same name (1982). Typically, the government resisted changes which might strengthen the role of Parliament too much or divert the priority given to bringing costs under control. FMI was an advance on 'Raynerism', combining the virtues of the efficiency scrutinies with the sophistications of MINIS. It was not a new direction but intended to change the financial culture of Whitehall. Specifically the FMI attempted to establish a system whereby managers at all levels had clearly defined objectives, plans and standards of achievement; access to comprehensive information systems to provide relevant essential data especially concerning costs; clearly defined responsibilities in relation to the use of allocated resources and general efficiency; and full support especially in terms of access to expert advice and training when necessary. In some ways this could be seen as a return to the Fultonian ideas about accountable management and the experiments with Management by Objectives. An interesting aspect was the recognition that flexibility was necessary and that real change needed to be generated from within departments and not only imposed from the top.

Just as Rayner had a unit, so did the FMI. This time the Financial Management Unit, a small organization comprising civil servants and outside management consultants, usually from major private firms with experience of working with government. Members were typically, but not exclusively of an accountancy orientation. The unit had flexible membership, some staying only for particular projects, and others working on a part-time basis. It generally had six or seven full-time members as its core. Each unit was intended as a temporary catalyst with a life expectancy of one year but this might be prolonged to enable it to assist in the implementation of proposals and plans. Through the FMI the 'virtues' of business practice, especially the identification of 'cost centres' in all areas of work, were to be finally transplanted into Whitehall.

Reports on progress since have pointed to bureaucratic resistance and recently to an acknowledgement that whilst savings have been made difficulties have also been discovered or rediscovered. The real potential for saving is still, of course, related to policy rather than management as Michael Heseltine, among others, reminded this government. The very existence of bureaucracies and programmes originates in political decisions and at the 'micro' level, no manager can be held solely accountable for the efficiency of his programme of work. Most of the old barriers still persist; this government has done little to change the situation. Ministerial responsibility still protects the civil service manager; there is no 'hire and fire' in Whitehall; little freedom of choice regarding supplies of materials and service; little freedom of choice of subordinates; few real incentives or sanctions available, despite some tentative moves towards less formalized promotion procedures and merit pay schemes, following recommendations by the Megaw Committee (1982).

It must be acknowledged that throughout this period there was caution and a growing concern that the new culture could create a management likely to equate 'cheaper' with 'better'. Such a crude criterion of success was not universally endorsed. For example, William Plowden questioned how far the relatively simple techniques relating to the facts about costs and outputs – numbers of staff, numbers of applications dealt with – were capable of being developed to deal with far more complex questions about *outcomes* (Plowden, 1985, p. 399).

Nevertheless, this particular 'wind of change' still blows. My emphasis on the Rayner–FMI partnership has been deliberate. This central 'guiding light' effectively epitomizes the new philosophy and highlights the sophistication of an approach which can effect and motivate all manner of practical changes while surmounting that greatest barrier to change, attitude. The intellectual and political climate has shifted compared with previous periods. Earlier assumptions about the role of government have receded in some quarters. Hayek, Friedman, Hoskyns[3] and the accountants are the new 'visionaries' of some politicians currently in office.

What they have tended to overlook or subordinate in their thinking has been the import of trends in ministerial–civil servant relationships for the conventions of responsibility and account-ability and the professional norms of officials. Constitutionally, ministers are collectively and individually responsible for policy and the conduct of their departments. Senior civil servants, however, although increasingly categorized and perceived as managers, remain confidential policy advisers.

In practice their influence on policy goes far beyond mere advice but if the permanent career character of the civil service is to be maintained, with politically sensitive and experienced officials nor-matively expected to keep ministers 'out of trouble', providing they act legally and constitutionally, it is essential that the image of party political neutrality be preserved. A service too closely identified with the policies of any one government, especially when ideo-logical differences are widening, could not be trusted to serve an opposition party which subsequently came to power. In the view of some commentators, civil servants should serve not only a par-ticular government but ultimately have a higher obligation to serve the state or Crown, acting in accordance with clearly defined professional norms.

When one party is continuously in office for more than ten years both the neutrality and trust aspects of relationships are apt to become strained, especially when ministers are strongly committed to doctrines they expect officials to identify with rather than query. Officials with doubts or reservations are likely to find their career prospects blighted. The situation is exacerbated when ministers resort to dubious or questionable tactics to escape parliamentary and public accountability. The civil service is, after all, a *public* service. The Ponting and Westland affairs illustrate some of the issues.

Without information, or with inaccurate, partial or misleading information, Parliament cannot secure ministerial accountability. In the Ponting case documents were leaked to an MP, who passed them on to the Commons Foreign Affairs Committee. They indi-cated that ministers had misled the House with respect to the sinking of the *Belgrano* during the Falklands War. Ponting's identity being discovered, he was charged under the Official Secrets Act but acquitted by a jury which paid scant attention to opinions expressed by the presiding judge. According to Ponting. who subsequently resigned from the civil service, his actions were justified by the overriding need for the Commons to have access to reliable infor-mation which did not threaten national security (Norton-Taylor, 1985).

The Westland affair also involved 'leaking', complicated by

ministerial and inter-departmental conflicts. Ordered by her minister, Leon Brittan, to leak to the Press Association carefully selected parts of a confidential letter, the Chief Press Officer of the Department of Trade and Industry, Colette Bowe, initially resisted but obeyed when the Prime Minister's Press Secretary, Bernard Ingham, indicated she should do so (Linklater and Leigh, 1986, p. 137). The aim was to undermine the position of Michael Heseltine, the Secretary of State for Defence. When the source of the leak became known Brittan resigned, no disciplinary action being taken with respect to the press officers concerned.

Relationships between ministers and civil servants have undoubtedly undergone change in the 1980s and this is further evidenced by the difficulties confronting civil service and other public sector unions.

As far as the civil service unions are concerned it is significant that according to Brian Towers (1987, p. 240) the largest civil service union, the Civil and Public Servants Association (CPSA), has been growing in size, indicating that public sector employment has remained buoyant, reflecting high densities and 'burgeoning union consciousness'. Certainly this burgeoning consciousness has been evident in the NHS in recent times, and has not only been associated with low pay and deteriorating working conditions but with the nature of the services and levels of funding generally. Public sympathy for nurses and other health service workers and professional groups representing for example, teachers and social workers has not and is not likely to extend to the less visible civil service unions. According to William Brown (1986, p. 167), public services have long made use of motivational mechanisms which rely on vocational commitment and career progression. Lack of motivational mechanisms in the form of reduced funding, uncertainty about the future and direction of career progression have tried the patience of committed professions like nursing and teaching. If these groups depend upon vocational commitment and career progression, this is also – and especially – true of civil servants.

In view of the fact that public sector unions supplement direct negotiations with employers by sponsoring MPs, lobbying government departments and lobbying ministers directly (Leopold and Beaumont, 1986, p. 34), civil service unions are placed in a particularly difficult situation since they are entirely public service and work directly for central government.

Questions of loyalty, career progression, job security and lines of accountability are factors affecting the terms and conditions of all employed in the civil service. These questions are likely to be raised if the government proceeds with its intention to implement the proposals of the Efficiency Unit Report on the Civil Service, *Improving Management in Government, The Next Steps* (Report of the Efficiency Unit, 1988). The report argued that most top civil servants were still mainly concerned with ministerial priorities and policy formulation rather than service delivery. There were few external pressures on departments to improve performance and the large size and diversity of the civil service made it difficult to manage as a single entity. The report recommended the separation of many executive functions from Whitehall leaving relatively few 'policy-makers' to run ministries and the establishment of agencies to run many civil service functions. While the implications for higher ranking civil servants engaged in more strategic policy-making roles are less significant, the imapct on the vast majority of civil servants, in particular those in the largest civil service unions (CPSA and SCPS) will be more dramatic. It is likely that there will be different criteria determining the pay and conditions of civil servants working in those sectors of government departments not hived off from those transferring to agencies. There may well be variation in salaries, career prospects and lines of accountability. On the other hand it is possible that there will be less likelihood of the use of review bodies or imposition of cash limits for pay, if, as suggested, the agencies would have considerable financial autonomy. However, in view of the banning of trades unions at GCHQ and the fact that the civil service unions have not so far been consulted over the report, it is more likely that the civil service unions will come out of the reform of central government weaker than before.

Conclusion

The third-term Thatcher government does not intend to 'rest on its laurels' or merely consolidate. The findings and recommendations of the Efficiency Unit have found favour with the government and the Prime Minister in particular. If implemented the civil service of the mid to late 1990s could be very different from the one we are familiar with today. On the other hand, it could be argued that any radical reform will require the support and compliance of senior civil servants and the civil service unions.

One particularly thoughtful observation culminating in a comprehensively argued 'blue print', is summarized in a recent article (Metcalfe and Richards, 1987).[4] The authors acknowledge achievements but shortcomings are highlighted too. The argument is that somehow the initiatives have 'run out of steam', the civil service machine having mounted a successful rearguard action. The call is for 'management' to be promoted above the executive level and perceived in 'broader strategic terms'.

Whether in fact any such changes will occur only time will tell, but even in terms of the Thatcherite perspective based on a private sector approach, the recent changes could be seen as deficient, since they lag behind the more imaginative approaches of the best business practices. All this presupposes that the Thatcherite aims are simply to improve efficiency, to mould a new and acceptable 'bureaucracy'. However, it must be remembered that the very essence of a state bureaucracy is anathema to this ideology. What has been presented as a healthy diet with a slimmer, fitter body as the aim could degenerate into anorexia nervosa and that could have serious consequences.

Notes

1   Recent sources illustrating some aspects of this are L. Chapman, *Your Disobedient Servant* (Chatto & Windus, 1979); and H. Young and A. Sloman, *'No Minister': An Enquiry into the Civil Service* (BBC, 1982).
2   There are many articles and reports on this topic. A good starting point is C. Painter (1975), 'The Civil Service: Post-Fulton Malaise', *Public Administration*, vol. 53, pp. 427–41. This article also provides references for contemporary books, articles and reports on the same issue.
3   The views of Sir John Hoskyns should be known by students as should the gist of the so-called Hoskyns/Wass debate. A convenient resumé and anlaysis can be found in an excellent article by G. K. Fry (1984), 'The Attack on the Civil Service and the Response of the Insiders', *Parliamentary Affairs*, vol. 37, no. 4, pp. 353–63.
4   The full 'blue print' is given in Metcalfe and Richards's book, noted in the Further Reading list.

References

Brown, William (1986), 'The Changing Role of Trade Unions in the Management of Labour', *British Journal of Industrial Relations*, vol. 24, 2 July.
Carey, (Sir) Peter (GCB) (1984), 'Management in the Civil Service', *Management in Government*, pp. 81–5.
Delafons, J. (1982), 'Working in Whitehall: Changes in Public Administration 1952–1982', *Public Administration*, vol. 60, Autumn, pp. 253–72.

Dror, Y. [1968] (1983), *Public Policymaking Re-examined* (Transaction Books: NJ, USA).

Fry, G. K. (1969), *Statesmen in Disguise* (London: Macmillan).

Fry, G. K. (1986), 'The British Career Civil Service Under Challenge', *Political Studies*, vol. 34, pp. 533–55.

Fulton Report (1968), *Report of the Committee on the Civil Service*, Cmnd 3638 (HMSO).

HMSO (1958), Sixth Report of the Estimates Committee, *Treasury Control of Expenditure*, HC 254–1.

HMSO (1970), *The Reorganization of Central Government*, Cmnd 4506.

HMSO (1982), *Efficiency and Effectiveness in the Civil Service*, Cmnd 8616.

HMSO (1982), *Efficiency and Effectiveness in the Civil Service: Third Report from the Treasury and Civil Service Committee, Session 1981–82*, HC 236.

HMSO (1987), *Civil Service Statistics 1987*, Government Statistical Service (HMSO).

James, S. (1986), 'The Central Policy Review Staff, 1970–1983', *Political Studies*, vol. 34, pp. 423–40.

Kellner, P. and Crowther-Hunt, (Lord) (1980), *The Civil Servants: an Inquiry into Britain's Ruling Class* (London: Macdonald Futura Publishers).

Leopold, J. and Beaumont, P. (1986), 'Pay Bargaining and Management Strategy in the Civil Service', *Industrial Relations Journal*, vol. 17, no. 1, Spring.

Linklater, M. and Leigh, D. (1986), *Not With Honour* (Sphere: London).

Megaw Committee (1982), *Report of the Inquiry into Civil Service Pay*, Cmnd 8590–1 (HMSO).

Metcalfe, L. and Richards, S. (1987), 'The Efficiency Strategy in Central Government: an Impoverished Concept of Management', *Public Money*, June, pp. 29–32.

Nash, P. (1981), 'We Tried Before, but without the Clout', *Management Services in Government*, pp. 137–44.

Norton-Taylor, R. (1985), *The Ponting Affair* (Woolf: London).

Plowden Report (1961), *The Control of Public Expenditure*, Cmnd 1432.

Plowden, W. (1985), 'What Prospects for the Civil Service', *Public Administration*, vol. 63, Winter, pp. 393–414.

Rayner, Sir Derek (1983), 'The Business of Government', *Administrator*, March, pp. 3, 5–6.

Stewart, J. D. (1974), *The Responsive Local Authority* (London: Charles Knight).

Towers, B. (197), 'Trends and Developments in Industrial Relations', *Industrial Relations Journal*, vol. 18, no. 4, Winter.

Further Reading

Keeling, D., *Management in Government* (Allen & Unwin, for RIPA: London, 1972).

Garrett, J., *The Management of Government* (Penguin: Harmondsworth, 1972).

Garrett, J., *Managing the Civil Service* (Heinemann: London, 1980).

Kellner, P. and Crowther-Hunt (Lord), *The Civil Servants: an Inquiry into Britain's Ruling Class* (Macdonald Futura Publishers: London, 1980).

Fry, G. K., *The Changing Civil Service* (Allen & Unwin: London, 1985).

Gray, A. and Jenkins, W., *Administrative Politics in British Government* (Wheatsheaf, 1985).

Ponting, C., *Whitehall: Tragedy and Farce* (Hamish Hamilton: London, 1986).

Metcalfe, L. and Richards, S., *Improving Public Management* (Sage, 1987).

5 The Changing management of local government

HOWARD ELCOCK

Past stabilities and their decline

British local government was essentially a Victorian creation. It was formed from the chaos of boroughs created over the centuries by royal charters, parishes, commissions and boards responsible for the discharge of specific functions. These were brought together in multi-functional local authorities by three major pieces of legislation: the Municipal Corporations Act of 1835, the County Councils Act, 1888 and the Local Government Act, 1894. Local government was hence Parliament's creation and – like all of us – it is subject to the changing views represented in our sovereign Parliament. The Queen in Parliament can alter the powers and functions of local authorities; increase, reduce or eliminate their powers, as well as creating or abolishing them at will. Nevertheless, until recent years, the local government world was stable, even sometimes a little stagnant. Most local authorities had similar managerial styles and structures which were based on assumptions that the areas they controlled, as well as their roles, functions and powers, were unlikely to be challenged or radically changed. These managerial similarities existed despite a wide variation in local political and social cultures which influenced the environments within which local authorities operated but not usually their managerial and administrative structures and procedures (Bulpitt, 1987; Stanyer, 1976).

Until the late 1960s, a local authority consisted of a varying number of functional departments, each of whose chief officers reported to a committee of councillors. A large city council might well have had around thirty such departments and committees, which were responsible for discharging the many and varied responsibilites allocated to the authority by statute. There was little overall co-ordination of the activities of these departments and committees. The council's Chief Officer would be its legal adviser – the Clerk – who had his own specialist responsibilities and was head of his own administration department. As for councillors, the only point at which they could systematically assess or compare what the different committees were doing was when they received the minutes of all the committees a few days before each meeting of the full council, which had to ratify the committees' decisions. Not surprisingly, few councillors were able to undertake this task and significant co-ordination occurred only when a strong party group of councillors sought to exercise at least some degree of control over the authority's overall policies (Wiseman, 1963).

The preparation of the authority's budget was similarly disjointed. It would begin by each department preparing estimates of what it needed to spend in the coming financial year. The departments would include all possible expenditures, as well as all proposals for new services or the expansion of existing ones. When the estimates were collated and compared with the resources available to the authority in the forms of government grants and other income, it almost invariably became apparent that not all the proposed expenditure could be accommodated unless the authority levied an unreasonably high rate. The treasurer and finance committee would then demand reductions, usually on a uniform percentage basis, so that the rate to be struck would be acceptable to councillors and the public. Such pressure for reductions would be particularly acute in election years.

In general, local authority committee and departmental structures, as well as their procedures and practices, were similar throughout the country and before 1973, experiments with new forms of management or policy-making were few and far between. However, in the 1960s Newcastle upon Tyne and Basildon appointed city managers to oversee policy and administration. A number of other authorities appointed management consultants to review their structures, procedures and practices.

A second enduring feature of the local government system has been that central governments have consistently sought to restrict the autonomy of local authorities, producing periodic warnings that the life was being squeezed out of local government (Glen, 1949; Griffith, 1961). So regular did these warnings become that the local government policy community was in danger of 'crying wolf' too often, which may have reduced its credibility when a real threat appeared. Civil servants appear to have a generally low opinion of local government and have therefore not, perhaps, been as careful to protect it from ministerial intervention as they might have been (Crossman, 1975).

Governments interfere with local authorities for three main reasons. The first is their desire to implement their parties' major policy commitments. Thus the Labour governments of the 1960s and 1970s were determined to remove selection from state secondary education throughout the land and to this end acted with increasing severity to compel local education authorities to reorganize their secondary schools on comprehensive lines. Likewise, successive Conservative governments have restricted local authorities' autonomy in housing, for example, by compelling them to charge their tenants 'fair rents' as defined in the 1972 Housing Finance Act, or more recently obliging them to sell council houses to sitting tenants who want to buy them.

A second reason for central pressure on local government is the Treasury's desire to ensure that local authorities do not act in ways that run counter to the government's economic and financial policies. In particular, they should not exceed the expenditure targets laid down for them by the Treasury and the Department of the Environment, and where applicable the Scottish, Welsh and Northern Ireland Offices. Since 1979, the government has sought to regulate not only the total of local government spending but also that of individual local authorities, which has produced spectacular clashes with several local authorities, notably Lothian Regional Council (Crompton, 1983), Liverpool City Council (Parkinson, 1985) and Edinburgh City Council.

Lastly, governments intervene to ensure that local government services are provided at acceptable levels throughout the country. Local authorities vary very considerably in the amount they spend per head of the population on each of the services for which they are responsible: the highest spender commonly devotes between 30 and 50 per cent more money per head to the provision of its major services than the lowest spender (Elcock, 1986a, p. 60). The adequate provision of services is assured in part by departmental inspectorates, of which Her Majesty's Inspectors of Schools and Colleges are probably the best-known, and by the provision of general and specific grants to encourage service provision and to equalize the resources available in the richer and poorer parts of the country.

In recent years many established local government policies and practices have increasingly been disturbed by central intervention, particularly since Margaret Thatcher came to office. These pressures are of three kinds: increasing restrictions on expenditure, culminating in the imposition of 'rate-capping' in Scotland in 1982 and in England and Wales in 1984. Selected local authorities are now restricted as to the maximum rates they can levy. Secondly, the last two decades have witnessed, in local government as in most other aspects of British government, increasingly frequent and often radical structural changes. Comprehensive reorganization between 1965 and 1968 in London, between 1972 and 1974 in the rest of England and Wales and between 1973 and 1975 in Scotland, was presaged by a twenty-year debate about what form restructuring should take. These reorganizations were followed first by an attempt by Callaghan's Labour government to adjust the allocation of functions between country and district councils in the late 1970s ('organic change') and then by the abolition of seven of the largest English local authorities by the Thatcher government in 1986. Such frequent and drastic changes hardly provide a stable environment for managers and policy-makers. Lastly, changes have been imposed on the management of individual services, such as 'fair rents' and compulsory council house sales, as well as the encouragement, and later the compulsion, to put many local authority services out to competitive tender. Some functions are likely to be removed from local authority control altogether, including large parts of education when the central government lays down a 'core' curriculum covering between 80 and 90 per cent of school timetables and itself takes over control of polytechnics, other colleges and some schools. All this demonstrates that the environment in which local government managers must operate has become both complex and unstable. They have had to change their methods very greatly in order to cope with this instability and complexity (Stewart, 1986).

Structures and functions of local authorities

Before we can discuss in detail the development of local authority management over the last twenty years, we need to set out briefly the structure of the local government system and the functions of the different kinds of local authority. Over most of the country there are two tiers of local government: county and district councils in England and Wales, regional and district councils in most of Scotland. Unitary local government exists in the three Scottish Islands authorities, as well as in Greater London and the six English metropolitan counties since their county councils were abolished in 1986. Since abolition, the metropolitan district councils have been supplemented by a complex and confusing structure of joint boards which now control some of the services formerly provided by the abolished councils. In many rural areas and small towns, parish and town councils provide a third tier of small local government units which have relatively few powers but are important as bodies representative of local interests and opinions.

In Northern Ireland, 26 district councils administer a very limited range of functions. Many of the services provided by local authorities in Great Britain are provided in Northern Ireland by centrally appointed boards. This emasculation of local government by severely restricting its role was one of a series of measures taken after the Stormont Parliament was prorogued and direct rule from Westminster imposed in 1972. The intention was to reduce the extent of discrimination on religious grounds which existed in the province's public administration and in particular to reassure the minority Roman Catholic community that determined action was being taken by the government to end discrimination against its members.

The functions and powers of local authorities have been allocated in four ways. Many services are provided exclusively by one tier of local government: thus housing is always a district function. A second group of functions is split or shared between the tiers. Refuse collection is a district function but its disposal is the responsibility of the county council, wherever one exists. Where there is no longer a county council, refuse disposal is usually undertaken by a joint board. A third group of functions is concurrent. The same powers, for example to subsidize theatres or provide public entertainments, are vested in both tiers. Lastly, there are some functions which are undertaken under the direction of joint committees or boards of councillors drawn from several local authorities. As a consequence of the abolition of the Greater London Council and the metropolitan county councils, these are now a prominent feature of local government in England's largest cities but they exist elsewhere too – either where a responsibility is shared between a number of local authorities, such as joint police forces, or where several authorities have decided that a function would be better provided jointly rather than by each of them severally.

These functions and powers must also be classified in terms of what they are intended to achieve and at whom they are directed. In discussing local government management, it is helpful to think of its functions under four headings. The first and most dominant group of functions, in terms of the proportion of the budget it absorbs and the number of people employed in them, are the services provided by local authorities for their citizens: education, social services, refuse collection and disposal, together with many others. The second group consists of the uniformed emergency services – the police and the fire service – which are also services provided for citizens but which pose particular problems of public accountability and of integration into wider local authority management activities. Chief constables and fire chiefs are notoriously reluctant to participate in management team meetings or to accept joint use of resources like computers or repair workshops with other departments.

A third group of functions is concerned with the management of the authority's resources. Local authorities spend millions of pounds of public money and are often accused of wasting it. Their activities constitute between a quarter and a third of total public spending. They also employ thousands of people, frequently being the largest single employing organization in their areas. Most public services are by their nature labour-intensive. Thirdly, local authorities own a great deal of land and property – they are often the largest landowners in their areas. These resources must be used honestly and efficiently and substantial departments of finance, personnel and estate management exist for this purpose. Lastly, local authorities are concerned with planning, which can best be defined as the task of reducing uncertainty about the future (Edison, 1973). This includes the preparation of strategic structure plans, which are policy statements in the context of which local plans are prepared and individual planning applications determined. The importance of planning has been considerably reduced since 1980 and the abolition of structure plans has been mooted by the Secretary of State for the Environment (Department of the Environment, 1986). Nevertheless, substantial elements of the town and country planning systems are likely to survive and be a significant preoccupation for local authorities.

Developing patterns of local authority management

Local authorities are therefore large, powerful organizations with extensive and varied responsibilities. However, until the 1960s little conscious thought was given to their management. The service departments and professions each had their own traditions and values and there were few, if any, formal mechanisms for co-ordinating their activities, or ensuring that they were using their resources efficiently. This led to criticisms of inefficiency, lack of co-ordination (for example, Donnison, 1962) and occasional allegations of dishonesty or corruption. A few local authorities experimented with managerial innovations like city managers or streamlined committee structures but most continued in their established ways until the reorganizations of the early 1970s.

New thinking about management in local government was stimulated by John Stewart's seminal work, *Management in Local Government: a Viewpoint* (1971). Subsequently the government appointed two committees to propose management structures for the new local authorities to be established between 1972 and 1975. The Bains Committee (1972) made recommendations for English and Welsh authorities, with the Paterson Committee (1973) doing the same job in Scotland. These committees proposed new structures and procedures which were strongly influenced by the corporate management advocated by Stewart and others. Some of corporate management's advocates proposed it with an evangelical fervour which evoked a corresponding scepticism from local government practitioners – a scepticism already activated by the general failure of the Maud Committee's (1967) recommendations on the management of local government to win acceptance. Nevertheless, most of the new local authorities adopted some or most of the ingredients of corporate management.

The central theme of any discussion of the pros and cons of corporate management in local government is the tension between *differentiation* and *integration*. Differentiation is the separation of an organization's functions into largely autonomous sub-units, while maintaining at most weak co-ordinating mechanisms at its centre. The traditional local authority is a classical example of differentiation, with little communication between departments – let alone active co-ordination. In local authorities, this differentiation has been reinforced by the specialist professionalism of many of their staff. Most local government officers train as professionals, sitting the examinations of such professional bodies as the Royal Institute of British Architects, the Chartered Institute of Public Finance and Accountancy, the Law Society or the Royal Town Planning Institute. Until recently, few local government officers were graduates. They have thus been educated both into a specialized body of knowledge and an established set of professional values, which may be common to the public and private sectors (Dunleavy, 1980; Laffin, 1986). During their careers, they are both influenced by and active in their professional bodies. Although these do not exercise the collective bargaining functions of trade unions, they provide services and protect the professional interests of their members;

hence they may absorb attention and energies that might otherwise be devoted to trade union activity.

Most professional local government officers belong to the National and Local Government Officers' Association (NALGO), while manual staff belong either to trade unions which also represent other public sector workers, such as the National Union of Public Employees (NUPE), or to general unions like the Transport and General Workers' Union (TGWU) or the General, Municipal and Boilermakers' Amalgamated Trade Union (GMBATU). There are thus no trade unions which cover local government alone. The influence of these unions on local government officers is relatively marginal but they do carry out effective collective bargaining for most grades of local authority staff – especially the manual and routine white-collar grades.

One consequence of the domination of local government by specialist professionals is that they tend to be unaware of the activities and values of other professions. At worst, such professionalism can become 'disabling' in that it leads to the loss of effective public accountability of the staff concerned to councillors and the public, as well as to unresponsiveness (or worse) to their customers' needs and wishes (Illich *et al.*, 1977; Elcock, 1983).

By the early 1970s a number of trends were producing pressure for integration in local authorities – the establishment of stronger mechanisms for co-ordinating their activities and effective management of their resources. Among these pressures was the recognition that health and welfare services must be better co-ordinated as institutional care began to give way to care in the community. Hence the Seebohm Committee (1968) recommended the creation of generic social services departments to manage previously separate social work, community health and welfare activities. Secondly, there were pressures for greater efficiency, in particular to reduce the duplication of facilities like repair workshops. Related to this was the realization that central purchasing of supplies would reduce costs for local authorities because they would be able to secure larger discounts from suppliers. The achievement of greater efficiency has also necessitated much negotiation with trade unions, especially at the local level, for the introduction of new working arrangements and to remove restrictive practices. The need for these changes has been intensified with the introduction of competitive tendering for many local authority services. 'In-house' tenders can only succeed if unit costs are reduced and since most local government services are labour-intensive, this can be achieved only by changing working practices and increasing productivity.

Thirdly, the range of management techniques available for improving performance and efficiency, especially in the personnel field, encouraged local authorities to establish or strengthen central management services or personnel and other resource management departments. The role of personnel officers has been reinforced by the need to negotiate changes in salary structures and working practices with trade unions and by increased militancy among public sector workers in the 1970s. Lastly, the arrival of the mainframe computer, which was both too expensive and too powerful to be monopolized by a single department, added to the pressure for integration. However, the more recent development of microcomputers is having the opposite effect, because these machines can be used by individual departments or sections. This may produce the 'polo effect' – an organization with a vigorous periphery but little central management (Pitt and Smith, 1984).

The consequence of all these pressures was a largely abortive attempt to encourage integration in the old authorities by the Maud Committee on the Management of Local Government (1967) and the engagement by a number of local authorities of management consultants to recommend changes in their structures and procedures. These consultants commonly recommended co-ordinating committees and the appointment of Chief Executive Officers (Greenwood and Stewart (eds), 1974); views which were endorsed by the Bains (1972) and Paterson (1973) reports.

In consequence the traditional pattern of local authority management has increasingly been replaced by what Greenwood and Stewart (1974) called a federal structure, in which the departments' activities are co-ordinated and managed by increasingly influential central organs. This federal or corporate approach to management can be characterized in terms of six developments, some or all of which have appeared to a greater or lesser extent since 1973 in most local authorities. The first three of these developments have chiefly affected councillors' roles and work, the last three those of officers and staff.

First, most local authorities have appointed Policy and Resources Committees of councillors, which are charged with taking overall control of the council's policies and management. They are usually fairly large committees, containing between a quarter and a third of the council's total membership. Opposition members are usually included but a few authorities have established one-party policy and resources committees where control of the council itself is securely in one party's hands. Policy and Resources Committees play one of three roles, according to Greenwood *et al.* (1978). Some simply comment on the service committees' minutes but most are given the right to comment on any new proposals coming from service committees. A few authorities have 'interventionist' policy and resources committees which themselves initiate policies for implementation by the service committees and departments. The one-party policy and resources committees are most likely to play this 'interventionist' role.

Policy and resources committees usually have reporting to them sub-committees responsible for the management of the authority's finances, personnel and land, as well as a performance review sub-committee, which is charged with assessing how effectively and efficiently the council is achieving its policy objectives. The concept of performance review was slow to win acceptance in local government after its advocacy by the Bains Committee but has gained considerably in importance in recent years.

The third integrative development mainly affecting councillors has been a reduction in the number of committees a local authority establishes, coupled with a widening of each committee's span of control. A single committee may now control two, three or more service departments, although this development has been inhibited to some degree by statutory requirements to establish certain committees, notably education, social services, housing and police committees. However, the fire brigade may be controlled by a public protection committee which also deals with emergency planning and consumer protection, while the leisure services committee will often control libraries, museums, art galleries and arts provision. Most local authorities now have planning and transportation committees which deal with highways and public transport as well as town and country planning. Councillors therefore sit on fewer but larger main committees. However, these committees have tended to spawn large numbers of specialist sub-committees and working parties. One county council, created in 1973, had established 52 formal sub-committees to report to its 14 main committees within the first two years of its existence (Elcock, 1986a, p. 262).

At officer level, the most significant single innovation has been the appointment by most local authorities of a Chief Executive Officer with responsibility for co-ordinating the authority's staff, as well as giving policy and management advice to the council. A few authorities never appointed a Chief Executive and a few more have disposed of them, often in controversial and rancorous circumstances but most have established and maintained the office. The Widdicombe Committee (1986) recommended that all local authorities should be legally required to appoint a Chief Executive, who would be removable only by a vote of two-thirds of all the authority's councillors, but this (like most of Widdicombe's recommendations) has yet to be implemented. Although the majority of chief executives are lawyers by training, the old legal monopoly of the chief post (the old Clerkship) is gradually being eroded by members of other professions – notably accountants, planners and engineers (Lomer, 1977).

The second development at officer-level – the establishment of a management team of chief officers – constitutes one of the Chief Executive Officer's main responsibilities. Two bones of contention have commonly arisen here. The first is the question of which officers to include in the team. Too many will render it ineffective, but excluding some Chief Officers gives offence and causes demoralization in departments which feel that they have been accorded only second-rate status because their chief is not a management team member. The second is the reluctance of some Chief Officers, commonly those responsible for the largest service departments, to take the time necessary to prepare for and attend management team meetings or to accept that officers from outside their own departments have anything useful to contribute to the management of their services. Education officers, directors of social services, chief constables and chief fire officers are especially likely to take such an attitude because of the size of their departments and their traditions of professional autonomy. They will often resent what they see as ignorant and unhelpful invasions of their own management tasks by other management team members or staff from central management units.

Lastly, as with committees, local authorities have tried to reduce the number of their departments by subsuming a number of related functions under a single chief officer. A few authorities have experimented with multi-functional directorates, where several chief officers report to a single director who alone is a management team member, but this does not seem to have been very successful (Greenwood *et al.*, 1978). The trend towards large, multi-functional departments was encouraged by the creation of generic social services departments in 1971 as a result of the work of the Seebohm Committee (1968), as well as by the Bains Committee's advice that no local authority needs more than about six departments. Most authorities still have more than this but far fewer than was generally the case before reorganization.

These changes in the internal structures and processes of local authorities have been accompanied by a growing acceptance that local authorities have a 'governmental' role to play in the affairs of their areas (Greenwood and Stewart, 1974). This entails accepting that an authority's responsibility is not confined to the discharge of its statutory functions but includes a wider remit to protect and enhance the welfare of its area's inhabitants. An early instance was the declaration by the Royal Commission on Local Government that local authorities have 'an all-round responsibility for the safety, health and well-being, both material and cultural, of people in different localities' (Redcliffe-Maud, 1969). This wider role perception has been encouraged by Section 137 of the 1972 Local Government Act, which empowers local authorities to spend up to the product of a two-pence rate for their areas on any activity which, in the council's opinion, is in the interests of some or all of the area's inhabitants. A number of local authorities have used this power to develop extensive local economic development programmes (Shaw, 1987) or to make grants to a wide range of local voluntary organizations in order to assist disadvantaged or minority groups. Use of this discretionary power was given a major fillip by the arrival in power in a number of local authorities of the 'New Urban Left' in the early 1980s (Gyford, 1985), but as a consequence it became highly controversial. The Widdicombe Committee was charged, among other things, to investigate these activities but in its report (Widdicombe, 1986), the committee proposed that the Section 137 power should be strengthened – a recommendation which is unlikely to be implemented since it does not conform to the desire of Mrs Thatcher and her colleagues to curb the campaigning and other discretionary activities of local authorities.

In management terms, the development of the 'governmental' local authority has tended further to strengthen the roles of the policy and resources committee, as the point at which co-ordinated action can be initiated, as well as those of the leader of the council, the Chief Executive Officer. Some council leaders may now be perceived as 'local prime ministers' (Cousins, 1985) and have to be full-time politicians. Chief Executives, as the heads of their authorities' paid staff, have to co-ordinate major policy initiatives to rescue local industries which have fallen on hard times or attract major new investments to the area, for example. Leaders and Chief Executives will often spend much of their time establishing links with other organizations in their local authority areas, including private firms, the nationalized (or privatized) industries, government departments and other agencies. Where a local authority has a strategic planning role, it may become a 'reticulist' organization which manages a wide range of such links (see Friend, Power and

Yewlett, 1977). This will probably absorb much of the time of its Leader, Chief Executive and senior Planning Officers.

Both the trend towards integration within local authorities and the adoption by many of them of the 'governmental' stance, have been further encouraged by the extension of organized party politics to almost all local authorities in the years since reorganization. In many cases, the local authorities established in 1973 brought towns and cities, with highly developed party machines and disciplined party groups on the council together with rural areas in which party organization had previously been loose or non-existent, most councillors sitting as Independents. The party organizations moved in to contend for control of the new councils, with the result that the percentage of seats which were not contested fell rapidly, as well as many Independent councillors being pressured into accepting party whips or being defeated by partisan candidates at election time.

There are now very few local authorities whose politics are not dominated by more or less disciplined 'groups' of councillors belonging to one of the major political parties. These groups and even more their executive committees, provide an additional integrative mechanism, especially in policy terms. Usually, the group executives meet shortly before the Policy and Resources Committee to determine the line party members will follow at the committee meeting. Party groups also enhance the roles of leaders, committee chairmen and their 'shadows', all of whose roles tend to become akin to those of front-benchers at Westminster. The leader and the committee chairman must expound the ruling party's policies to the officers and explain the officers' professional views to their colleagues in the group. On party-controlled authorities, this intermediary role is crucial and makes the chairman's agenda meeting, held before the agenda for each committee meeting is sent out, very important. It also entails an increasing number of more or less informal meetings between the leading members of the ruling party group and the council's senior officers (Greenwood, 1983; Elcock, 1986a, p. 106; Elcock and Jordan, 1987), as well as much contact with officers of the authority's trade union branches.

However, one essential difference between central and local government remains, even in the most partisan local authorities: the officers are charged to serve the whole council, not just the current ruling party (as is the case with the civil service). The importance of maintaining this principle was stressed by the Widdicombe Committee as a result of its investigation of the impact of party politics on local government. In particular, the committee reviewed the increasing practice of making political appointments of staff to support leading members of ruling party groups; they concluded that to do this was desirable as long as a clear distinction was maintained between these political appointees and the authority's permanent staff, who must serve and advise ruling and opposition party members alike. Widdicombe, however, gave local authority procedures, even in controversial areas such as this, a generally clean bill of health – somewhat, one suspects, to the government's dismay.

The 1980s: New pressures, new methods

By 1979, most local authorities had firmly established their post-reorganization administrative structures. Some made abrupt changes – for example, Birmingham City Council dismissed its Chief Executive Officer and abandoned much of its much-vaunted corporate management structure when the Conservatives won control of the council in 1978 (Haynes, 1980). The election of the Thatcher government brought new pressures, as did the control of a number of local authorities in the early 1980s by a new breed of Labour local politicians – John Gyford's (1985) 'New Urban Left'. Public service trade unions had also become more militant in the previous few years – a development to which the New Urban Left was sympathetic. Trade unionists hence became more closely involved in local authority management structures – sometimes to the extent of being given representation on local authority committees. More recently, the rise in electoral support for the Liberal–SDP Alliance produced an increasing number of local authorities on which no one party had an overall majority. This too has presented councillors and officers alike with new policy and managerial problems (Blowers, 1977; Haywood, 1977; Leach and Stewart, 1986). These three new pressures – the Thatcher government, the rise of the 'New Urban Left' and the increasing number of 'hung' or 'balanced' councils, have created new waves of managerial development.

One major impact of the public spending cuts which have been demanded in most years since 1976 – a demand which has intensified since Mrs Thatcher's election in 1979 – has combined with the government's decisions first to encourage, now to compel, local authorities to submit many of their services to competitive tendering, to produce changes in working practices and industrial relations. This has involved extensive and sometimes difficult negotiations with trade unions, both locally and nationally but unions and managers have had to accept that they must co-operate in reducing costs in order to maximize the chance of 'in-house' tenders succeeding against private sector competitors. It is not at all clear, however, that letting tenders for service provision to private con-tractors had produced better services or lower costs in the National Health Service or local government.

Another recent trend in local authority management is an increas-ing preoccupation with ensuring that decisions and services are acceptable to the public. Public participation in decision-making has been encouraged, especially in town and country planning since the Skeffington Report, *People and Planning*, was published in 1969. More recently, an increasing number of local authorities have begun to undertake detailed surveys of consumer reactions to the services they provide (Fenwick, 1986). Local authority procedures have also become more accessible to members of the public as a consequence of the Local Government (Access to Information) Act 1985, which severely restricts the extent to which local authority business can be conducted in private. Another effect, however, has been to increase the number of informal groups and procedures which are not subject to the requirements of the Act – so that real decisions are made informally behind closed doors and then ratified at formal meetings held in public.

They have also begun to try to make their services more accessi-ble and attractive to the public. In particular over the last decade or so many authorities have decentralized control over service pro-vision to units responsible for small neighbourhoods. In the mid-1970s the Department of the Environment encouraged a range of area management initiatives (Harrop *et al.*, 1978; Webster, 1982) and a number of social service departments began to develop 'patch' structures in which much responsibility for service provision has been devolved to neighbourhood teams. The arrival of the 'New Urban Left' in the early 1980s produced wider initiatives in which service provision was devolved to neighbourhood offices con-trolled by neighbourhood committees. Walsall Metropolitan Borough Council commended such an initiative after Labour won control of the council in 1982. It proved so popular that when Labour lost control to a Conservative and Liberal coalition, the borough's new rulers dared not abolish the scheme. Since then, many more local authorities have developed decentralization schemes (Hoggatt and Hambleton, 1987). Sometimes, however, these schemes have been resisted or even blocked by local trade union branches, whose members resist the changes in working practices involved in decentralization, especially where they involve their members having more contact with the public.

These initiatives may briefly and inadequately be characterized as being of three types. First, departmental decentralization, in which a single department devolves much of the responsibility for service provision on neighbourhood teams or offices. This approach has been particularly prevalent in the social services, where it seems to have had considerable success (Payne, 1979; Hadley *et al.*, 1984; Elcock, 1986b). Secondly, several departments can combine to provide local advice and services from area or neighbourhood offices (Hambleton, 1979). Lastly, partial control over such neighbourhood offices has been vested by some local authorities in neighbourhood committees, consisting of ward councillors and other community leaders. This creates a political dimension to decentralization. Corporate and political decentralization encourage collaboration between locally based staff from different departments, thus generating corporate management 'from below' to supplement the corporate management 'from above' – in terms of integration at the top of the organization – through policy and resources committees, chief executive officers and so on (Hoggatt and Hambleton, 1987).

The Thatcher government repeatedly claims that its proposals to oblige local authorities to put more services out to competitive tender, to give school governors more power, to give tenants the right to buy their council houses, and to allow them a choice of landlord, are all ways of increasing local services' responsiveness to the public. Previously, control tended in practice to be vested in public service professionals who sometimes held paternalistic attitudes towards their clients. Also, trade union shop stewards turned some local authority manual organizations into inefficient units riddled with restrictive practices. The government's reforms may reduce these evils and increase local authority services' responsiveness to the public. Time will tell.

Lastly, we must consider the impact on a local authority's management of the election of a council on which no one party has an overall majority. Parkinson (1985) argued that three-party politics on Liverpool City Council in the 1970s produced a decade of inertia. Councillors were unwilling to take unpopular decisons like raising the rate or reorganizing the secondary schools to cope with rapidly falling rolls in the inner city areas. By contrast, in Avon and Lancashire county councils, after Labour lost control in the 1985 elections while remaining the largest party, its members continued to make policy at least until very late in the first budgetary cycle determined by the 'hung' council. Even then – and in Avon's case amidst a great deal of controversy – the budgets were altered only at the margin (Barlow, 1987; Clements, 1987). The election of 'hung' councils thus had little effect, at least in the short term, on the substance of these authorities' budgetary policies. It is a nice point whether the uncertainty concerning committee decisions in 'hung' authorities increases or reduces officers' influence (Blowers, 1977; Haywood, 1977; Elcock, 1986a). On balance, it probably increases councillors' influence. Finally, 'hung' councils need to develop procedural conventions if the authority's business is to be carried on; Cheshire County Council's conventions were commended to other authorities by the Widdicombe Committee, while Lanca-shire's Chief Executive was instrumental in securing cross-party agreement on procedures after the council became 'hung' in 1985 (Barlow, 1987).

Conclusions: Politics, management and the future

This short account of local government management as it has developed since reorganization, illustrates one of the crucial differ-ences between public and private sector management: the import-ance of politics and political events in determining the content of the management task (see Kingdom, 1986; Elcock, 1986c). The struc-tures and procedures of the traditional local authority were deter-mined by the ultimate accountability of all of the authority's employees to the council and its committees. The constitutional convention that politicians determine policy and officers carry it out is a myth but it is nevertheless a centrally important influence on how public servants – including local authority officers – are expected and expect to behave. This is reflected in some of the traditions of the local government service, including the deference shown to councillors and the rule that every letter sent to a coun-cillor must be signed with the chief officer's name. The traditional local authority was usually an honest, relatively efficient but not creative organization. Its staff were narrowly confined by formal rules and departmental specialisms; their creativity was stifled by bureaucratic rules and hierarchical control – mostly in the name of accountability to councillors.

The development of corporate management arose largely from non-political imperatives, such as the development of an increas-ingly wide range of finanical and personnel management techniques but its development was also a result of political and other criticism of failures of co-ordination within and between local authorities. The reports on the Maria Colwell and subsequent child abuse tragedies, for example, have repeatedly highlighted lack of inter-departmental or inter-organizational co-ordination as a major reason for failure to prevent disaster. In any case, the establishment of disciplined party groups on nearly all councils after 1973 gave a powerful fillip to integration, since the changes in structures and procedures which followed the Bains and Paterson Reports were reinforced by party groups, their executive committees and the consequent increasing prominence of leaders and committee chairmen as policy-makers.

More recently, integration has been further developed because of the need to tighten control of local authority budgetary processes, in order to meet or resist central government demands for expenditure reductions. By contrast, the rise of the 'New Urban Left' has accelerated progress towards internal decentralization. However, this can be, in its own way, a form of integration, since it enables or obliges staff from different departments to work together at the fieldwork level – hence it is 'corporate management from below'. There is also a trend towards greater awareness of consumer views and more sensitivity towards their needs, wishes and reactions – especially those of racial and other minorities. Lastly, the government's commitment to competitive tendering is likely to alter local authorities' roles fundamentally, from being bodies providing public services themselves to being responsible mainly for the oversight of services provided on their behalf by private companies.

In all these developments, politics has been crucial in determining the evolution of local authority management, in two ways. First, it determines the national and local value frameworks within which local authority managers must operate. Secondly, those value frameworks influence the ways in which local authorities' structures and processes must develop in order to implement them.

In 1970, local government was a settled, uniform, perhaps somewhat complacent set of institutions. Now, management structures vary considerably between authorities and are subject to change as a result of the uncertainties and pressures with which local authorities must now cope. Local authority management has never before been so exciting a subject – indeed, some practitioners probably find it too exciting – but over it all hangs the threat of extinction by the increasingly heavy hand of central control. Some services and institutions are soon likely to be removed from local authority control altogether. New national controls are threatened, including the core curriculum in schools, compulsion to put services out to tender and an ever more severe financial regime. The introduction of the community charge (poll tax) is likely to reduce what remains of the financial autonomy of local authorities. However, local government has been deemed to be on its death-bed many times before. R. A. W. Rhodes's (1981) analysis of central–local government relations demonstrates that local authorities possess resources with which they can evade or resist the centre's efforts to control them. Although the balance of power is gradually tipping towards the central government's way – and has been doing so for a long time – the vitality of local authorities, together with their financial, political and information resources, as well as their legal prerogatives, will long survive Mrs Thatcher's tenure of office – unless she abolishes them all.

References

Bains, M. (1972), *The New Local Authorities: Management and Structure*, Department of the Environment.

Barlow, J. (1987), 'Lancashire County Council' in H. Elcock and G. Jordan (1987), pp. 37–49.

Blowers, A. (1977), 'Checks and Balances: the Politics of Minority Government', *Public Administration*, vol. 55, pp. 41–55.

Bulpitt, J. (1967), *Party Politics in English Local Government* (Longman, Green).

Clements, R. (1987), 'Avon County Council' in H. Elcock and G. Jordan (1987), pp. 25–36.

Cousins, P. (1985), 'Local Prime Ministers', *Teaching Public Administration*, vol. 4, pp. 44–50.

Crompton, P. (1983), 'The Lothian Affair', *Scottish Government Yearbook* (Edinburgh University Press).

Crossman, R. H. S. (1975), *The Diaries of a Cabinet Minister: Volume 1, Minister of Housing and Local Government* (Hamish Hamilton/Jonathan Cape).

Department of the Environment (1986), *The Future of Development Plans: a Consultation Paper*.

Donnison, D. V. (1962), *Health, Welfare and Democracy in Greater London*, London School of Economics and Political Science.

Dunleavy, P. (1980), *Urban Political Analysis* (Macmillan).

Edison, T. (1973), *Local Government: Management and Corporate Planning* (L. Hill/INLOGOV).

Elcock, H. (1983), 'Disabling Professionalism: the Real Threat to Local Democracy' *Public Money*, vol. 3, pp. 23–7.

Elcock, H. (1986a), *Local Government: Politicians, Professionals and the Public in Local Authorities* (Methuen).

Elcock, H. (1986b), 'Going Local in Humberside: Decentralization as a

Tool for Social Services Management', *Local Government Studies*, July/August, pp. 35–49.

Elcock, H. (1986c), 'Public Administration or Public Management?', *Teaching Public Administration*, vol. 6, Summer, pp. 22–30.

Elcock, H. and Jordan, G. (eds) (1987), *Learning from Local Authority Budgeting* (Avebury).

Fenwick, J. (1986), *West City Consumer Survey 1985: First Report*, Newcastle upon Tyne City Council.

Friend, J. K., Power, J. M. and Yewlett, C. J. L. (1977), *Public Planning: the Inter-Corporate Dimension* (Methuen).

Glen, J. H. W. (1949), *Changes in the Structure of Local Government*, Institute of Municipal Treasurers and Accountants.

English Local Government', *Public Administration*, vol. 61, pp. 149–68.

Greenwood, R. and Stewart, J. D. (eds) (1974), *Corporate Planning in English Local Government* (C. Knight/INLOGOV).

Greenwood, R. *et al* (1978), 'The Politics of the Budgetary Process in English Local Government', *Political Studies*, vol. 25, pp. 29–47.

Griffith, J. A. G. (1961), 'The Future of Local Government', *Municipal Review*, pp. 804–9 and 818.

Gyford, J. (1985), *The Politics of Local Socialism* (Allen & Unwin).

Hadley, R., Dale, P. and Sills, P. (1984), 'Teaming up for Change', *Social Work Today*, 3 December, pp. 16–18.

Hambleton, R. (1979), *Policy Planning in Local Government* (Hutchinson).

Harrop, K. *et al.* (1978), *The Implementation and Development of Area Management* (INLOGOV).

Haynes, R. (1980), *Organisation Theory and Local Government* (Allen & Unwin).

Haywood, S. (1977). 'Decision-making in Local Government: the Case of an Independent Council', *Local Government Studies*, vol. 3, pp. 41–55.

Hoggatt, P. and Hambleton, R. (1987), *Decentralization and Democracy: Localizing Public Services*, School of Advanced Urban Studies.

Illich, I. *et al.* (1977), *Disabling Progressions* (M. Boyars).

Kingdom, J. (1986), 'Public Administration: Defining the Discipline', *Teaching Public Administration*, vol. 6, Spring, pp. 1–13; Summer, pp. 1–21.

Laffin, M. (1986), *Professionalism and Policy in Central–Local Relations* (Gower Press).

Leach, S. and Stewart, J. D. (1986), 'The Hung Councils', INLOGOV, Local Government Training Board.

Lomer, M. (1977), 'The Chief Executive in Local Government' *Local Government Studies*.

Parkinson, M. (1985), *Liverpool on the Brink* (Policy Journals).

Paterson Report (1973), *The New Scottish Local Authorites: Organisation and Management Structures*, Scottish Development Department.

Payne, M. (1979), *Power, Authority and Responsibility in Social Services Departments* (Macmillan).

Pitt, D. and Smith, B. C. (1984), *The Computer Revolution in Public Administration* (Wheatsheaf).

Redcliffe-Maud Report (1969), *Report of the Royal Commission on Local Government in England*, Cmnd 4584 (HMSO).

Report of the Maud Committee (1967), *Management of Local Government* (HMSO).

Rhodes, R. A. W. (1981), *Power-Dependence Theories in Central–Local Relations* (Gower Press).

Seebohm Report (1968), *The Local Authority and Allied Social Services* (HMSO).

Shaw, K. (1987), 'Training for Local Economic Development: A Contribution to Educational Institutions', *Discussion Papers in Local Government* (Local Authority Management Unit, Newcastle Polytechnic).

Skeffington Report (1969), *People and Planning* (HMSO).

Smith, T. A. (1966), *Town and County Hall: Problems of Recruitment and Training*, Acton Society Trust.

Stanyer, J. (1976), *Understanding Local Government* (Fontana/Collins).

Stewart, J. D. (1971), *Management in Local Government: a Viewpoint* (Charles Knight).

Stewart, J. D. (1986), *The New Management of Local Government* (Allen & Unwin).

Webster, B. (1982), 'Area Management and Responsive Policy-making', in S. Leach and J. D. Stewart (eds), *Approaches in Public Policy* (Allen & Unwin), pp. 167–98.

Widdicombe, D. (1986), *The Conduct of Local Authority Business* (HMSO).

Wiseman, H. V. (1963), 'The Working of Local Government in Leeds', *Public Administration*, vol. 41, pp. 51–69 and 137–55.

6 The management of law and order

GEORGE POPHAM

Introduction: context and complexities

The management of law and order can only be comprehended when its political, economic and social connections are appreciated. The formulation and enforcement of law are pre-eminently the concern of the state, the focus of political activity and study, but neither state nor law can be divorced from economic phenomena, such as property, contracts and markets, which influence their functions and character. Also relevant are social factors, such as class and ethnic relations, regional and cultural diversity, living standards, the educational system and even the age structure of the population. Furthermore, the normative aspects of law link it to ethical values, involving such contested notions as justice, rights, liberty and equality. These complexities converge within comprehensive doctrines or schools of thought, labelled 'conventional wisdoms' by Berki (1986, ch. 4), which provide differing perspectives and simplified models of 'reality'.

Doctrines are not the exclusive preserve of political parties or activists but are selectively adopted, often inconsistently, by apparently apolitical individuals, academics, professional and other groups, and media controllers, creating an overall climate of public opinion which, in varying degrees, constrains the strategic and operational management of policing, the preoccupation of this chapter. Schools of thought differ in their assumptions regarding the causes of crime and disorder, prescribing or implying alternative measures. Briefly outlining them, focusing on the broad orientations of conservatism, liberalism, socialism and marxism, indicates some of the problems and attitudes involved.

Perspectives on law and order

Conservatism

According to Berki (p. 199) the conservative stance on law and order is the epitome of conventional wisdom, adopted by the 'establishment', upper and middle classes, the overwhelming majority of the legal profession, businessmen, military and police. The greater part of the working classes, inhabiting the most crime-prone localities and the most frequent victims, may well lean towards an 'authoritarian populism' which mirrors conservative demands for firm policing and strict retributive punishment.

Objective studies regarding the views of police officers are hard to come by, partly owing to Home Office reluctance to permit inquiries which could throw doubts on police impartiality. Given the large number of officers involved, in excess of 120,000, there are clearly individual variations at all levels. Reiner, however, referring to available academic evidence, concludes that police sympathies are 'pretty apparently right of centre' (in Punch, 1983, p. 130; also Reiner, 1978, chs 8 and 11 *passim*).

The essence of conservative thought on law and order, particularly in radical right versions, is individual responsibility. Most citizens are perceived as orderly and law-abiding. A minority, however, fail to control the antisocial proclivities inherent in human nature. Individual circumstances play a part but do not excuse criminal or disorderly conduct. Self-discipline is necessary. According to Sir Robert Mark (1977, p. 76), a former Metropolitan Police Commissioner, most social violence stems from 'ordinary human characteristics; selfishness, greed, ambition, lust and so on', rather than from the social conditions seized on by apologists. Just retribution will hopefully discourage repetition and deter potential offenders. The liberty of the majority must be protected within the established order (see Aughey and Norton, 1984, p. 145).

By their conformity, the bulk of the population are assumed to acknowledge the legitimacy of existing social and political institutions which slowly and naturally evolve, subject to modification by recognized constitutional methods. Nothing is considered more abhorrent than the disruption produced by political dissidence and belligerent strikes. A minority of malcontents, extremists, militants and deviants, however, threaten tranquillity, national security and even the moral fibre of society, employing conspiratorial, violent, extra-parliamentary methods. Their actual or possible conduct is such that they are rightly subject to security checks and police intelligence gathering, essential for the preservation of the rule of law which they threaten.

In conservative thought, the police require adequate resources to deal with miscreants but should limit costs significantly by maintaining good relations with the law-abiding majority. Furthermore, the impartial enforcement of law, together with professional expertise, justifies police enjoying unusual degrees of freedom from political direction and control by elected representatives.

There are more subtle and sophisticated versions of conservatism, deriving from the organic and elitist philosophy of Burke. Some adherents may justifiably protest that the radical right, temporarily in the ascendant, traduce the true faith. For example, individualism may be offset by 'one-nation' concern for the poor and underprivileged. Nevertheless, all factions or sects perceive the rule of law as essentially a matter of protection, not only against criminals and political extremists, but also against the possible abuse of power by ministers and officials, including the police.

Liberalism

There is some common ground between conservatism and liberalism. Both, for example, are wary of state bureaucracy and trade unionism. In the twentieth century both have accepted welfare state provision and limited economic interventionism, though conservatism, in its Thatcherite mould, has ideologically reverted to the values of mid-nineteenth-century Manchester school liberalism, preaching the virtues of individualism, capitalism and laissez-faire. Liberalism, too, favours the capitalist order but in a more human form.

If the strength of conservatism lies in numerical support, liberalism nevertheless enjoys vocal and practical expression by influential elements in society. In matters of law and order they include 'enlightened' judges and 'progressive' chief constables as well as occupational groups associated with the 'soft embrace' of the state – social workers, probation officers, psychiatrists, and some academics and church leaders, many of whom have access to the mass media or more restricted means of communication.

The liberal persuasion is more tolerant towards movements regarded askance by conservatives, such as CND and Greenpeace, as well as towards aberrent non-conformist individuals. This is manifested in the policies and operational decisions of liberal police chiefs, typified by the former Chief Constable of Devon and Cornwall, John Alderson, who claimed to be continuing the 'firm but friendly' tradition of British policing.

Liberalism makes greater allowance than conservatism for the impact of individual circumstances and social conditions on criminal behaviour, with the 'victims' of crime extended to include the families of offenders. Unruly conduct is deplored but partially attributed to social deprivation, sometimes compounded by aggressive and provocative policing. The report on the Brixton disorders of 1981, by Lord Scarman, the embodiment of judicial liberalism, exemplifies this disposition. Deterrent and punitive measures are recognized as necessary but penal policy is to be predominantly infused by the principles of reform and rehabilitation.

Class conflict is repudiated by liberalism, together with 'the bureaucratic elitism of scientific socialism and the social elitism' attributed to conservatism (Ingle, 1984, p. 166). The hallmarks of liberalism are hostility towards an over-centralized state and a marked preference for group pluralism and participative community politics. It follows that the style of policing most favoured is community policing, as encouraged by Alderson and ex-Superintendent Webb in Handsworth, both Liberal-Alliance candidates on their retirement. The recruitment of more special or part-time constables is also advocated as a means of citizen involvement.

Liberalism, then, seeks the humanization of the capitalist order, not its abandonment, with corresponding import for criminal justice and policing strategies. Socialism and marxism, on the contrary, seek to transform society – to institute a different order.

Socialism

Socialism shares conservative and liberal commitment to change by parliamentary means. It accepts the machinery of the state, the civil service, the judiciary, armed forces and police as politically neutral, even if most senior personnel exhibit conservative backgrounds and leanings. There is a realization that socialist permanent secretaries, generals, judges and chief constables are highly improbable, posing some difficulties. It is nevertheless assumed that state elites are open to the rational arguments of moderate Fabian socialists, seeking only gradual limited change, for efficiency's sake. Moreover, professional integrity and constitutional propriety ensure subservience to a properly elected government.

The peaceful evolution of capitalism into a qualitatively different socialist society is therefore considered possible. The legal sovereignty of Parliament and the political sovereignty of the electorate are maintained. Defiance on the part of a minority of reactionary capitalists, if it took the form of illegality, would be dealt with by due process of law and armed force if necessary.

Socialism goes further than liberalism in attributing crime and disorder to social causes. As one writer puts it, 'poverty, deprivation, ignorance and inequality are the ingredients from which criminals are manufactured' (Elcock, 1984, p. 149). The Haldane Society of Socialist Lawyers echoes this, rejecting the contention that 'crime is limited to a peculiar criminal class', set apart from normal people (Blake, p. 9). Individual psychology is acknowledged but only as a subsidiary factor.

The social and economic causes of crime must therefore be attacked; crime itself is more a symptom than the actual disease. The ills allegedly generated by capitalism, endemic class conflict, regular cyclical unemployment, maldistribution of wealth and income, low wages, inadequate housing and run-down inner cities, can be 'cured' by state action. Even when a Conservative government is in office much can be achieved by socialist local authorities, imaginative officials, radical social workers, trade unions, pressure groups and continual proselytizing by left-wing intellectuals and academics.

Although generally uncritical of routine policing, socialists are apt to deprecate trends towards over-reactive and coercive styles in the handling of strikes and certain marches and demonstrations. At least on occasion, confidence in police impartiality comes into question and they are portrayed as pro-employer and hostile to anti-apartheid, anti-nuclear and similar 'progressive' cause groups. Solutions are sought in greater degrees of accountability to elected local Police Authorities. When socialist Labour governments have been in power, however, the managerial efficiency anticipated from greater centralization has tended to override local control.

Marxism

There are so many controversies between its adherents that it is difficult to summarize marxism without risking charges of misrepresentation. According to one commentator, marxism 'has become a theoretical mode' and 'a framework for debate, rather than a rigid orthodoxy' (Shaw, 1984, p. 179). Nevertheless, it provides yet another model or paradigm which has some explanatory value even for those who remain sceptical concerning some of its features.

According to Marx's collaborator Engels (1892, p. 159), by the mid-nineteenth century, industrialization and the expansion of the industrial proletariat had made the English nation 'the most criminal in the world'. Doubtless the more efficient policing necessitated by the growth of cities contributed to the inflation of crime statistics. Present day marxists still regard the economic system as fundamental in determining power relationships between classes, reflected in the character and application of law, but doctrinal revisions, associated with changed perceptions of the state, attach great importance to ideological domination and political action.

For marxists, the state in capitalist democracies exists to safeguard and perpetuate capitalism. It does so partly by socializing certain costs of production through public expenditure; for example, by allocating funds to maintain the infrastructure or by grants and subsidies to producers in the form of inducements or tax concessions. In addition, it utilizes a combination of coercion (the police and armed forces) and consent or legitimization, varying the proportions according to circumstances (O'Connor, 1973, pp. 5–10; Gough, 1979, ch. 5).

Legitimization is vital because, as a non-marxist author remarks, unless the mass of the public feels a 'moral obligation to observe established law, the law may come to be unenforceable' (Atiyah, 1983, p. 98). It will certainly become difficult and costly to impose. The most obvious example is Ulster, where legitimacy is undermined by the co-existence of Protestant and Catholic communities, with separate sub-cultures and organizations, divided national loyalties towards the UK and Ireland, and lack of Catholic confidence in political institutions and the impartiality of the Royal Ulster Constabulary. On the mainland, even though the electoral system is widely recognized as unrepresentative, legitimization is largely successful. Nevertheless, the degree of legitimacy varies in different periods and according to social class, ethnicity and region. Legitimization is not spontaneous but has to be cultivated and there are always potential problems, especially in times of economic recession.

Coercion has an inverse relationship with legitimization – it declines as the latter increases and increases as legitimization weakens. If legitimization is successful problems of policing tend to diminish. Moreover, coercion is difficult to reconcile with consensual democracy so the significance of the state as the organizer of consent and legitimacy is enhanced (Hall, 1978, p. 201).

According to marxists, the state is not ultimately neutral but it enjoys considerable independence in deciding policies to serve the long-term interest of the capitalist order (presented as the common or national interest). Enlightened self-interest, and legitimization, may require concessions to the pressures of organized labour. The state's autonomy is 'relative', however, because it cannot contemplate economic collapse, on which revenues depend, or any abandonment of the pursuit of profit, irrespective of the party in office.

Legitimization is more easily secured when general living standards are rising but, according to marxism, profits derive from increasing the productivity of labour while restricting its total income to less than the market value of what is produced or supplied. Exploitation and class conflict are endemic but contained in prosperous times by legitimizing social services, affordable out of expanding tax revenues.

The system is subject to recurring crises, however, though they may be widely separated in time. World competition squeezes wages, leading to ineffective total demand and rising unemployment. This is exacerbated by monopolistic trends and the 'rationalization' of work-forces, together with constant technological innovation which displaces labour. The subsequent escalating costs of social security provision give rise to charges of government 'overload' and waste and business interests claim tax burdens are undermining international competitiveness.

If the frontiers of the welfare state *are* rolled back (and the relative autonomy of the state suggests this is not absolutely certain) class conflict, poverty and inequality increase, undermining legitimacy. Greater dependence on force becomes necessary and police forces are allocated additional resources. Whether such an analysis can be plausibly applied to Britain in the 1980s is a moot point (see Hillyard and Percy-Smith, 1988) but it is decidedly the case that the first half of the decade witnessed increased government concern over law and order, together with enhanced interest in effective and efficient policing management.

The management of policing: Resources and their utilization

Moving from general perspectives to the more immediate concerns of policing management, one encounters such matters as budgetary allocations; coercive and persuasive styles; optimum force size and technological innovation; formal and informal organization; hierarchical authority and discretion; internal controls, such as policy committees and policing by objectives; relationships between forces and other organizations; consent, complaints and public relations; community policing; efficiency, effectiveness and crime statistics; local accountability, professional autonomy and centralization.

There are 43 police forces in England and Wales, established by the Police Act, 1964. The Metropolitan and City of London forces are each headed by a Commissioner, the 41 provincial forces by a Chief Constable. Scotland has a further 8 forces, Northern Ireland has the Royal Ulster Constabulary. There are also other forces, such as the British Transport Police and Ministry of Defence Police. Limited space here confines attention to the 43 forces in England and Wales.

To be effective, forces need the capacity to carry out their manifold tasks. This largely depends on the adequacy of their resources. The financial and other resources allocated to law and order are determined by the priorities of government, particularly central government in Britain. In the first half of the 1980s it was assumed by government that police forces needed to be more generously resourced in order to combat a reputed crime wave and industrial unrest. The need to restore law and order was a major issue in the general election of 1979, taken up by the media and vigorously pressed by such bodies as the Association of Chief Police Officers and Police Federation, leading to charges of politicization.

Police managers are probably inclined mentally to transform political problems into problems of administration, such as resourcing, in line with managerial or bureaucratic ideologies (Mannheim, 1960, p. 105). The fact of the matter is that policing cannot be taken out of politics. Chief Constables and other senior officers have to be politically aware and appreciate that throughout budgetary processes, central and local, the backing of ministers, councillors, administrators, pressure groups and media is essential. The political environment is therefore vitally important.

In the 1980s the share of law and order as a proportion of public expenditure has risen appreciably, at a time when strenuous efforts have been made to reduce government spending, except in the run-up to elections. While total social security payments ineluctably rose as unemployment escalated from just over 1 million in 1979 to over 3 million by 1983, housing expenditure fell by more than 50 per cent. Rising unemployment, together with burgeoning housing and other social problems, did not augur well for crime rates, however well-managed and resourced police forces might be. Research suggests that youths are three times more likely to commit crime when unemployed, especially if they come from large households, have low-income parents, and live in poor housing (Farrington D. P. *et al.*, 'Unemployment, School Leaving and Crime', *British Journal of Criminology*, vol. 24, no. 4). By implication, income redistribution, better housing and full employment are more effective ways of reducing crime than the recruitment of additional police.

Between 1979 and 1986 spending on police rose from £1.1 billion to £2.9 billion, a real increase of 36 per cent, and the number of officers in England and Wales grew by some 10,000 to almost 120,000. In 1961 total strength had been 75,600 (Bradley, Walker and Wilkie, 1986, p. 15). Throughout all ranks pay doubled (*New Society*, 14 November 1986). In addition, in 1981 the 43 forces in England and Wales were employing over 37,000 civilians, many on work previously undertaken by the more highly paid police, such as dealing with inquiries from the public, operating communications systems and serving summonses.

Additional resources did not stem increasing crime or improve overall clear-up rates. Between 1979 and 1987 reported crime in England and Wales rose by over 50 per cent, yet clear-up rates fell from nearly 36 per cent in 1985 to 31 per cent in 1986. The relevance of such statistics for assessing the efficiency and effectiveness of police management is nevertheless difficult to determine. Forces may differ in the way they classify, define and record crimes, thereby affecting impressions of performance. Tying increases in pay or manpower to 'evidence' of greater efficiency, as the Home Secretary has suggested (*Guardian*, 12 April 1988) is therefore contentious.

The Commissioner of the Metropolitan Police pointed out in 1987 that figures were inflated by, amongst other things, increased use of credit cards, unemployment, a consumer-oriented society and the diversion of officers from crime prevention and detection to public order duties, presumably in response to government pressure. He cited the Wapping printing dispute in particular (*Daily Telegraph*, 17 March 1987). With 81 per cent of households possessing a telephone, as compared with 45 per cent in 1973, the reporting of offences has probably increased at a faster rate than actual breaches of the law. Given that about a third of all crime is committed by boys under the age of 17, it is sometimes assumed that the low birth rates of the 1970s will bring about an apparent improvement in efficiency in the 1990s (*The Economist*, 21 March 1987, pp. 38–9).

This has been described as over-simplistic because there are many complicating factors, including the long-term effects of structural unemployment (Lea, Matthews and Young, 1987). Nevertheless, a fall in reported crime from an average annual rise of 6 per cent (with marked yearly variations) to only 1 per cent for 1987/88 was mainly attributed to a decline in the number of mid-teenage boys by

100,000. According to one authority, however, the smaller number of teenagers were probably committing *more* crimes, whilst another suggested that the most reliable indicator was the figure for serious offences, nearly always notified to the police. These jumped sharply, violent crime rising 12 per cent, sex attacks by 11 per cent, robbery 9 per cent and attempted murder by 83 per cent (*Sunday Times*, 27 March 1988; on crime statistics generally see Slatter, 1986, ch. 5).

Government willingness generously to resource police forces was never unqualified and Chief Constables were made aware of the obsession with cutting public expenditure and obtaining 'value for money' (an arcane phrase) even before the defeat of the miners' strike of 1984–5, an objective pursued with scant regard to cost (Home Office, 1983). By 1988, the official side of the police negotiating board, the Home Office and Police Authorities, was proposing the ending of various allowances, such as the reimbursement of national health charges and the rates element in housing allowances. The chairman elect of the Police Federation complained that this was a poor reward for standing up to flying pickets and rioting mobs (*Guardian*, 1 April 1988).

The pay awards of the early 1980s encouraged recruitment but had a considerable impact on financial resources since manpower pre-empts 85 per cent of force budgets (Bradley, Walker and Wilkie, 1986, p. 28), stimulating Home Office pressure for more civilian employees. Taking into account cash limits, overtime bills, additional legal responsibilities, greater public consultation and increases in reported crime, resourcing – which to managers in other public services appeared distinctly liberal – looked less so from within.

The number of officers each force requires differs according to its geographical area, population, crime rates, road mileage, number of shops and other criteria. There are considerable variations in size, complements being decided by the Home Office after negotiations with Chief Constables and the Local Police Authorities charged with maintaining adequate and efficient forces. Determining the optimum size for a force is further complicated by the desirability of maintaining communal links.

When substantial numbers of ethnic minority groups are concentrated in particular districts or divisions legitimation problems intensify. Attempts to deal with this by ethnic recruiting drives have so far yielded only meagre results. In May 1987 it was reported that there were fewer than 1,000 black and Asian officers in England and Wales out of a total strength of 122,000. The Metropolitan

Police had 359, slightly more than 1 per cent of its complement; the West Midlands Police had 135 or 2 per cent, the highest per cent non-white (*Guardian*, 14 May 1987).

Management entails the control of material as well as human resources. Apart from buildings, ranging from police stations to training establishments, resources for policing relate mainly to force, mobility, communications, surveillance, and information storage and retrieval. The character as well as the scale of resources is significant because they encroach on civil liberties and therefore pose ethical problems of utilization.

In conformity with the tradition of enhancing legitimacy by minimizing provocation, the uniformed officer on routine duty is provided only with a discreetly concealed truncheon as a weapon. Assignments are not invariably routine, however, and in the past police equipped with cutlasses and other arms have confronted strikers, protesters or rioters (Geary, 1985). Mounted police are an effective means of crowd control but their presence may be inflammatory and conjure up images of the cavalry when used on a substantial scale to control strikes or demonstrations.

In common with other organizations, police forces have to adapt to change. The increase in armed robberies, terrorism and mass protests has resulted in police armouries which can comprise handguns, rifles, automatic weapons, CS gas and plastic bullets. In what circumstances such resources are to be obtained and used and on whose authority, are contentious issues (Mainwaring-White, 1983, ch. 5). It is not simply a matter of operational independence or professional judgement since, apart from the connection with styles of policing in liberal democracies, the inept handling of a situation may convert it into a major political issue. When Police Authorities have opposed a Chief Constable's request for CS gas the Home Secretary has made it available, symptomatic of the blurring of control and responsibility.

Just as the railways and the telegraph profoundly affected the nature and mobility of both crime and policing in the nineteenth century, so the car, telephone, radio, computer, closed-circuit television, fibre optics, telescopic lens and electronic listening devices have revolutionized policing in the twentieth century. The consequences are disquieting in a democracy because they make possible covert styles of operational management. Efficiency and effectiveness may be secured at the expense of liberty when those who espouse unorthodox views are liable to have their telephones tapped and their activities closely monitored.

The possession of expensive capital equipment has additional managerial consequences. First, it demands intensive use if it is to be cost-effective; this encourages the creation of larger, more remote forces, as well as collaboration between them. Secondly, centralization becomes attractive as a way of minimizing expense, leading to the establishment of national units and loss of local control. Thirdly, the skills needed to operate equipment foster specialization. Size, centralization and specialization, plus the multiplicity of tasks laid on police in complex technological societies, raise formidable problems of organization.

Organization: Bureaucracy and behaviour

The use of resources is intimately connected with organizational forms of behaviour. Police forces are commonly perceived as bureaucracies of a disciplined, quasi-military character, meeting the Weberian 'ideal type' criteria of hierarchy, specialization and integration, rule-bound and impersonal in their functioning. Weber himself, however, drew attention to the dysfunctions of actual bureaucracies, with their delays, rigidities, excessive paperwork and obfuscation. Furthermore, theorists have commented on their dual character, formal authority being modified by informal behaviour, associated with customs, routines, personalities, conflicts of interest, dispersal of actual as opposed to ostensible power, and work cultures.

Each force is unique but all conform to the bureaucratic model. There is invariably an integrating headquarters. At the apex of the hierarchy are the Chief Constable, his Deputy and one or more Assistant Chief Constables. In the Metropolitan Police the equivalent ranks are Commissioner, Deputy Commissioner and Assistant Commissioner. The Chief Constable or Commissioner typically presides over a Policy Committee, determining the main decisions on overall strategy and policy. The precise nature of headquarters organization varies with the size and complexity of the force and, subject to span of control, is liable to change (on organization generally, see Jones, 1980, chs 3 and 4). At Scotland Yard, headquarters of the Metropolitan Police, the four Assistant Commissioners currently head departments concerned with Territorial Policing, Special Policing, Personnel and Training, and Management Services. A civilian Receiver, a member of the Policy Committee, is responsible for departments dealing with Civilians, Finance and Contract Supplies. The 8 areas of the Territorial Policing Department encompass 75 divisions (Greater London Council, 1986, pp. 11–12).

In provincial forces, divisions vary from a minimum of two to six or more. Each has its own headquarters and a number of sub-divisions which are presumed to be reasonably self-sufficient though they differ considerably. In an urban setting a sub-division might comprise a fair-sized town with a population of between 80,000 to 120,000. Clearly then, there are different levels of management and a variety of problems.

In spite of increased numbers of police it has proved difficult to provide uniformed foot patrols, nostalgically associated with the service role and hence legitimation. The 'bobby on the beat' is today a comparatively rare phenomenon, only 10 per cent of the time of officers up to the rank of inspector being spent on foot patrol in the Metropolitan Police (Smith and Gray, 1985, p. 309).

Manpower is deployed in diverse ways, often in reaction to current events. After the 1981 riots, many officers in the Metropolitan Police were transferred to District Support Units. Others were diverted to the Royalty and Diplomatic Protection Group in the aftermath of terrorist action. Reductions in overtime, to conserve cash, together with additional rest days negotiated by the Police Federation, representing the work-force, have depleted manpower. Given the amount of paperwork and rule bound procedures imposed by law with respect to investigations, charges and court cases, reports of occupational stress and absenteeism are scarcely surprising.

Government reluctance to provide ever more resources has compelled police managers to innovate. For example, to improve clear-up figures and effective use of manpower the Metropolitan Police, after pilot experiments, is quantifying the solvability of crimes. Only those scoring more than three on the basis of information available are followed up by detectives. Thus the partial description of a suspect scores one point but the number of a get-away car is worth four. Concentration on solvable crimes releases uniformed officers from temporary, largely futile duty in plain clothes, making them available for preventative street patrols. The pilot experiment produced modest improvements in clear-up rates and doubling of arrests by detectives (*Guardian*, 23 March 1988).

In common with public sector managers generally, Chief Constables have made use of a battery of managerial techniques. A high proportion of Chief Constables are members of the British Institute of Management and evidently see themselves, in part, as managers of a special type (see 'Managing the fight against crime', *The Economist*, 13 February 1988, p. 27; also Grimshaw and Jefferson,

1987, ch. 7, on Management Teams). Those more sceptical with respect to managerial nostrums have had them prescribed by the Home Office. Policing by objectives, adapted from management by objectives, may be cited as an example.

Policing by objectives appears to be the epitome of technical rationality, substituting for the profit motive in resource allocation. Following an assessment of past performance, objectives are set out broadly in a brief policy statement. These are translated into specific goals for divisions and departments and 'action plans' formulated. Organizational changes are instituted if necessary and full use made of automated information systems and evaluation. In devising action plans, consultations with community groups are prescribed and the views of all ranks canvassed. Implementation and evaluation are the final stages (Butler, 1984, chs 8–11).

In a sense policing by objectives constitutes a form of rational legitimization, given the consultation involved. Nevertheless, the value judgements of the unelected Chief Constable and his policy committee prevail. The opportunity costs of the chosen objectives, the foregone alternatives, may not be specified and agendas are likely to be influenced by subjective preferences.

Techniques appeal to those attracted by the ostensible certainties of quantification who may overlook or devalue important qualitative considerations. They form part of an ideology of 'management science', a value system exalting technical rationality. 'Efficiency and effectiveness' is its catchphrase. It has been pointed out, however, that if 'efficiency' involves confining value to what can be estimated in money terms, often on the basis of creative accounting, 'effectiveness' entails consideration of human and social consequences, leading towards the ethical values of critical legitimization (Jones, S. and Silverman, E., 'What Price Efficiency?', *Policing*, vol. 1, no. 1, Autumn, 1984).

In theory, objectives determined by those at the top of bureaucratic organizations are put into effect. Within actual bureaucracies, however, matters are complicated by problems of communication. Upward transmission of information is often filtered and downward instructions may not have much impact whatever systems of monitoring or reporting are employed. Messages in both directions are open to distortion, resistance, unreceptiveness, misunderstanding and interpretation according to interest or convenience (Dunning and Hochstedler, 1982; Katz and Kahn, 1978, ch. 14).

Occupational groups evolve their own cultures, at various levels, and the police are no exception (Reiner, 1985, ch. 3; Smith and Gray, 1985, ch. 14). The values and priorities of sergeants and constables, too numerous to supervise closely, tend to differ from those of more senior ranks. Objectives set from above may undergo change in the course of implementation or be secured by dubious means which can threaten legitimate authority (Holdaway, 1983, chs 4 and 8). Furthermore, because of the plethora and ambiguities of law and policies, limited resources, and the uniqueness of individual situations, the lower ranks exercise considerable discretion. Constables are prime examples of the 'street level bureaucrat' (Pike, 1985, ch. 4; Lipsky, 1980).

Discretion is not just available to junior officers, however, freedom of manoeuvre being essential at all levels for effective management. On the other hand, it lends itself to discrimination and manifest bias in the enforcement of law, encouraging differing group perceptions of the law's legitimacy. Corporate crime, for example, has not received the attention it merits (Box, 1983). It remains to be seen what difference the newly established Serious Fraud Office will make. On the other hand, it is alleged that there is widespread racial prejudice in some forces, with ethnic minorities disproportionately charged or deprived of adequate police protection against racial harassment. This has clear implications for legitimization, public relations and policing by consent.

Public relations: Policing by consent

The successful management of policing depends on external relations to an extent probably greater than in any other sphere, public or private (Bordua, 1967, ch. 2). Without voluntary information and co-operation from other agencies and the general public, forces confront virtually insurmountable obstacles in their pursuit of efficiency and effectiveness.

They start with considerable advantages. Most people seek the protection they offer, particularly those who reside in disadvantaged areas where crime rates are high. Opinion polls regularly indicate a favourable image of police as an occupational group. Public support is also fostered through the day-to-day provision of services of a helpful and pacific nature, the return of lost property, for example. This may be reinforced by voluntary efforts, such as organizing or assisting in the running of youth clubs. In addition, public relations departments cultivate the media, schools and populace in increasingly sophisticated fashion.

As with the state, however, distinctions may be drawn between the manifest and the latent characteristics of policing. Public relations may be natural and spontaneous or artificial and contrived. Ulterior motives can involve public relations departments in deception, cover-ups and symbolic actions designed to foster a favourable image. According to the National Council for Voluntary Youth Service, in a report on 'Youth Work and the Police', some officers working in youth groups have recruited young people as informers using threats and promises of immunity (*Guardian*, 10 April 1988). They are probably a minority but a close-knit body of professionals is prone to mislead the laity or general public.

The term 'public', conveys a misleading impression of homogeneity. In reality the public comprises various classes and groups and relations with each differ markedly. This has implications for 'consent', since what is acceptable to one category often antagonizes another. Of the groups posing special problems of public relations for police one may cite by way of illustration ethnic minority youth, striking trade unionists and members of movements such as CND.

The precarious nature of relationships with ethnic minority youth, subject to disproportionate unemployment and deprivation is evidenced in numerous studies (for example, Smith and Gray, 1985, ch. 15; Cowell, Jones and Young, 1982; Scarman, 1982). Since the riots in Brixton, Toxteth, Handsworth, Moss Side and Tottenham in the early 1980s attempts have been made to establish a rapport, including the efforts to recruit more non-white officers referred to earlier. Such disturbances may be sparked off or exacerbated by police action and raise complex problems of operations management. The roots of the matter, however, lie deeper in society, with the police to some extent merely reflecting more widespread but generally latent attitudes.

The monitoring of potential trouble spots has become increasingly sophisticated, Chief Constables profiting from experience. Recognition of warning signals and pre-emptive action may in future prevent or contain disturbances. They can be denied media attention if they do not get seriously out of hand ('Riots Nipped in the Bud', *Guardian*, 17 October 1984; 'Indicators put Midland Police on Riot Alert Three Times', *Guardian*, 18 August 1986; 'Senior Police Taught to Nip Riots in Bud', *Daily Telegraph*, 19 May 1986). Disorder is of course a symptom of social malaise and alienation which effective police management can suppress but not cure.

One way of improving mutual understanding and evoking public support has been sought in community policing, practised over a long period by particular forces and favoured in the Scarman report (see Gordon, 1987, ch. 4). Its advocates associate it with 'policing by consent' (Brown, 1982) and also contend that its applicability extends beyond ethnic relations.

'Community policing' and 'policing by consent' are ambiguous terms, open to varying interpretations. As presented by former Chief Constable Alderson, community policing is a comprehensive style of strategic and operational management, involving a majority of officers, directly or indirectly, in continuous collaboration and consultation with various local departments, organizations and groups, ideally with parallel national arrangements (Alderson, 1984, pp. 217–29; Moore and Brown, 1981; Baldwin and Kinsey, 1982, ch. 8; Centre for Contemporary Studies, 1984).

The aim is to identify and tackle problems jointly but multi-agency approaches to issues, though common and often unavoidable, raise many problems. They include interdepartmental conflicts and clear identification of responsibility and accountability. Moreover, inter-agency relationships, such as those between police forces and social service or education departments, take different forms and pose dilemmas involving the accommodation of differing values and interests (Thomas, 1986, chs 1, 2 and 7). Although diplomatic skills are called for, Chief Constables are in no doubt that the police should be paramount. For this reason the terms 'consultation' and 'liaison' are preferred to 'joint responsibility'.

Community policing interpreted as consultation relies mainly on the establishment of committees at various levels, divisional, sub-divisional or area, with members nominated by Chambers of Commerce, ethnic associations, local churches and other bodies. Consultative committees received legislative backing in the Police and Criminal Evidence Act, 1984. Critics, including some senior police officers, claim time-consuming committees divert manpower and attention from clearing up crime and undermine the equal enforcement of certain laws, such as those relating to 'soft' drugs (Waddington, 1984, ch. 5). In complex organizations like police forces, departments and officers specializing in community relations may appear to absolve other units and colleagues from pursuing good relations with various sections of the public. Differing priorities, and intentional or unintentional lack of communication between units, such as those concerned with drugs and community liaison, can cause confusion and provoke incidents. There are apparent conflicts of value between 'hard' and 'soft' styles of policing though some commentators claim that when circumstances seem to require it community police quickly revert to the organizational norm of toughness. Much depends on which mixture of hardness and softness is signalled by the Chief Constable and his immediate policy advisers as likely to be the most effective.

Supporters of community policing contend it is highly compatible with democracy, involving a form of social contract and public consent. Sceptics hold it can be manipulative and largely symbolic, exploited to legitimize policies which are really determined by Chief Constables, whose autonomy remains sacrosanct.

Ostensibly catering for participation, community policing may act as a surrogate for accountability to elected Police Authorities, whose potential control over policy is repudiated even by liberals such as Alderson. The membership of liaison or community committees is not truly representative but based on patronage (a burgeoning and worrying trend in public sector management). An inquiry into the disturbances at Tottenham, for example, reported that the chairman of the Haringey Police and Consultative Group acknowledged that it lacked a 'black element'. With some 1,200 organizations to draw on, however, problems of size, unity and representativeness are considerable (Gifford, 1986, pp. 208–9). Even at national level registering consent remains shot through with complexities, though this does not seem to concern the public, rendering legitimization that much easier (Raphael, 1976, pp. 94–6; Pateman, 1985, ch. 5).

Relationships with picketing strikers differ from those involving ethnic minorities. When picketing is small scale and peaceful, strikers and police normally co-operate harmoniously. In such circumstances police may recall their predominantly working-class origins and demonstrate a certain degree of sympathy, if not identify, with 'fellow workers', even though they themselves have surrendered the right to strike. The police appear neutral as between employers and workers. In larger scale politically sensitive situations it is difficult, if not impossible, for police to appear impartial, especially if a strike threatens public order or the tranquillity to which they and the government attach top priority.

According to some accounts, junior ranks generally hold rather unsophisticated views with respect to complex strikes, perceiving their role as purely instrumental, requiring the enforcement of unambiguous laws, in accordance with clear guidelines. From their more elevated position senior officers appreciate that laws permit discretionary options which can enhance effectiveness but also affect their legitimizing image of impartiality (Kahn *et al.*, 1983, ch. 5). The character of policing crucially depends on how discretion is used and for what ends.

These are periods when the neutral stance, if not openly abandoned, strains credibility (instances are provided in Morgan, J., 1987; Stevenson and Quinault, 1974, introduction and ch. 4; Stevenson and Cooke, 1979; Geary, 1985). Since mass picketing closed the Saltley Coke Depot in Birmingham in 1972, there have been several occasions when the policing of strikes has been intensely political. From the police point of view industrial disputes have been managed more effectively. The miners' strike of 1984–5 and the printers' dispute at Wapping in 1986 are the most notable examples. It is more open to question whether the methods employed could be described as efficient given the intimation of central government, at the height of events, to disregard financial costs. Costs also include a deterioration in good relationships between police and many trade unionists for some time to come.

The favourable image of police has also been put at risk generally through the employment of methods which vitiate civil liberties (National Council for Civil Liberties, 1984). They include the alleged indiscriminate actions of Special Patrol Groups, the excessive mobilization of Support Units; the utilization of the National Reporting Centre to deploy police contingents outside their own areas, and the erection of road blocks interfering with free passage on the highways during the miners' strike. There have also been well-substantiated allegations of unauthorized telephone tapping and the storing of intelligence about CND and other activists who have never broken the law or been charged (Du Quesne and Goodman, 1986, pp. 78–105; Campbell and Connor, 1986; Hain, 1986; Fine and Millar, 1985; Hewitt, 1982). Policing practice has necessarily replicated a more authoritarian and abrasive style of government.

It may be contended that the law being imprecise and discretionary, police have not necessarily exceeded their legal powers. Some allegations are uncorroborated and complaints procedures ignored. Nevertheless, there is widespread concern over the operations and styles of policing and dissatisfaction with the present system of control and accountability.

Accountability: Centralization, localism and autonomy

The tripartite system for controlling police forces, laid down in the 1964 Police Act is confusing, lending itself to centralization and the autonomy of Chief Constables at the expense of Local Police Authorities.

The Home Secretary is responsible and accountable to Parliament for the Metropolitan Police, no Local Police Authorities being involved. He is also accountable to Parliament for promoting the efficiency of provincial forces in England and Wales. The distinction between the words 'responsible' and 'accountable' is significant, though seldom precisely defined. According to constitutional theory, he refrains from issuing overt directions concerning police operations. Nevertheless control is effectively exerted through funding, veto powers over the selection and dismissal of Chief Constables, the Inspectorate of Constabulary, the numerous documents and guidelines drawn up by Home Office officials, coded but well-understood hints and public pronouncements.

Provincial forces are also accountable to Local Police Authorities, comprising two-thirds county councillors and one-third magistrates. Joint authorities exist when the area of a force takes in more than one county. Police Authorities are charged with securing the maintenance of adequate and properly equipped forces. They appoint and dismiss Chief Constables, subject to the Home Secretary's endorsement. They determine the force's budget, the Home Office meeting half the cost, but expenditure incurred by statute or central government regulations must be met. As the greater part of expenditure relates to pay and the Home Secretary finally determines salaries and the size of forces, budgetary control is perhaps more apparent than real.

Chief Constables enjoy a unique degree of autonomy, purportedly to guarantee the amorphous notion of the rule of law (on the rule of law see Harden and Lewis, 1986, ch. 2). Much is made of answerability to the courts as a safeguard against the abuse of power. Reiner (1985, pp. 189–90) is not reassuring on this point. The Director of Public Prosecutions is generally reluctant to institute cases against police, allegedly because juries tend to expect particularly convincing prosecution evidence. Civil actions are costly and seldom successful. Though writs of habeas corpus can be sought to end illegal detention and judges may exclude police evidence secured contrary to law, the judiciary tend to grant police considerable discretion in the interpretation of law, strengthening their position with respect to other forms of scrutiny and redress.

An Independent Police Complaints Authority exists but it suffers from a credibility gap. All complaints go initially to the force in question. The majority, involving allegations of discourtesy or inconsiderate behaviour, can be negotiated without further reference. Cases concerning death or serious injury must be reported to the Authority. The personnel of the PCA, not themselves police officers, are appointed by the Prime Minister. Complaints against one force are, however, actually investigated by an officer from another force, supervised by a member of the PCA.

The extent and nature of such supervision is unclear. The investigating officer submits a confidential report to the PCA. In due course the PCA issues a statement. This can be highly unsatisfactory from the complainant's point of view. For example, statements on the break-up of a 'peace' or 'hippy' convoy in Wiltshire and on police action at Manchester University, both incidents occurring in 1985, condemned the excessive police force employed. In the first case no individual officer was identified as a culprit. In the second, although there were 33 individual and 71 general complaints, only 3 officers were subsequently charged, 2 with perjury and the other with assault. Against this two students and one other person were charged with attempting to pervert the course of justice.

Given the high degree of professional solidarity which prevails there is scepticism concerning investigative processes and the adequacy of supervision. The Law Society, National Council for Civil Liberties and the Police Federation have all expressed dissatisfaction with the system (Gostin, 'A Common Cause for Complaints', *Guardian*, 12 March 1984; also see Sir Cyril Philips, *Policing*, vol. 1, no. 1, Autumn, 1984).

Deaths caused by police action, or occurring while people have been in custody, have provoked considerable disquiet over the years; some are still the subject of speculation in spite of inquests and court findings (see Scraton and Chadwick, 1987, ch. 7). Policies concerning the use of firearms are controversial but are treated as operational decisions, to be determined by Chief Constables rather than Police Authorities. An officer who accidently killed a child, although suspended for a time, was promoted shortly afterwards. Some shootings, sometimes of innocent people, whilst not resulting in deaths, have caused serious injury and, to put it mildly, damaged public relationships.

The more frequent arming of police has much to do with terrorism and events in Northern Ireland from which the mainland cannot be isolated (see Hillyard, 1987, ch. 10, pp. 304–8). When questions of national security and secret intelligence are involved open government and accountability are clearly more difficult to attain. Secret government, however, is incompatible with democracy (Dearlove and Saunders, 1984, ch. 5, pp. 137–65; Leys, 1986, ch. 14, pp. 299–309). Over-sanitized accounts of policing management are at best misleading and undermine the vital importance of applied ethics (Richards, 1985, ch. 2). The Sampson-Stalker report on an imputed RUC policy of 'shoot-to-kill' has so far merely resulted in promises of possible disciplinary action. The sudden removal of Mr Stalker from leading that inquiry, on unfounded charges of unprofessional conduct, remains perplexing and scarcely instils confidence in systems of accountability.

Well-publicized conflicts between Chief Constables and Police Authorities reinforce doubts about the adequacy of public accountability. Amongst other things these have concerned the issuing of arms, the use of CS gas, the deployment of manpower outside the force's area during strikes, to the neglect of local crime, and the storing of intelligence on citizens who have done no more than write to the local press in support of peace movements. In all these instances Chief Constables have acted without reference to their police authority, or successfully appealed to the Home Secretary.

Although the Chief Constable is obliged to submit an annual report to the authority, its form and content are his to decide. Operational independence and professional expertise are invoked to justify autonomy. Control by laymen, it is argued, would not only be inefficient but would open the door to political interference. As no police authority could rightfully direct police to act illegally, however, there is no reason why the relationship of a Chief Constable with his authority should differ markedly from that of, say, a Chief Education Officer with his county council. Control by elected laymen is a means of avoiding government by permanent officials, including the powerful individuals who head police forces. In this instance there is a reversal of the constitutional norm, with elected representatives advising a decison-taking Chief Constable.

There are nevertheless many problems associated with the composition and functions of Police Authorities. Radical critics would remove appointed magistrates as incompatible with democracy, particularly as they sometimes hold the balance of power in authorities with no clear party majority. Some would like to see reconstituted authorities challenge Chief Constable monopoly of operational decisions on the ground that these are often essentially political, rather than professional or technical. Others, dubbed reformist by Morgan and Swift, would not go so far, believing that existing powers are adequate but need to be used more vigorously, a position adopted by Scarman (Morgan and Swift, 1987, p. 261).

It is sometimes asserted that Police Authorities lack drive because they fail to attract the more prominent or experienced local politicians, who seek greater prestige and political influence by specializing in other areas, such as education or housing. Some members are uncertain as to their role or what constitutes knowledge relevant to policing. Monitoring performance and securing value for money pose special difficulties because wages and related expenses, outside Police Authority control, pre-empt budgets and crime statistics are open to varying explanations and interpretations. The powers and status of the Chief Constable tend to devalue those of Authority members to an unusual degree (Day and Klein, 1987, pp. 118–19).

It would be surprising, however, in such a highly centralized country as Britain, if Chief Constables really enjoyed the degree of independence ascribed to them. The Home Secretary and his department control 50 per cent of police budgets and lay down tight financial constraints. Through the Inspectorate of Constabulary uniformity and collaboration are encouraged if not assured. Circulars, regulations and 'advice' abound. Training is increasingly organized on a national basis. The Home Secretary takes an active interest in the appointment of Chief Constables, who cannot be removed without his approval. He has regular contact with the Association of Chief Police Officers. He can call for reports and institute investigations and inquiries into particular incidents and problems. He is in fact already the police authority for the largest force in the country (Lustgarten, 1986; Spencer, 1985).

This suggests that there is little prospect of overt change in the tripartite system. The strengthening of central control over policing is part of a more general national trend which looks set to continue. Nevertheless, initiatives on crime prevention, labelled 'crime concern', are under way and these have implications for the management of policing. Based on French experience the aim is to tackle social conditions which breed crime ('Foreign Bodies', *Guardian*, 18 November 1987). Collaboration between the Home Office, Department of Employment, Department of Trade and Industry and Department of Environment is envisaged, logically demanding a corresponding degree of co-operation between police forces and other agencies at sub-national level and closer association of Police Authorities with relevant local government committees. Given the already considerable involvement of Customs and Excise, the Post Office, Transport and other authorities, it is apparent that managing law and order involves much more than the efficient managing of police.

References

Alderson,J. (1984), *Law and Disorder* (London: Hamish Hamilton).
Atiyah, P. S. (1983), *Law and Modern Society* (Oxford: OUP).
Aughey, A. and Norton, P. (1984), 'A Settled Polity; the Conservative View of Law and Order', in P. Norton (ed.), pp. 137–48.
Baldwin, R. and Kinsey, R. (1982), *Police Powers and Politics* (London: Quartet).
Berki, R. N. (1986), *Security and Society* (London: Dent).
Blake, N. (n.d.), *The Police, the Law and the People* (London: Haldane Society).
Bordua, D. J. (1967), *The Police: Six Sociological Essays* (New York: Wiley).
Box, S. (1983), *Power, Crime and Mystification* (London: Tavistock).
Bradley, D., Walker, N. and Wilkie, R. (1986), *Managing the Police* (Brighton: Harvester).
Brown, J. (1982), *Policing by Multi-Racial Consent* (London: Bedford Square Press).
Butler, A. J. P. (1984), *Police Management* (Aldershot: Gower).
Campbell, D. and Connor, S. (1986), *On the Record* (London: Michael Joseph).
Centre for Contemporary Studies (1984), *Community Policing* (London: CCS).
Cowell, D., Jones, T. and Young, J. (1982), *Policing the Riots* (London: Junction Books).
Day, S. and Klein, R. (1987), *Accountabilities* (London: Tavistock).
Dearlove, J. and Saunders, P. (1984), *Introduction to British Politics* (Oxford: Polity).
Dunning, C. M. and Hochstedler, E. (1982), 'Satisfaction with Communication in a Police Organisation', in J. R. Green (ed.), Managing Police Work: Issues and Analysis (London: Sage).
Du Quesne, T. and Goodman, E. (1986), *Britain an Unfree Country* (London: Heterdox).
Elcock, H. (1984), 'Law, Order and the Labour Party', in P. Norton (ed.), pp. 149–64.
Engels, F. [1892] (1969), *Condition of the Working Class in England* (London: Granada).
Fine, B. and Millar, R. (1985), *Policing the Miners' Strike* (London: Lawrence & Wishart).
Geary, R. (1985), *Policing Industrial Disputes 1893–1985* (Cambridge: CUP).
Gifford, Lord (1986), *The Broadwater Farm Inquiry* (London: Karia).
Gordon, P. (1987), 'Community Policing: Towards the Local Police State'.
Gough, I. (1979), *The Political Economy of the Welfare State* (London: Macmillan).
Greater London Council (1986), *Guide to the Met.* (London).
Grimshaw, R. and Jefferson, T. (1987), *Interpreting Police Work* (London: Allen & Unwin).
Hain, P. (1986), *Political Strikes* (Harmondsworth: Penguin).

Hall, S. (ed.) (1978), *Policing the Crisis* (London: Macmillan).

Harden, I. and Lewis, N. (1986), *The Noble Lie* (London: Hutchinson).

Hewitt, P. (1982), *The Abuse of Power* (Oxford: Martin Robertson).

Hillyard, P. (1987), 'The Normalization of Special Powers: from Northern Ireland to Britain'.

Hillyard, P. and Percy-Smith, J. (1988), *The Co-ercive State* (London: Fontana).

Holdaway, S. (1983), *Inside the British Police* (Oxford: Blackwell).

Home Office (1983), *Manpower, Effectiveness and Efficiency in the Police Service*, Circular 114/83, November.

Ingle S. J. (1984), 'Alliance Attitudes to Law and Order', in P. Norton (ed.), pp. 165–78.

Jones, J. M. (1980), *Organizational Aspects of Police Behaviour* (Farnborough: Gower).

Kahn, P., Lewis, N., Livock, R. and Wiles, P. (1983), *Picketing* (London: Routledge & Kegan Paul).

Katz, D. and Kahn, R. L. (1978), *The Social Psychology of Organizations* (New York: Wiley, 2nd edn).

Lea, J., Matthews, R. and Young, J. (1987), *Law and Order: Five Years On* (Middlesex Polytechnic).

Leys, C. (1986), *Politics in Britain* (London: Verso).

Lipsky, M. (1980), *Street Level Bureaucracy* (New York: Russell Sage).

Lustgarten, L. (1986), *The Governance of Police* (London: Sweet & Maxwell).

Mainwaring-White, S. (1983), *The Policing Revolution* (Brighton: Harvester).

Mannheim, K. (1960), *Ideology and Utopia* (London: Routledge & Kegan Paul).

Mark, Sir Robert (1977), *Policing a Perplexed Society* (London: Allen & Unwin).

Moore, C. and Brown, J. (1981), *Community versus Crime* (London: Bedford Square Press).

Morgan, J. (1987), *Conflict and Order: Police and Labour Disputes in England and Wales 1900–1938* (Oxford: OUP).

Morgan, R. and Swift, P. (1987), 'The Future of Police Authorities', *Public Administration*, vol. 65, Autumn.

National Council for Civil Liberties (1984), *Civil Liberties and the Miners' Strike* (London: Yale Press).

Norton, P. (ed.) (1984), *Law and Order and British Politics* (Aldershot: Gower).

O'Connor, J. (1973), *The Fiscal Crisis of the State* (London: St James).

Pateman, C. (1985), *The Problem of Political Obligation* (Oxford: Polity).

Pike, M. A. (1985), *The Principles of Policing* (London: Macmillan).

Punch, N. (1983), *Control of the Police Organization* (Cambridge, Mass.: MIT).

Raphael, D. (1976), *Problems of Political Philosophy* (London: Macmillan).

Reiner, R. (1978), *The Blue-Coated Worker* (Cambridge: CUP).

Reiner, R. (1985), *The Politics of the Police* (Brighton: Harvester).

Richards, N. (1985), 'A Plea for Applied Ethics' in Thackrah, J. R. (ed) *Contemporary Policing* (London: Sphere).

Scarman, Lord (1982), *The Scarman Report* (Harmondsworth: Penguin).

Scraton, P. (ed.) (1987), *Law, Order and the Authoritarian State* (Milton Keynes: Open University Press).

Scraton, P. and Chadwick, K. (1987) 'Speaking ill of the dead: Institutionalised Responses to Death in Custody', in P. Scraton (ed), pp. 212–36.

Shaw, M. (1984), 'Marxism and the Problem of Law and Order in Britain', in P. Norton (ed.), pp. 179–92.

Slattery M. (1986), *Official Statistics* (London: Tavistock).

Smith, D. J. and Gray, J. (1985), *Police and People in London* (Aldershot: Gower).

Spencer, S. (1985), *Called to Account* (London: NCCL).

Stevenson, J. and Quinault, R. (1974), *Popular Protest and Public Order* (London: Allen & Unwin).

Thomas, T. (1986), *The Police and Social Workers* (Aldershot: Gower).

Waddington, P. A. J. (1984), 'Community Policing', in P. Norton (ed), pp. 84–99.

7 National Health Service management

KEITH BARNARD

Introduction

The emergence of management in the National Health Service has been marked by three discernible phases. From the 1960s until the mid-1970s there was considerable interest in 'scientific managment' starting with the adoption of work study techniques to improve operational efficiency among domestic staff. The second, overlapping phase, running from the mid-1960s to the late 1970s, emphasized planning methodologies, first for designing new hospitals and subsequently for service development strategy. The third phase of management since 1979 can be seen to have discarded the hitherto prevailing assumption that processes would necessarily produce the desired results, thus bringing to prominence an approach which owes much more than its two preceding phases to commercial management principles.

The objective now is to emphasize responsible financial management and value for money, or more colloquially, to 'remove the fat' from the system, a system which proponents argue has grown fat because of the lack of any consistent internal or external discipline. A recurring debate over the last three decades, that is since the first experiments of borrowing workshop techniques from industry, has been whether the National Health Service was sufficiently 'different' from other organizations – particularly industrial enterprises – to justify a unique approach to its management. Under the successive Thatcher governments we have seen the most sustained effort to ensure that National Health Service managers have to face the same kind of pressure and disciplines as their colleagues in the market sector of the national economy. This belief that the National Health Service needed essentially the same kind of management as commercial enterprises was given its most fundamental assertion in the Griffiths proposals for general management in the National Health Service which were implemented from 1984 onward (Griffiths Report, 1983). Now, some three years later, the organizational world of National Health Service management seems so different that many of its practitioners find it difficult to conceive of management before Griffiths. Whether it is Griffiths as such which is responsible or the other government-induced pressures alluded to earlier, is a matter for judgement, and it is still too soon to know whether some basic relationships within the health care system have changed, notably the distribution of power between government, health authorities with their delegated powers, managers, and the medical profession. For this reason, and because for most of the life of the National Health Service it has been seen as a different kind of enterprise requiring its own management approach even if it did borrow from others' experience, it can be fairly said that National Health Service management needs to be understood through its history. This is the approach adopted in this paper.

Management of the National Health Service

Although in popular usage we refer to the National Health Service as one of our universal services in the United Kingdom, in fact in terms of organization and management there are not one but four national services reflecting the constitutional fact that the United Kingdom is composed of England, Wales, Scotland and Northern Ireland. Each national service is the responsibility of a different minister – the three national Secretaries of State and, for England, the Secretary of State for Social Services. By the same token there are four Departments of State involved in managing the services, the Scottish, Welsh and Northern Ireland Offices and the Department of Health and Social Security (DHSS), each acting in the name of their minister.

It is, of course, the case that for many government functions, the United Kingdom is one country not four; and in fact both political culture and hence public administration are seen to be centralist in their essential character. But the national Departments have been set up – the Scottish Office in the nineteenth century and the other two much more recently – partly as responses to a particular political situation in each case and partly as a recognition of the intrinsic sense of difference warranting separate administration or national management. Each Secretary of State has social services in his or her portfolio and in the case of health, it is a direct responsibility. The national sense of identity is reflected in the Health Service where a number of administrative differences can be seen in terms of the kind of national and local institutions established and in the managerial terminology employed. Sometimes, particularly in the case of the former, the administrative structure is justified by geographic and demographic factors; often in the latter case of terminology, one suspects a need to appear different from the English.

Differences between the countries can be instructive, not least in identifying alternative means of discharging a number of administrative functions, and there is pressure from time to time for each to adopt successful or seemingly attractive features operating in one of the other countries. But a detailed comparison goes beyond the scope of this chapter which will concentrate on Britain, easily the largest country in terms of both geography and population.

In any event, access to the health service is universal throughout the United Kingdom for all British citizens[1] irrespective of residence, and despite administrative differences, between the four countries. The values, goals and objectives underlying the health service system are the same. These were laid down in the original statute, the National Health Service Act 1946. Although the Act and subsequent related legislation were consolidated in the National Health Service Act of 1977, the original intentions have remained unchanged. The Act requires the relevant Minister to promote a comprehensive health service designed to secure improvement in the physical and mental health of the people through prevention, diagnosis and treatment of illness. Specifically, Section 3 of the 1977 Act states, 'It is the Secretary of State's duty to provide . . . to such extent as he considers necessary to meet all reasonable requirements . . . facilities for the care of expectant and nursing mothers and young children as he considers are appropriate as part of the health service . . . such facilities for the prevention of illness, the care of persons suffering from illness and the aftercare of persons who have suffered from illnesses as he considers are appropriate as part of the health service'.

The Royal Commission on the National Health Service, set up in 1976 to review the functioning of the Service, reporting in 1979, summarized their understanding of the objectives of the National Health Service as:

- to influence individuals to remain healthy;
- to provide equality of entitlement to health services;
- to provide a broad range of services of a high standard;

- to provide equality of access to these services;
- to provide service free at the time of use;
- to satisfy the reasonable expectations of its users;
- to remain a national service responsive to local needs.

While both the legislation and the Royal Commission's perceptions are capable of more than one interpretation operationally, the underlying philosophy of the National Health Service is clear enough and it is one which has been shared by political parties in government and opposition across the political spectrum.

It must be said that since 1979 this last assertion might be made with slightly less conviction than hitherto, with left and right adopting opposite stances on the desirability of non-public, that is private provision and non-tax or health insurance funding of services. Opposition parties have been less inclined to believe that the government really espouses the old values, and are more prone to regard steps to introduce competition or contracting out of particular services not as worthwhile efforts to improve the efficiency of the National Health Service, but as scarcely veiled attempts to undermine the fabric of the service itself and make a privatized alternative to the National Health Service a self-fulfilling prophecy. Whatever the truth of such suspicions, eight years and two dramatic re-elections after the right gained power, the National Health Service is still showing the same essential shape even though details have changed.

Health services system structure

Notwithstanding the emergence of a private sector in the late 1970s and 1980s (covering broadly those coming to the country for medical treatment, United Kingdom citizens insured for private treatment, usually surgery, and nursing care for the elderly in private nursing homes) it is the public sector organizations which dominate the system. On any reasonable assumptions or calculations well over 90 per cent of the population make use of the National Health Service.

As indicated above, the legislation obliges the minister to develop a system for the whole population. In fulfilling this obligation, his principal tasks are first to secure funds from the Treasury, subsequently to be approved by Parliament as one of the government's spending programmes; secondly to allocate the funds to the National Health Service to run the services it provides; thirdly to issue general policy guidance which he expects the National Health Service to interpret and implement in each geographical area according to local circumstances; and fourthly to monitor the National Health Service to ensure that local services are functioning effectively and efficiently in line with his policies. Since the regulation of the private sector is also within the minister's sphere of responsibility, there is clearly one focal point for health policy.

This raises an interesting boundary question for the so-called health sector of the economy and society. If one talks of health management or health planning, it is often no more than a loose usage substituting for health 'services' management and planning, which in turn may mean more precisely 'medical' care. This ambiguity has persisted for the life of the National Health Service. In the 1930s and up to the Beveridge Report of 1942, talk of reform of the then prevailing arrangements included references to a state medical service and a national hospital service. Afterwards it was a National Health Service from the 1944 White Paper onwards. Admittedly, as already cited, the National Health Service Act enjoins the minister to do many things, but in practice the emphasis in terms of financial expenditure and human resources has always been on treatment, mostly in hospitals and on the first contact services, usually with general medical practitioners. These treatment activities were traditionally (especially in the United States) referred to as medical care and subsequently (in the United Kingdom from the early 1970s) arguably less accurately, as health care. So the health sector is normally taken to mean the arena of health services, otherwise medical care, otherwise health care. The concept of national health [sic] policy was to gain currency from the mid-1970s highlighted by the World Health Organization (WHO), the technical agency for health in the United Nations system. WHO policy statements[2] highlight the need for a range of initiatives to promote and maintain health, implying the necessity for the health sector to collaborate with other sectors. This broadening of the concept from health care to health policy had been anticipated in a specific way in the United Kingdom.

When the position of Secretary of State for Social Services was first created in 1968, the intention was that he would be the minister directly responsible for health and social security. Two ministries with those titles were combined as the Department of Health and Social Security, which he was to head. It is generally perceived that this co-ordinating role has not been actively discharged by successive Secretaries of State and it may well be that the role was contested by other ministries and their ministers. There is some evidence to support that assumption. In 1970 when the Central Policy Review Staff (CPRS) was created, one issue which exercised it was the need for a joint approach to social policy. It was an acknowledgement that social problems would often span the boundaries of government departments. In such cases the solution would be a policy requiring inter-departmental collaboration, with organizational and budgetary consequences. It is a reasonable inference that if the Secretary for Social Services had been able to exercise his co-ordinating role, the CPRS would not have deemed it important to press the matter.

By 1975 the CPRS had aroused the interest of ministers sufficiently for the publication of their proposals to be sanctioned by the Labour government. They appeared in a monograph, *A Joint Framework for Social Policies* (HMSO, 1975), having previously been extensively leaked to the press as a joint approach to social policy (JASP). At the time, JASP promised an imaginative breakthrough in public administration and policy formulation. In the event the ideas of the joint approach did not survive prolonged exposure in the arena of government administration, perhaps not really surprisingly, since it did not directly address the *de facto*-autonomy of individual departments. The central importance of professional and administrative territoriality in public administration is much more clearly seen now than then. Most of all it was not an issue of sufficiently overt political importance to attract the continuing interest of ministers. Indeed the whole question of the machinery of government at national and local levels, which attracted considerable ministerial interest and managerial effort in the early years of the 1970s, was no longer a matter of concern by the end of the decade, except in so far as there was a reaction against the 'growth of government' accompanied by a search for savings in public expenditure. It remains to be seen whether the high visibility of social problems such as AIDS and the decline of the inner cities, both manifestly requiring inter-departmental/inter-sectoral responses, will revive an interest in the machinery of government, or will be seen in the first case as a matter of information dissemination and in the second, as stimulation of the local economy.

Since the failure of JASP to command serious attention, there has been no further public attempt to co-ordinate social policy in the same over-arching fashion.

Department of Health and Social Security (DHSS) and the National Health Service

The distribution of functions between the ministries gives the Secretary of State for Social Services three major responsibilities.

- Social Security: the administration of various income maintenance schemes laid down by statute through a nation-wide network of local offices of the DHSS which is managed in a simple hierarchial fashion in the name of the Secretary of State.
- Personal Social Services: the Secretary of State does not provide directly any of the services so labelled (help for various categories of people in need or distress which may take the form of domicillary support or institutional care) but gives policy guidance and exercises a range of controls over the providing local authorities.
- The National Health Service: mainly covering the medical services as already indicated. These are provided formally in the name of the Secretary of State but in a fashion which may be described as a hybrid of the other two, Social Security and Social Services. The Secretary of State appoints corporate bodies, Regional Health Authorities (RHAs), which are in law both his agents and also quasi-autonomous. RHAs in turn appoint District Health Authorities for each local area which similarly enjoy an ambiguous relationship with a higher tier, in their case, the RHA. Government initiatives, however, have suggested that on balance, ministers are keen to emphasize the accountability of subordinate to superior tiers rather than autonomy.

The functional limits to the National Health Service as they now operate were first laid down in a public government discussion document (Green Paper) in 1970 (HMSO, 1970), and the position adopted then was subsequently taken up in legislation. The National Health Service would include those services where the skill of the personnel was medical or medical-related (for example, nursing). All staff with other skills (such as, social work) would be employed by other agencies and their work would be the responsibility of that agency on which would fall the obligation to make their services available. At the same time other agencies could no longer directly employ health workers, but the District Health Authority was charged with providing medical advice whenever required by the various local authority departments, including Social Services and Environmental Health.

National Health Service administration: Overview of the hierarchy

Reference has already been made to the functions of the Secretary of State and the DHSS and their relationships with National Health Service authorities and local authorities. In effect, the DHSS is run as two departments which only become one at the highest level. In practice there is Social Security, and there are Health and Personal Social Services which are treated together in terms of developing government policy and priorities. This is in recognition of the close relationships between the social and health needs of many often highly dependent groups in society such as the elderly and the handicapped. Government thinking on such issues, that is its intentions and expections of the responsible agencies, is encapsulated in policy guidance circulars and other documents which are issued from time to time to both health and local authorities, even though the DHSS enjoys an immediate corporate relationship only with the National Health Service.

In essence then, the role of the DHSS is to give advice to ministers and subsequently implement government policy. Over the years it has become clearer that it is the 'corporate head office' of the National Health Service. Although the Secretary of State has the necessary powers of direction in reserve, the DHSS normally operates through persuasion, exhortation and to some extent inducement. Its key instruments are its approval of major capital developments proposed by the service, its control (in association with the professions) of the expansion of medical manpower, and its allocation of virtually all financial resources to the service. Against the background of those controls, DHSS requests the National Health Service 'field' authorities to review and make proposals for the provision and development of services in line with government policy and priorities and within the financial assumptions they have been given. Subsequently ministers and their officials review how far the National Health Service has moved in accordance with the guidance they have been given. The most explicit acknowledgement of the 'head office' function was the creation of the National Health Service Management Board and the Supervisory Board within the DHSS in 1984, implementing the recommendations of the Griffiths Report (see below).

The DHSS corporate link with the National Health Service is through the fourteen Regional Health Authorities (RHAs). The boundaries of each region have been drawn with regard to a variety of physical, social, demographic and political geographical factors, but a dominant technocratic or professional criterion has been that each region has within it at least one university medical school with its associated teaching hospitals which are part of the National Health Service hospital provision for that locality. The RHA has a strategic role in the management and development of the National Health Service. Its tasks are to interpret and consider the application of national policy according to regional circumstances; to prepare after full consultation with local level interests a long-term strategic plan; to plan directly the capital developments and medical manpower expansion which arise out of the strategic plan; to make financial allocations to District Health Authorities (DHAs) to run local services and to require DHAs to prepare local operational plans in accordance with the strategic plan and make realistic financial assumptions. Lastly RHAs are expected to monitor DHAs' performance. Except for a limited range of activities where technical considerations or expected economies of scale so determine, RHAs are not involved in the management of operational services which are reserved to DHAs. Their control over major capital developments and the location of specialist medical manpower are key factors determining the shape and scale of hospital and other services that a particular DHA has to manage.

National Health Service organization as an evolution

The structure of the National Health Service set up by the National Health Service Act of 1946 had separate administrations below the Ministry of Health for hospitals, a range of personal health and environmental services (provided by the local government authorities), and the general medical, dental, pharmaceutical and opthalmic services provided by private practitioners referred to as independent contractors. This tripartite structure (Figure 7.1) was arrived at, partly under the influence of previous history, partly by what was acceptable to the medical profession, and partly by the organizational necessities of launching the National Health Service.

The influence of history on the choice of structure, continued through later reorganizations, can be seen very clearly. It is perhaps most evident in the transformation into National Health Service Executive Councils of the local insurance committees which had been set up to administer the pre-1946 limited National Health Insurance scheme providing access to general medical practitioner services for lower paid workers; and in the status of the practitioners providing these services, not employees, but independent contract-

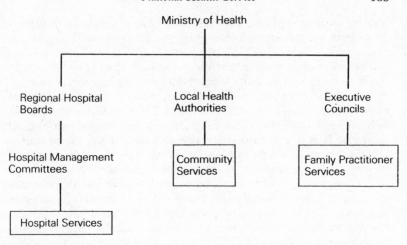

Figure 7.1   *The structure of the NHS*, 1948–74 (England).

ors employed to provide services. The local government authorities, together with the voluntary bodies, lost all responsibility for
hospitals when they were nationalized, but kept the public health
and other responsibilities which they had been acquiring since the
last century. While the arrangements for the management of hospitals – grouping hospitals irrespective of previous ownership – represented innovation, the idea of regionalization for strategic development and supervision had been previously advocated and put into
effect during the Second World War.

The acceptability of proposals to the medical professions should
be self-evident, since their co-operation is essential. When the
National Health Service was inaugurated this was highlighted by
the 'cat and mouse' game played by the Minister of Health, Aneurin
Bevan, and the medical profession which created suspense as to
whether GPs would agree to work within the National Health
Service. In the event they did, but the whole episode marked out the
enduring symbiotic nature of the relationship. Government needs
the skills of the medical profession and generally the latter is content
with the National Health Service, provided its special status is
preserved. This includes the opportunity to express opinion at every
managerial and administrative level, thereby influencing policy and
organization; and secondly, exercising without restriction professional judgement in the treatment of patients. The history of the
National Health Service, subject to change, has been one of fairly
comfortable co-existence between government and profession,

leaving unanswered the question: how can a work-force with a monopoly of technical skills, involving life and death issues, be managed?

The question is more explicitly raised now than in days past. In the beginning expectations were firmly underpinned by a 'service ethic' which supposedly guided the professional behaviour of reasonable men and women. It implied a style of self-management backed up by a keen sense of hierarchy and respect among all workers. It was not necessarily appreciated that the medical profession, clinical decision-makers managing the treatment of patients, would exercise an important influence on the use of resources or that their research discoveries, together with technological developments, would add to costs. On the contrary there was optimism that the cost would decline as the service tackled the backlog of ill-health that had gone untreated before the National Health Service. This fallacy was soon exposed by Roberts (1952) who argued that built-in factors ensured that costs would rise. His reasoning, later absorbed into the mainstream of belief, was the so-called 'infinity of demand', based on rising public expectations, technological innovation and an ageing population. There was relatively little understanding or conception of hospital costs, the lion's share of the total budget, and consequent alarm when the pre-National Health Service estimates appeared to have been seriously miscalculated. Many assumptions were subsequently made about expensive bureaucracy and abuse of a 'free' public service. The eventual response to the trend of rising expenditure was for the government to set up in 1953 the first comprehensive study of the way the National Health Service worked – the Guillebaud Committee – which looked at both cost and organization. A study on costs commissioned by the committee (Abel-Smith and Titmuss, 1956) showed that increases from 1949/50 to 1953/54, when calculated at constant prices, were much more modest, at £11 million, than that at current prices, £59 million. While as a proportion of GNP, cost had actually fallen from 3.75 per cent to 3.25 per cent.

In terms of organization and improvements to management the committee reviewed possible improvements to the existing structure, the most attractive politically, according to one's ideological persuasion, being either to turn the National Health Service into a corporation, in the style of the BBC or the trading nationalized industries, or alternatively, to absorb it into local government. Both ideas were unacceptable, the first because it was inconceivable, at that time, that there would be no direct ministerial accountability to Parliament; the second because it was widely felt to be impractical and has been an option argued for unsuccessfully in Cabinet when the 1946 legislation was prepared. The committee pragmatically concluded that the National Health Service was doing a good job and should be left to consolidate its position (Guillebaud Report, 1956).

In retrospect it can be seen more clearly that the Guillebaud Report took the first steps towards constructing an agenda of management issues which has remained relevant ever since. The issues can be stated simply. If the National Health Service cannot reduce the cost of ill-health to society by its very existence, an assumption which lay behind its creation, but costs can be controlled by financial devices, principally by imposing a ceiling on its budget, what then constitutes an adequate service? What means should be employed to determine the best use of resources, whether viewed geographically, as allocations to medical specialities such as accident surgery, cardiology or psychiatry, or availability for particular population groups, such as children or the elderly? Which is the best way to manage resources, and assess their impact in terms of improved patient health, rather than merely in terms of productivity measured by numbers treated? Issues of control over finance and manpower, or central supervision or local discretion, of formal and informal mechanisms for co-ordination and integration of services, have continued to exercise the minds of managers at the DHSS and in the Health Service. Nor do there appear to be any solutions of lasting validity or acceptability.

Explanations of the failure to find a 'right set of solutions' for the National Health Service are sought by academic and political observers in various root causes – for example, the absence of a market, the fundamental error of providing free services through a cumbersome bureaucratic machine; in the self-interested behaviour of its work-force, medical, managerial and ancillary; and in the nature of capitalist society. Such explanations are rarely seen as helpful to managers as they respond to the challenges of keeping their organizations functioning. If they are not to be accused of disregarding such theories, they may be indicted for not always heeding the lessons of experience. The arguments reviewed by Guillebaud surfaced again within ten years as the reorganization debate gathered pace in the 1960s.

Guillebaud, a government initiative, had been sceptical about structural change while clearly recognizing the importance of management and the further development of the service. In 1958 the medical profession itself, marking ten years of the service, initiated its own review with the Porritt Committee, which reported in 1962 (Porritt Report, 1962). By then other important developments had occurred. Various measures had been taken or were in preparation regarding the recruitment, training and career development of administrators (Lycett Green Report, 1963). More visible than this was the government's commitment to a major capital building programme for hospitals published in 1962, as *A Hospital Plan for England and Wales*. (Welsh 'independence' came later in 1964; a separate Scottish plan was published.) This was, however, more than a building programme. It envisaged replacing the existing hospital provision with District General Hospitals of 600–800 beds serving populations of 150,000 to 200,000. A coherent pattern of health service provision would emerge, based on the concept of a district: the district being in effect the hospital's catchment population with the main hospital being the district's focal point, supported by complementary services provided by general practitioners and local authorities. Although views on hospital size, design and function were to change over time, this district concept had a lasting impact on National Health Service thinking. Not only did it signal discussion about the scale of local organization, but by recognizing the need for links between hospitals and other providers of services, it focused attention more sharply on issues of integration and co-ordination. These were to become matters of dominant importance as the decade progressed. The Porritt Report was also important in shaping the debate to come.

Porritt's contribution was to propose administrative unification at local level, replacing the tripartite structure. This was less radical than at first appeared. For beneath the one health board envisaged for each area, the structure relapsed into the tripartite distinctions of 1948, with the addition of a fourth element, occupational health, which was developing outside the National Health Service. Initially Porritt was given a cool reception, perhaps because the conclusions of Guillebaud had remained in the mind. The importance of Porritt was that it provided the vocabulary for debating organizational restructuring reform.

Concurrent with the implementation of the 'Hospital Plan' and the message of Porritt, there was growing interest in patients' needs and the quality of the services they were receiving. Two developments were particularly significant. First, the Institute of Economic Affairs, dedicated to the promotion of universal market solutions, published a monograph, *Health through Choice* (IEA, 1961), citing shortcomings in the service and indicating how they could be remedied by privatization. Secondly, the emergence of patients' pressure groups, one claiming the title 'The Patients' Association';

these bodies were also critical. The National Health Service responded by challenging the validity of the economic arguments and the legitimacy of the consumer groups.

The first half of the 1960s was an era when organizational restructuring seemed the answer to many problems in many spheres of production. In the field of hospital administration economies of scale were sought by the amalgamation of Hospital Management Committees to form so-called 'jumbo' groups. But the argument became more fundamental, though argument is perhaps not the appropriate term. A tide of opinion started to flow strongly for problem solving through administrative change. One organization in any locality, rather than three, would ensure that so-called rational decisions would be made about resource allocations and planning, permitting the proper co-ordination of services to meet professionally defined patient needs.

There was little surprise when in 1967 the minister announced his intention to review the structure of the service. It was now politically acknowledged that what had been an effective political compromise in 1948 was not ideal; that it carried the risks of fragmented services in any locality, and depended almost entirely on the motivation of individuals to promote effective co-ordination. By the late 1960s, ten years after Guillebaud, such potential or actual disadvantages were important enough to warrant major reorganization. Over the first twenty years of the National Health Service, awareness of changes in patterns of morbidity and care, organizational experience and the growing magnitude of the resources involved, all increased the pressure for restructuring.

The minister's response (HMSO, 1968) was a Green Paper inviting reactions and debate. It suggested that there should be about 40 to 50 area boards, each with a membership of 15 or 16 persons. They would be accountable to the minister and responsible for issues of policy. Efficiency was seen as more important than broad public representation. It was closer to a 'board of directors' model than the representative democracy model manifested in elected local government. It was also clear in the Green Paper, *pace* Porritt, that the internal organization should not perpetuate the tripartite structure but be set up for management functions – planning, personnel, supplies, finance and a secretariat servicing the Board. The possibility of some form of incorporation with local government was not ruled out, since a Royal Commission on Local Government was concurrently deliberating.

Although the Green Paper did little more than clarify the prevailing arguments and proposals for change, it received a decidedly

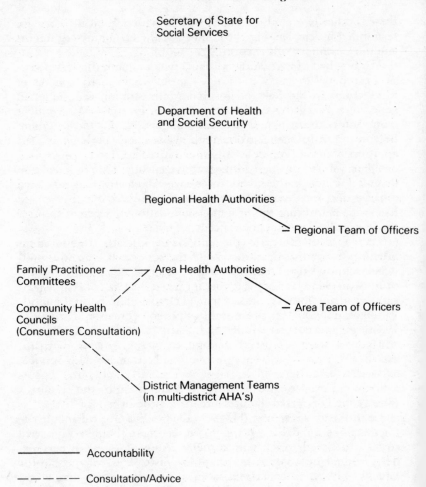

Figure 7.2   *The structure of the NHS, 1974–82 (England).*

hostile reaction. This illustrated a more general lesson in public administration: that all proposals for change, once articulated formally, become threatening in a way which they cannot be while they are the subject of mere speculation and debate. However broad-based the coalition favouring change appears to be, each specific part of the proposed package will spawn its vocal opponents. In the case of the Green Paper, three issues became the focus of criticism. First, the absence of a regional tier between the local level of planning and operational management, argued for partly on technical grounds; secondly, the severe reduction in the number of lay representatives whether elected or nominated; thirdly, the fear that the area boards would be so big as to be remote from the public as consumers.

A change of minister – the first Secretary of State in the combined health and social security department – brought the promise of revised proposals. These appeared in a second Green Paper (HMSO, 1970) which introduced a regional tier, albeit in a relatively weak form; with a clearly defined set of tasks to be performed on behalf of the proposed ninety area authorities. The second Green Paper acknowledged demands for localized and consumer-sensitive organization and management. It also recognized the strength of feeling among the medical profession and hospital staff against absorption into the structure of local government. Through platform references to sparing the National Health Service from 'parish-pump politics' it was made clear that any reorganization would be in parallel with, not part of, local government; but since co-operation was necessary between the National Health Service and a number of local authority services, the geographical boundaries of each should be 'coterminous' as far as possible.

Although these second Green Paper proposals were never enacted, because a change of government occurred soon after, much of the envisaged structure was preserved in the proposals effected by the next government in the *National Health Service Reorganization Act 1973* (HMSO, 1973). Two principal features were the deliberate strengthening of the regional tier, creating an overt line of command from the Secretary of State through the Regional Health Authority (RHA) to the Area Health Authority (AHA), and the conscious separation of consumer representation from management function through the establishment of Community Health Councils (CHCs). Management was seen as a professional specialist task and links with consumer interests but one part of the network of external relations to be maintained (Figure 7.2). One may also note that although no longer constitutionally independent, being linked formally to AHAs, the general practitioner services retained their administrative identity with Executive Councils, renamed Family Practitioner Services. Their formal subordination to the AHA was an irritant but had little or no practical effect. In 1985 they were given fully independent status, with a duty to collaborate with health authorities.

By the mid-1970s the National Health Service was a mature public sector organization. This was itself no small achievement since it was fashioned out of a host of local patterns of provision with mixed public and private ownership. There was a decided shift in the organizational climate away from *administration* towards *management*, the distinction, as defined by Keeling (1972), being that administration was the application of rules and management the harnessing and deployment of resources to a purpose. After the 1974 reorganization implementing the 1973 Act, responsibility for the planning and operation of local services rested with District Management Teams (which will be considered later). Let us first consolidate our understanding of the issues in National Health Service management, because by this time the service as it exists today had been fashioned.

The late 1960s and early 1970s had seen the government responding to a growing demand, essentially from within the National Health Service, for administrative unification as a precondition for better organization and quality of services. The sequence of Green Paper and other government statements focused on the following questions: How centralized did a centrally funded service have to be? What degree of autonomy could be allowed to National Health Service officers, in the interests of effective, efficient management? How many tiers were needed to secure the necessary linkages between the political tasks of the responsible minister and the professional tasks of clinicians and other health workers? What role should there be for elected public representatives as appointees to health authorities? What should be the nature of links with other social services?

The solution adopted in the 1973 Reorganization Act comprised a multi-tier form rather than the single-tier system of the first Green Paper, with a line of command which meant delegated rather than devolved authority to National Health Service bodies; separation of consumer representatives from management (rejecting a possibility raised in the second Green Paper) but formally guaranteeing their right to be consulted and heard; and an ostensible substantial operating autonomy to multi-disciplinary officer teams in the management of the service at each level. It was held that these arrangements, although focusing on management, would enhance opportunities to provide a better quality of patient care. These proposals reflected a preoccupation with 'more rational' decision-making. Within complex, technologically based organizations it was necessary to find a way of identifying key decisions, whereby the centre could control the general direction of the whole organization while delegating as much operational decision-making as possible to subsidiary units, acting in accordance with centrally determined policy and their awareness of local conditions. A formal corporate planning and management system was seen as an effective means of achieving this, whereby policy guidance and resource assumptions were passed from the centre to the operational level and plans based on these were submitted to the centre for scrutiny and endorsement. However, it remained a matter of continuing debate how far this approach could be taken. Within a large complex service like the National Health Service, pressure will be exerted on decision-makers by a wide array of interest groups representing, or purporting to represent, both providers and recipients of service, and some of these efforts will have an effect. The increasing specialization of care expanded the range of interest groups among both health workers and consumers, while competition for allocating limited resources between equally desirable objectives, highlighted the political context of choice and the limitations of conventional corporate planning. Indeed, if the corporate metaphor is taken further, it will show the National Health Service to be a conglomerate, with little or no real opportunity to strip either assets or liabilities. Only the radical right would see it otherwise.

So the 1974 reorganization took place against a set of conflicting trends and assumptions. Current management thinking put forward a picture of professionally trained officials making rational decisions within a well-defined corporate structure. The political reality was a picture of interest groups, with varying degrees of power, applying pressure on the decision-makers to make sure that their interests were protected. The optimistic, perhaps unrealistic, assumption was that these interests would be contained by incorporating them within the formal structure and machinery of consultation and co-operation.

Management after the 1974 reorganization

The response to the problems and opportunites was a compendium, *Management Arrangements for the Reorganized National Health Service* (HMSO, 1972). The general aim was to ensure a comprehensive and fully integrated Health Service in which care should be provided as far as possible locally, with due regard to the health needs of the community as a whole. More specific objectives which it was felt that the management arrangements ought to promote were:

- co-ordination of all personal health services with each other and with local government services; and planning services in relation to the 'needs' of the people to be served;

- the more effective working of professional practitioners through the provision of structure and systems to support them administratively, and means for them to contribute more effectively to National Health Service decision-making;
- more uniform national standards of care, but with encouragement for innovation and the rapid implementation of improved approaches to health care at local level.

To give practical effect to these aims the proposed management arrangements were based on certain general organizational principles. For example, it was intended that:

- the health care professions should be integrally involved in planning and management at all levels, but without infringing the principle of clinical autonomy;
- individual and collective responsibilities must be clearly defined and allocated as between authorities and officers and as between members of officer teams;
- there should be maximum decentralization and delegation of decison-making, but within policies established at national, regional and area levels. There should be a matching accountability upwards with performance judged against previously agreed plans, and control of expenditure against budgets based on plans.

It may be remarked that most of these principles echo those of classic corporate management systems. Indeed they were an amalgam of the advice of international management consultants McKinseys, with their vast experience of corporate planning and management in other spheres and some limited UK health sector experience, and the 'Glacier' School of organizational thought of Professor Jacques, of Brunel University, which placed great emphasis on formal structures and delineation of roles. However, the first principle suggests a potential conflict still pertinent today, between management concern for control and order and the professional values of freedom, judgement and independent action.

In acknowledging clinical autonomy, the *Management Arrangements* conceded that the National Health Service would have to be managed differently from other organizations. In particular, emphasis was placed on collegiate management and advisory and consultative machinery. The growth of specialization among clinicians and other staff, with resultant functional interdependence, reinforced this need. These characteristics were crystallized in the endorsement of consensus as a cardinal principle of team management. Subsequently the pathology of consensus management excited as much comment as any other feature of the National Health Service, such as the cluttering of agendas with issues that had no place there and the failure of team members to accept the implications of this mode of decision-making and implementation.

But concern over consensus was paralleled in other major features of the new organizational arrangements. The new framework allowed decentralization of decisons but with strategic direction from above. In practice where could or should decisions be made? What sounds an attractive principle was not always operationally unambiguous and the right to decide was not always uncontested. No less contentious was the managers' insistence that consultation did not imply acceptance of the views offered. Those consulted often could not understand why they were asked only to be ignored. Thus it emerged that the decision process, which was intended to focus on the most appropriate use of resources became commonly perceived as being easily frustrated by political and human factors, even though many had apparently been anticipated when the decision-making system was designed.

Given all the features of the 1974 reorganization, it was possible to present them as having a defensible logic. They had surface 'reasonableness' yet quickly became subjected to fierce criticism. Perhaps it was not surprising. The change-over from the old to the new authorities was particularly disturbing for many senior officials who were expected to learn instantly new roles and ways of working. There was a vacuum effect of 'sucking up' of talent into the new administrative superstructure which denuded the operational levels of the services of experienced managers. The change destroyed the well-established network of influence and information to which medical staff had become accustomed and knew how to exploit. The destruction of that network, the complexity of the new arrangements, and the diffusion of responsibility, left senior medical staff extremely frustrated and fierce opponents of the structure. Before long they were making that opposition very public.

The 1974 structure had been advocated as the basis for future rational management whereby decisions on priorities and resource allocation could be based on well-informed assessment of 'needs'. Arrangements encouraging consultation and collaboration with interested parties and other agencies would enable agreement to be reached on the 'right' policies to be followed. The underestimation of sectional conflicts (intensified by the slowing down in the growth of resources) and the sheer complexity of management, demonstrated the apparent naivety of the reforms.

It will remain a matter of speculation whether, given time, the 1974 arrangements could have been made to work or would have evolved satisfactorily. The government elected in 1979 was already committed to introduce legislation simplifying the structure. The first modifications became effective in April 1982; more radical changes were to follow.

In view of the high hopes that were entertained for the 1974 reorganization it is appropriate to consider criticisms and assess the organization of the 1974–82 National Health Service. On the positive side there was the introduction of a corporate planning system in 1976, a necessary concomitant of the structural changes. If unification had been essential to create the conditions for rational comprehensive decision-making at national, intermediate and local levels, a National Health Service planning system was required, so that the objectives of better care could be pursued in a systematic way. Short-term action plans were to be drawn up in the context of longer-term strategy and priorities. Two related developments occurred. The year 1976 also saw the first comprehensive statement of government policy and priorities for the health services and the related personal social services provided by local authorities (DHSS, 1976). The statement was issued as a consultative document and was modified the next year (DHSS, 1977) in the light of reactions. It was an attempt at giving an explicit corporate policy lead and an appropriate follow-up to the organizational changes. The second development in 1976 was the promulgation of the Resource Allocation Working Party's formula (RAWP) for redistributing financial resources so that less well-funded regions (identified on a per capita basis and adjusted for various health related factors) levelled up to others (DHSS, 1976). The economic situation rendered redistribution between regions a politically contentious issue.

One other positive development after 1974 was the opening up of the National Health Service to public debate. This may not have been universally welcomed by the National Health Service staff, who were sometimes suspicious of the media and community and consumer representatives. But the 1974 structure built in watchdog bodies in every district, the CHCs, and although they had not executive functions, they had a right to ask questions and make their views known. The authorities had an obligation to provide information and respond to criticisms. Clearly CHCs varied in their effectiveness in heightening public awareness and influence on management. Overall, however, their creation was an important step forward in community participation (NPHT, 1974).

On the negative side, the reorganized service, set up with optimism about the future, soon found itself in an era of increasing financial and resource restraint. The initial emphasis on planning had encouraged expectations of growth and development. The whole ethos of reform had been based on expectations of expansion, not retrenchment. Now the government contended planning was logically connected with scarcity, undermining its appeal. Secondly, partly owing to constraints, there were many instances of heightened tensions between the tiers in the Service–Region/Area, Area/District. Typically this manifested itself as the superior tier chastising the lower for overspending its budget and getting the retort 'we are not overspent, but underfunded'. More fundamentally, it was an inevitable result of hierarchical corporate structures, whereby superior levels seek order and control, fearing irresponsible behaviour on the part of inferior tiers and lower strata are convinced that superior tiers have no real understanding of operational realities; a classic instance of tension between autonomy and control very common when all finance emanates from a central point.

Stress was exacerbated by worsening industrial relations. For example, conflict developed between the government and the medical profession over the former's policy of private practice by removing private patient 'pay beds' from National Health Service hospitals. In the 1970s virtually every major staff group was involved in disputes involving policy. The general effect was a growing disaffection with the reorganization.

The government's initial response was to adopt the ploy of a Royal Commission on the Service. This did not placate the workforce, nor did the commission's report have any significant effect on the evolution of the service. This generally valuable review of the National Health Service, recommending adaptations to an organization basically perceived as a success, was delivered to the incoming Thatcher government of 1979. While in Opposition the Conservative party in Parliament had been carrying out its own investigation of the system.

The establishment of the commission failed to placate the medical profession because the Labour government proceeded with its plan to discourage private practice while it was deliberating. Salary inducements to forego the additional income offered by private practice were firmly rejected by consultants. The ideological debate over private practice was a trial of strength out of which the Labour government emerged without triumph. The outcome allowed private practice to remain at least at its existing level. Controls on private practice within the NHS, later introduced, simply boosted the growth of independent private hospitals, attracted commercial interest, and encouraged expansion of the independent private sector in general.

Clearly the growth of a private, commercial sector, was ideologically attractive to the incoming Thatcher government and it acted early on a commitment to dismantle controls on private practice which Labour had imposed. Nor did it discount radical change in the funding of the National Health Service, linked to the substantial growth of private medical insurance. They did not act on this possibility, although it remained alive in the hearts and minds of the keepers of the party's ideological conscience.

The biggest commitment was to restructure the service along the lines of the analysis made in Opposition; this was broadly compatible with the aspirations of some doctors, particularly hospital consultants. The Conservative government quickly produced a consultative paper, *Patients First* (December, 1979) which, drawing on the Royal Commission's recommendations where it suited their purposes, argued for a simplified structure and maximum delegation of managerial responsibility.

A corollary of the structural modifications, particularly the replacement of Areas by District Health Authorities, was a simplification of the corporate planning system, which had been introduced in 1976. The argument was that the discipline of planning had proved itself but that it had become too bureaucratic in practice, with proliferating paperwork, a view widely shared within the service. So planning, albeit modified, stayed in the restructured National Health Service which came into commission in April 1982, when the District Health Authorities became statutory bodies.

The multi-disciplinary management teams which had been a central feature of the 1974 reorganization also stayed. This was a reaffirmation of what had become the orthodoxy of National Health Service management thinking, and marked out the National Health Service as requiring a different approach to management from that of, say, local government. Specifically, while the 1974 local government reorganization created the post of chief executive to lead an authority's corporate management, such a post was deemed to be inappropriate for the National Health Service, just as a

Scottish proposal from the Farquharson–Lang Committee in 1966 for a similar post had been rejected for the National Health Service in Scotland.

A number of reasons can be advanced for the prevailing National Health Service view. Hospital consultants were generally ambivalent about management: interest in the managerial responsibilities inherent in their role as commanders of resources varied greatly, and their attitude towards administrators was probably shaped largely by their success in obtaining the resources they requested from them, particularly to develop clinical or laboratory services. The relationship which normally mattered most to a senior consultant was the 'quasi-marital' relationship he enjoyed (or otherwise) with the ward manager, his ward sister.

Following the Guillebaud Report in 1956, a number of moves were made to strengthen the recruitment, training and development of administrators. The Salmon Report on *Senior Nursing Staff Structure* (Salmon Report, 1966) also emphasized administration, leading to the demise of the title 'matron' and the introduction of senior, principal and chief nursing officers. This was perhaps partly a recognition of the increasing number of male nurses moving into senior positions; it was also intended as a conversion of traditional nursing administration, where status and position counted most, into efficient nursing management, appropriate to the new, large general hospitals then being built.

Both favourable and hostile views were expressed by nurses about the Salmon reforms. They introduced a narrower hierarchical pyramid, replacing the flat structure of a central administration around the matron and a plateau of ward sisters with considerable operational autonomy. To the leadership of the profession, however, Salmon was an important landmark because it gave nursing a seat (through the post of chief nursing officer) at the decision-making table. The nursing view would be heard alongside that of the chief administrator and doctors at every meeting of the authority.

In 1967 Salmon was followed by the Godber Report (or 'Cogwheel' Report, after the motif on its cover) on the *Organization of Medical Work in Hospitals* (Cogwheel Report, 1967). This advocated greater cohesion among consultants through a collegiate pattern of organization, based on separate categories of specialist and related staff, co-ordinated by a medical executive committee (MEC). Implementation of these proposals was patchy but was on a scale sufficient to create a sense that team management was evolving. Relationships between the chairman of the MEC, the chief nursing officer and the chief administrator were clearly crucial for success. Moreover, the overall management function was assuming ever greater importance when the vogue in public administration was encouraging the creation of larger agencies and institutions.

Given the evolution of the service, it is understandable that in the post-1974 debate about senior management structure the notion of a chief executive should have been rejected in favour of a collegiate management team acting by consensus. The team had to agree decisions and abide by them (closely analogous with 'cabinet responsibility'). If they were unable to reach agreement they had to report their failure and request a decision from the chairman and members of the area authority, providing a strong incentive to agree amongst themselves. The reasoning behind the 1974 structure formally endorsed the practice of consensus management, but management teams were enlarged to include the treasurer, or financial manager, and the newly created community physicians (who replaced local government's medical officer of health). Two part-time members of the District Management Team represented the hospital consultants and the general medical practitioners in the area.

The success of teams inevitably varied. Concern was often expressed regarding inertia and the diminution of individual responsibility (despite efforts in the official documentation to distinguish between collective team and individual officer responsibility). It was soon clear that the administrator member of the team at each level (region and district) had a key role in achieving effective co-ordination and implementation of decisions. Some administrators consequently felt they should be acknowledged as chief executives but this obviously found no favour with the professional representatives. So the orthodoxy of consensus team management survived the 1982 restructuring.

It did not, however, survive the Griffiths Report a year later (Griffiths Report, 1983). Despite the organizational shake-up and the introduction of various devices to improve efficiency, including competitive tendering for domestic support services in hospitals and other premises and despite more explicit acountability through annual performance reviews of each level, ministers remained concerned about the use of resources and the quality of management. It was against this background that Griffiths and his small team of fellow businessmen were asked to review the service and advise the Secretary of State. That advice was duly tendered in a published letter to the Secretary of State, in October 1983. This summarized the team's *National Health Service Management Inquiry* which became known as the Griffiths Report.

Its recommendations were put out for consultation but essentially they were accepted immediately, representing a dramatic break with the orthodoxy which had been evolving over two decades. Gone was the automatic right for a profession to be represented in top management in each level of the service. Gone was what some had construed as a *de facto* right of veto on team decisions, because gone was the consensus mode of decision-making, together with teams and collective responsibility. Instead, responsibility for decisions and action was vested in one individual, the general manager, whose precise professional background would be irrelevant. It was part of the Griffiths view that suitable general managers should be recruited from outside the ranks of National Health Service staff, for example, from business or the armed services. It was not intended that existing administrators would simply be relabelled and proceed as before, though in practice they did fill most of the new posts.

The Griffiths general manager proposal is rooted in an objective that none of the previous reforms had achieved, effective managerial control of the service. Griffiths is a conscious abandonment of the traditional 'spirit' of the service, moving from a professional to a managerial culture. It directly challenges health professionals, attempting to diminish their 'control' and pressing them (particularly physicians) to concentrate attention on performance and use of resources, while at the same time regarding patients as consumers with their own tastes and preferences. It may be that the next few years will see the managerial taming of autonomous professionals exercising their monopoly knowledge. Other factors may also work in management's favour.

For instance, the sense of crisis in the health sector, with ever-increasing material demands, the consequence of an ageing population and technological innovations, puts increasing pressure on the medical profession to justify their resource claims by results. The more open discussion within the medical profession of concepts of audit and performance review, and especially resource management, coupled with the central role assigned to general management, suggests possible change in the relationship between clinicians and management. Other indications supporting such a hypothesis can be found in the consequences of the longer-term trend of increasing specialization and the dependency of the most prestigious specialities on technology provided or maintained by others, making them potentially vulnerable to greater external control.

Even so, their possession of essential knowledge and skill, their statutory monopoly to act as medical practitioners, their continuing high social status and public esteem, may ensure that they are still able to subvert an unwanted managerial initiative. In terms of Alford's analysis of health care politics (Alford, 1975), they remain the 'dominant interest' in the health care structure. But the managers with their motivation as (in Alford's terms) 'corporate rationalizers' may be in a stronger position while economic and political pressures grow. In which case, they are aptly seen by him as the 'challenging interest' in the structure. If they sustain that challenge it will mark a new era.

In spite of a formal hierarchy and conventional management patterns in the nursing and support services, where it matters, that is in medical practice, the health sector so far has been characterized by non-authoritarian relationships. The apparent contradiction between management, implying control, and the operating professional autonomy of physicians has been customarily resolved by casting managers in the role most acceptable to the professionals, that of 'facilitators'. The official documents of both the 1974 and 1982 National Health Service reorganizations make this explicit: 'success in improving health care' depends primarily on the people in the health care professions . . . management plays only a subsidiary part . . .' (HMSO, 1972); 'it is doctors, dentists and nurses and their colleagues in the other health professions who provide the care and cure of patients . . . it is the purpose of management to support them . . .' (*Patients First*). There is central control of such personnel policies as salaries and conditions of service, but to date little operational control over medical professionals. Guaranteed, full professional autonomy – clinical freedom to treat the patient – and the collegiate culture of senior medical staff have ensured protection. This is not to say that there have been no external constraints on the professional drive to develop and expand their activities. The politically determined rate of expansion of this tax-funded service and priorities in the allocation of resources whether human, material, or financial, have served as controls. Restriction of resources, naturally enough, has been a cause of resentment, particularly among those in the profession who have been less favoured. This kind of control has been very real indeed and is reflected clearly in the slower rate of growth of total financial resources for health care (percentage of GNP) than in most other developed countries, and in the relatively modest expansion of high technology procedures. However, these controls are self-evidently negative and do not directly interfere with professional work place behaviour.

Doubts about current efforts to create a managerial culture in the National Health Service must remain, even if such doubts will now be expressed more guardedly than hitherto. Earlier references in the chapter to the conditions favourable to trade union influence in the 1970s have a distinctly historical flavour in the late 1980s. Nothing could more clearly reflect the demise of the National Health Service unions representing manual workers than their lack of success in protecting the members from the effects of competitive tendering for support services. Even when an in-house tender for a service has been successful, it has almost invariably adversely affected the level of remuneration of the staff concerned. The diminution of union influence has been the result of a sustained political will, which continues to be evidenced in the central direction of the service. There is therefore a juxtaposition of a centralizing pressure from government in terms of policies to follow (such as competitive tendering with their local managerial implications, including the loss of immediate control when groups of staff are employed by an outside contractor) and an insistence on the individual manager taking responsibility. The Griffiths era for all its challenge to professionals, has certainly not made the managers' task easier. On the contrary, the decison to appoint general managers for limited terms, through renewable contracts, the emphasis on managerial performance assessment and performance-related pay, together with current ministerial interest in creating an internal market within the National Health Service, all increase pressure. This is confirmed when the domain theory of social service organizations is applied. The three domains of policy, of the health authority, the medical profession, and management, reflect different values and expectations. Only the management domain has a direct interest in organizational objectives and efficiency, but it does not have the ready means to influence the professional domain where many changes originate. Many questions must remain.

It was clear before the 1987 general election that general management would survive whatever the outcome. Had a different government been elected, other structural changes would have followed imposing a different set of pressures on the general managers. It is perhaps ironic that despite emphasizing short-term results, part of the Griffiths prescription (Figure 7.3) particularly proposals for new structures under the DHSS, National Health Service Supervisory and Management Boards, partly simulating commercial corporate organization, was designed to achieve 'consistency and drive over the long term'.

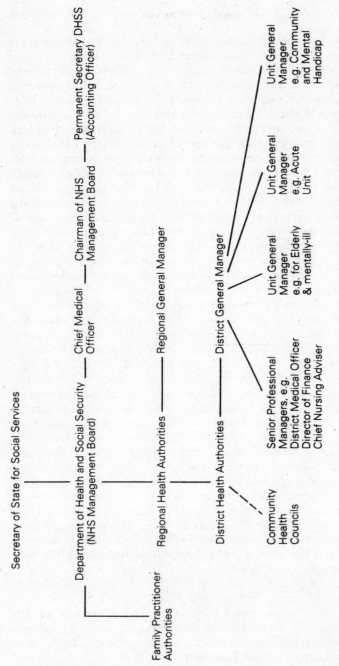

Figure 7.3 *The structure of the NHS: post-Griffiths (England).*

Students of the National Health Service must now monitor events to see whether the managerial means prove appropriate and effective in securing the social strategic objective of better care and better health; or whether a political objective will emerge (as some have predicted) of using the managing mechanisms eventually to take the health service out of the public sector. A further possibility, suggested by a working group set up by the Institute of Health Services Management (*The Economist*, 4 June 1988, pp. 31–2), is to separate the day–to–day running of the NHS from central government through the establishment of an independent National Board, run by a chief executive. Pay and conditions of service would be fixed by local managers in accordance with local conditions. Such suggestions are consistent with plans for many central government departments, based on the advice of Sir Robin Ibbs's Efficiency Unit.

Notes

1   There are reciprocity arrangements with European Economic Community and also certain other countries whereby citizens of one country have the rights of the citizens of the other country in terms of access to services. At the same time, providing medical care to others in need visiting the United Kingdom is now interpreted much more restrictively than was originally the case.

2   The most important of these was the Declaration of Alma Ata, the outcome of the international WHO/UNICEF Conference on Primary Health Care, Alma Ata, USSR, September 1978. All WHO policy subsequently stems from this.

References

Abel-Smith, B and Titmuss, R. M. (1956), *The Cost of the NHS in England and Wales* (Cambridge University Press).

Alford, R. (1975), *Health Care Politics* (University of Chicago Press).

Alma Ata (1978), 'Primary Health Care', *Health for All Series, no. 1* (WHO).

Anderson, F. (1984), 'Griffiths set to survive', *Health Services Journal*, 4 June.

Barnard, K. and Harrison, S. (1986), 'Labour Relations in the NHS', *Social Science and Medicine*, vol. 22, no. 11.

Beveridge Report (1942), *Social Insurance and Allied Services*, Cmd 6404 (HMSO).

Cogwheel Report (1967), *First Report of the Joint Working Party on the Organization of Medical Work in Hospitals*, Ministry of Health (HMSO).

DHSS (1971), *National Health Service Reorganization* Consultative Document.

DHSS (1973, 1973, 1974), *Reorganization of the National Health Service and Local Government in England and Wales: a Report for the Working Party on Collaboration between National Health Service and Local Government on its activities*, three reports.

Farquharson–Lang Report (1966), *Report of the Committee of the Scottish Health Services Council on Administrative Practices of Hospital Boards in Scotland* (HMSO).

Griffiths Report (1983), *National Health Service Management Inquiry Report* (DHSS).

Fulmer, R. M. (1978), *The New Management* (New York: MacMillan).

Fulton Report (1968), *The Civil Service: Report of the Committee*, Cmd 3638 (HMSO).

Guillebaud Report (1956), *Report of the Committee of Inquiry into the Cost of the National Health Service*, Cmd 9663, Ministry of Health (HMSO).

Harrison, S. (1982), 'Consensus Decision–Making in the NHS', a review in *Journal of Management Studies*, vol. 19, no. 4.

HC Social Services Committee (1984), *Griffiths National Health Service Management Inquiry*. First Report from the Social Services Committee Session 1983–84 (includes documents received in evidence and transcript of oral hearings), HC 209 (HMSO).

HMSO (1968), *The Administrative Structure of Medical and Related Services in England and Wales*, Ministry of Health (HMSO).

HMSO (1970), *The Future Structure of the National Health Service*, DHSS.

HMSO (1972), *Management Arrangements for the Reorganized National Health Service* (MARNHS), The Grey Book.

HMSO (1972), *National Health Service Reorganization – England*, Cmnd 5055, DHSS.

HMSO (1973), *National Health Service Reorganization Act* (CU 32).

HMSO (1975), *A Joint Framework for Social Policies*, Central Policy Reveiw Staff.

Hunter Working Party Report (1972), *Report of the Working Party on Medical Administration*, DHSS (HMSO).

Keeling, D. (1977), *Management in Government* (Allen & Unwin).

Lycett Green Report (1963), *Report of the Committee of Inquiry into the Recruitment, Training and Promotion of Administrative and Clerical Staff in the Hospital Service*, Ministry of Health (HMSO).

Maxwell, R. (1987), 'Reshaping the NHS', Policy Journals.

National Health Service Act 1946 (Ch. 81) and National Health Service Bill, Summary of the proposed new services, Ministry of Health, Cmd 6761 (HMSO).

National Health Service Act 1977 (Ch. 49) (HMSO).

Porritt Report (1962), *A Review of the Medical Services in Great Britain*, Medical Services Review Committee, Social Assay.

Roberts, F. (1952), *The Cost of Health* (London: Turnstile Press).

Royal Commission on the National Health Service (1979), *Report*, Cmd 7615 (HMSO).

Salmon Report (1966), *Report of the Committee on Senior Nursing Staff Structure*, Ministry of Health (HMSO).

Schulz, R. and Harrison, S. (1973), *Teams and Top Managers in the National Health Service* (Kings Fund).

Index

Page numbers in *italics* refer to figures.

The political responsibility of intellectuals addresses the many problems encountered in defining the relationship of intellectuals to the society in which they live. In what respects are they responsible for, and to, that society? Should they seek to act as independent arbiters of the values explicitly or implicitly espoused by those around them? Should they seek to advise those in public life about the way in which they should act, or should they withdraw from any form of political involvement? And how should their preoccupations with truth and language find practical expression?

The contributors to this volume seek to provide tentative answers to these questions. They come from a wide variety of disciplines, ranging from economics to linguistics and sociology to philosophy, and are drawn from both America and Eastern and Western Europe. The volume is given a particular interest by recent political upheavals in Eastern Europe, where many intellectuals have been confronted with sharply practical, sometimes dramatic, choices about their role in the political arena.